Sascha Albers, Bastian Schweiger, Markus Raueiser (Editors)

Strategy Case Book

Second Edition

KÖLNER WISSENSCHAFTSVERLAG
Köln 2015

Bibliografische Information Der Deutschen Bibliothek

Die Deutsche Bibliothek verzeichnet diese Publikation in der Deutschen Nationalbibliografie; detaillierte bibliografische Daten sind im Internet über http://dnb.ddb.de abrufbar.

Alle Rechte vorbehalten

© Die Autoren, Herausgeber und
  Kölner Wissenschaftsverlag
  Albers, Peters & Reihlen GbR
  Köln, 2015

http://www.primescience.com
http://www.koelnerwissenschaftsverlag.de

Das Werk einschließlich seiner Teile ist urheberrechtlich geschützt. Jede Verwertung außerhalb der engen Grenzen des Urheberrechtsgesetzes ist ohne Zustimmung des Verlages unzulässig und strafbar. Das gilt insbesondere für Vervielfältigungen, Übersetzungen, Mikroverfilmungen und die Einspeicherung und Verarbeitung in elektronischen Systemen.

Die Wiedergabe von Gebrauchsnamen, Handelsnamen, Warenbezeichnungen, usw. in diesem Werk berechtigt auch ohne besondere Kennzeichnung nicht zu der Annahme, dass solche Namen im Sinne der Warenzeichen- und Markenschutz-Gesetzgebung als frei zu betrachten wären und daher von jedermann benutzt werden dürfen.

Umschlaggestaltung: Anja Ternes
Printed in Germany

ISBN: 978-3-942720-84-7

Preface to the Second Edition

The concept of providing shorter, regionally anchored cases for strategy students (see the preface to the first edition below) has been vividly and positively received. As a response to this positive reception, we now offer the second edition of our case book. In addition to minor tuning and updates of the original cases, we have introduced four new cases (Borussia Dortmund, ThyssenKrupp, Kessels & Smit and Valve, and Strategic Planning at a University) in our portfolio that also contribute to a further diversification of our geographical spread:

	Case short title	Suggested strategy topics the case can be used for	Length (ca. wordcount)
1	Geo-Institut (A)	Resource-based View; Dynamic Capabilities	3060
2	Geo-Institut (B)	Industry Analysis	2620
3	German Lift Market	Industry Analysis	4200
4	Modomoto	Competitor Analysis, Competitive Dynamics	4020
5	Henkel Shared Services	Corporate Strategy and Structure	5380
6	Borussia Dortmund	Corporate Strategy	4726
7	Markus Schober GmbH	Growth Strategies, Post Merger Integration, Corporate Culture	3960
8	WOW Air Cargo	Cooperative Strategy	5980
9	Vaillant	International Strategy	3290
10	ThyssenKrupp	International Strategy	4865
11	Egrima	Strategy Process, Innovative Contexts	3900
12	Kessels & Smit and Valve	Strategy Process	4801
13	University Department	Strategy Process	
14	Online Food Retailing	Innovative Industry Contexts, Industry Analysis, Competitor Analysis,	5360
15	Kölner Stadt-Anzeiger	Mature Industry Contexts	5480
16	Reissdorf Kölsch	Mature Industry Contexts, Macrocultures	4230
17	Higher Education	Neo-Institutionalism, Industry Analysis	6940

We again hope you enjoy working with our case collection, and certainly welcome your feedback to casebook@koelnerwissenschaftsverlag.de.

Sascha Albers, Bastian Schweiger, Markus Raueiser

Sønderborg and Cologne
October 2015

Preface to the First Edition

Scholars and students of strategy know that there is no single, unanimous understanding of strategy, but that strategy is a multifaceted concept that will seem clear on one day and blurred on another. Accordingly, popular expositions on strategy follow either clear, and often simplifying definitions (most textbooks), different 'schools of thought'[1], or highlight 'tensions'[2]. The identification and formulation of strategy problems, the informed discussion about their nature, ways of dealing with them and concepts, tools and techniques to aid in this process is what many courses of Strategic Management are about. The learning experience and effectiveness of these courses is, according to our experience, benefitting from accessible, interesting, and relevant situations that companies have to deal with – and thus, students can relate to based on their own working experience, or will have to deal with sometime in the future. The use of case studies (i.e. goal directed, selective narratives of company situations) in strategy courses has turned into an important part of strategy classes around the world.

In line with this popularity of case studies, there is certainly no shortage of cases. Why then, did we feel the urge to come up with this book project and add to the mountains of (good) strategy cases that are available in other books and from other business schools? Three reasons have driven our effort.

First, many of the available and good strategy cases are often very long, laden with details (also beyond the necessary ambiguity that a strategic problem situation necessarily entails) and, at times, are too blurry to meaningfully connect theory and concepts with the described situation.

Second, despite the number and variety of available cases, at least for us, it has been an arduous exercise to find compelling and fitting case material for some specific, but less popular issues for master-level courses, that due to their degree of abstraction, greatly benefit from illustration and in-class discussions.

Third, while it is not difficult to get students interested in Apple, Google, and Facebook, it is often helpful to also give students some non-US companies at hand, or even companies that come from their home or study region.

The result of our efforts in addressing these motivations is the collection of case studies in this book. The 13 cases that we offer here are (mostly) shorter and crisper than a "standard" case; they therefore allow students a more direct approach to the case's core, and enable a more focused illustration, preparation and in-class discussion. With regard to the spectrum covered, the cases are – in principle - suited to support the discussion of theories, concepts and techniques of a master-level strategy course. The cases can be used for teaching concepts of sources of competitive advantage, strategy content, strategy process, strategy context and constructivist perspectives to strategy. Finally, with regard to the 'geographical motivator': all cases are about German companies, many of them from North Rhine-Westfalia. This represents our attempt to bring regional companies into the classroom since the initial setting of all of the co-editors was in or around Cologne (North Rhine-Westfalia). While this is a big advantage for us and our teaching, we acknowledge that this might not be of major interest elsewhere.

This point, however, also hints to the further development of this book in forthcoming editions. While we also strive to include further strategy topics, we will also widen the geographical scope of the cases covered here. One of the editors' affiliations is now in Denmark, which will yield new Danish cases. It is important to stress that we also welcome suggestions and contributions from other parts of Europe.

The following table illustrates the current case collection, the topics the cases can be used for, as well as their length (wordcount):

	Case short title	Suggested strategy topics the case can be used for	Length (ca. wordcount)
1	Geo-Institut (A)	Resource-based View; Dynamic Capabilities	3060
2	Geo-Institut (B)	Industry Analysis	2620
3	German Lift Market	Industry Analysis	4200
4	Modomoto	Competitor Analysis, Competitive Dynamics	4020
5	Henkel Shared Services	Corporate Strategy and Structure	5380
6	Markus Schober GmbH	Growth Strategies, Post Merger Integration, Corporate Culture	3960
7	WOW Air Cargo	Cooperative Strategy	5980
8	Vaillant	International Strategy	3290
9	Egrima	Strategy Process, Innovative Contexts	3900
10	Online Food Retailing	Innovative Industry Contexts, Industry Analysis, Competitor Analysis,	5360
11	Kölner Stadt-Anzeiger	Mature Industry Contexts	5480
12	Reissdorf Kölsch	Mature Industry Contexts, Macrocultures	4230
13	Higher Education	Neo-Institutionalism, Industry Analysis	6940

The preparation and publication of this book would not have been possible without the support of the authors, and many company representatives that spent their time talking to us about their firms and industries. We thank all of them and are looking forward to their input in revisions of the present cases or even in writing new cases. We also owe a thank you to our home institutions that allowed us to spend time and resources for the purposes of this book. These are the Danfoss Center of Global Business within the Department of Border Region Studies at the University of Southern Denmark, the Department of Business Policy and Logistics of the University of Cologne, and the Cologne Business School.

We hope you enjoy working with our cases – and would like to invite your feedback to casebook@koelnerwissenschaftsverlag.de.

Sascha Albers, Bastian Schweiger, Markus Raueiser
Sønderborg and Cologne
September 2014

NOTES

[1] See e.g. Mintzberg, H., Ahlstrand, B. W., & Lampel, J. 1998. *Strategy Safari: A Guided Tour Through the Wilds of Strategic Management*. New York: Free Press.
[2] See e.g. Wit, B. de, & Meyer, R. 2010. *Strategy: Process, Content, Context: An International Perspective* (4. ed.). Andover: South-Western Cengage Learning.

CONTENTS

Preface to the Second Edition v
Preface to the First Edition vi

I. Sources of Competitive Advantage

1 Geo-Institut Columbus GmbH (A) – Constantly Changing 1
2 Geo-Institut Columbus GmbH (B) – Extending the Market Position 11
3 Going Up or Going Down? - A Case Study of the German Lift Market 21
4 Modomoto vs. Outfittery - A Fierce Fight to free Men from their Shopping Pains 35

II. Strategy Content

5 Bringing Henkel Shared Services to the next Level – The Contribution of Shared Services to the Company Target Achievement 2012 49
6 You'll Never Walk Alone: Stakeholder Management and Corporate Strategy at Borussia Dortmund 67
7 The Takeover of Boxler – A Quantum Leap for Markus Schober? 83
8 The WOW Air Cargo Alliance 95
9 Business Strategy in Russia: Market Entry and Development of Vaillant 111
10 A Brazilian Love Affair – Did ThyssenKrupp's Internationalization Strategy Fail? 123

III. Strategy Process and Context

11 Searching for new Business Opportunities – The Strategy Process at Egrima Holding 139
12 Managing without Management – How Companies Succeed Without Hierarchy 153
13 Strategic Planning at a University Department – A Meaningless Endeavor or Just Done in the Wrong Way? 167
14 Online Food Retailing in Germany – Sleeping Giant or a Niche Market? 177
15 Kölner Stadt-Anzeiger and the Digital News Revolution 193

IV. Constructivist Perspectives

16 Reissdorf Kölsch: Regaining Momentum 213

17 Higher Education as Rocket Science: Private Business School Taking Off
    or Hitting the Ground? 225

Authors 245

1

Geo-Institut Columbus GmbH (A) – Constantly Changing

Bastian Schweiger, Roberto González Amor and Sascha Albers

It is Friday evening. After an exhausting week with 10 hearing appointments, Hermann Muermann is sitting in his company car on his way home towards Porta Westfalica. While crossing the border between Baden-Württemberg and Hessen, he is reminiscing about the conversations of the last week over and over again. How can he give his company its next spurt of growth? Is it time for product innovations? Or should the company reorganize the sales channels in order to leverage the established product portfolio?

Hermann Muermann is the managing director of the Geo-Institut Columbus GmbH, headquartered in Porta Westfalica, Germany. The firm is famous for its technologically advanced print relief technology, which enables the illustration of mountains and depths in geographic maps. The flagship product of the firm, beside the relief maps, is a relief globe with a diameter of 64 cm (25.12 inches). Since its foundation, the Geo-Institut has developed premium geographic products, which are mainly used in schools. Furthermore, they are popular with private and corporate clients.

After a difficult period of stagnating sales during the past few years, new paths have to be created to make the company grow again. The market has changed. Customer needs have changed. In Muermann's view, the time has come to establish new and innovative strategies and ideas.

THE GEO-INSTITUT COLUMBUS GMBH: COMPANY HISTORY

The Geo-Institut has concentrated on the development and production of geographical, political and technological relief maps and relief globes. It prides itself on its technologically and cartographically advanced relief printing method. Based on its high-quality products, the firm has managed to attract customers beyond Germany's borders in Central and Northern Europe, as well as in the USA.

Hermann Muermann's father-in-law, Ernst Knoll, founded the company in 1948 under the name Geoplastischer Verlag Ernst Knoll ("Geoplastic Publishing House Ernst Knoll") in Vlotho, a small town in northern Germany. Because of his employment as a surveyor, Ernst Knoll had a strong connection with geography. The idea to create relief maps came to his mind after receiving a request from the local primary school to paint maps of the surrounding area for their educational use. In 1948, Ernst Knoll produced his first relief maps out of cement. The cartographic information required for these maps was easily obtained from the land surveying office. The relief map facilitated teaching success in various school subjects. Besides the benefits it offered in geography lessons, it was also useful for application in history lessons (on migration or military campaigns), religious education (crusades, spread of the world religions) or even in biology classes (limits of vegetation, distribution of various animals). His passion for geography drove him to steadily improve his products. The rather unwieldy cement maps, for example, were replaced by flexible rollable rubber maps. Those maps had the advantage that they were easier to transport and store inside the school. In 1956, the next remarkable product innovation occurred in the form of relief maps made out of a plastic film. This innovation enabled the company to further increase its product quantity and quality.

Due to the increasing number of orders and new ideas which widened the product portfolio, Ernst Knoll decided to move into a bigger area in Porta Westfalica in 1969, where the company is still located today. Simultaneously, the firm changed its name to Relief-Technique. Over the years, Knoll and his employees acquired a high degree of competence in the production of relief maps that was appreciated by local and international customers. These competences, as well as the sophisticated production facility, were only used for newly introduced products. On the occasion of the relocation, Knoll remarked:

> "Our relief maps fulfil the highest quality and functional standards. Meanwhile, they are well known all over Europe. My employees in the development and fabrication department learned their business from scratch. For this reason, they know all the details of relief construction. These abilities have to be sustained, developed and realized in new products."

After careful consideration during the years that followed, in the mid-70s, Ernst Knoll, the thinker, presented his newest idea: a relief globe, which makes geography tangible. It makes the surface of the earth visible and tangible, and visualizes, for example, the Mariana Trench as well as the Himalaya mountains. This relief globe was supposed to become the flagship of the company. During the realization of this ambitious purpose, he had to overcome a number of complications. In the mid-80s, after more than 10 years of development, the relief globe was finally launched on the market. The development of the relief construction found its climax with this project.

At that time, the leadership of the family business had already transferred to the next generation. In 1982, the founder of the company, Ernst Knoll, passed the business on to his daughter Irmela and his son-in-law Hermann Muermann. Simultaneously, the firm was renamed, from Relief-Technique to the Geo-Institut. Besides the distribution of the new flagship product, the Relief Globe, Muermann had to face significant challenges in terms of its main customers: schools. The three-dimensional relief map, which was once the reason for the company's foundation and had found international clients in Great Britain, Belgium and Denmark, had to bear significant losses in sales during the mid-80s. As a result, the task for the new leading generation was clear: introduce new product innovations in order to compensate for losses in sales and open up new growth paths.

One result of the innovative product developments was a map of the surrounding school area, a milestone in recent corporate history. Hermann Muermann describes the product as follows: "The schools could individually choose a map extract of their surroundings, and afterwards teach local history." This product was the first product innovation in the history of the firm which was not based on the relief technique. Instead, the maps of schools' surroundings were sold in two variants: a large variant for front-style teaching and a smaller hand-out variant for every child in the class. That way, the expensive and long fabrication process of the relief maps was avoided, and, simultaneously, individual solutions for the schools as a real value-added were offered. These maps of schools' surroundings were a remarkable success: they generated considerable additional sales in Germany and abroad for years. But since 2000, the relevance of the map has decreased. Today, this product only plays a minor role in the product portfolio.

An important factor for the corporate development of the Geo-Institut was innovative production technology. At the beginning of the 1990s, the Geo-Institut generally manufactured sophisticated relief globes and maps entirely in-house. With the arrival of the computer and the corresponding software, the fabrication of the maps was later simplified and the personnel intensity reduced. The previously laborious, analogical production was simplified and the production process was accelerated. Overall, the technical development allowed for a reduction of production steps: the printing of large-sized maps was increasingly outsourced, in order to reduce investment in printing machines at the Geo-Institut. At present, only small-sized maps are still printed using internal printing machines. To develop specific map designs, the Geo-Institut uses external support by consulting independent designers or design studios. Although the relief globe is still produced manually, the biggest part of work at the Geo-Institut takes place at the computer (see **Figure 1.1**).

PRODUCTS OF THE GEO-INSTITUT COLUMBUS GMBH

The Geo-Institut's products aim to give customers unique insights into the world's geography. Fundamentally, the products can be separated into two groups: suitable teaching materials for schools and exclusive relief products for private and commercial customers. (**Figure 1.2** graphically summarizes the structure of the product portfolio.)

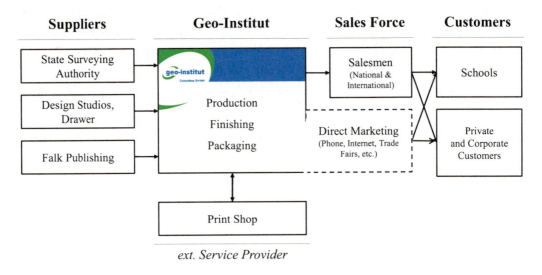

Figure 1.1: The value chain of the Geo Institut

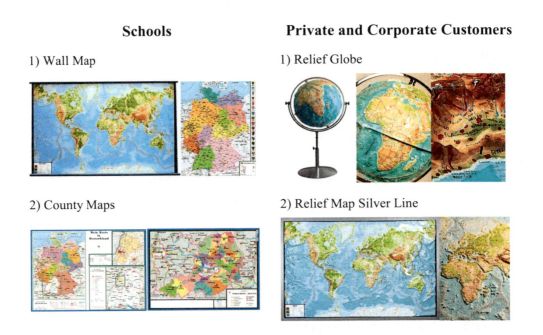

Figure 1.2: Product Portfolio by Customer Group

Teaching Materials for Schools

Market and customers. Mainly, the Geo-Institut distributes its maps to schools, and especially primary schools. "We are living on our sales to primary schools!" Hermann Muermann says. But the situation on the market for teaching material is becoming more and more tense. The financial margins of the states and municipalities, which cover 99 % of the costs in the German school system, are getting progressively smaller. A further complication for the Geo-Institut is that, compared to other school forms, primary schools on average receive the lowest spending per pupil (see **Figure 1.3**). Furthermore, with recent changes to the school curricula, geographical topics have become less important over the last few years. The Geo-Institut's competitors have also reacted with technological innovations in the teaching materials sector. Interactive wall maps, self-study discs and other media products are already available on the market or under development.

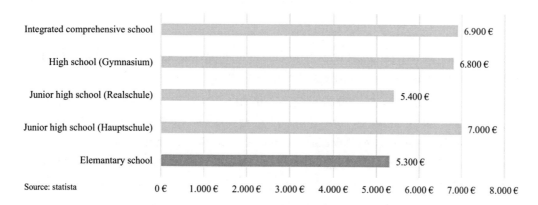

Figure 1.3: Expenditures per student by public school type in 2011 (in EUR)

Products. With the launch of the school area maps, a product not made through relief technique was introduced for the first time. Currently, the Geo-Institut produces almost exclusively maps without a relief structure as teaching materials. Two product lines are offered to schools: wall and hand-out maps, which visualize Germany, Europe or the whole world, and maps which describe a selected part of a government district (which part is to be displayed can be selected by the individual customer).

The wall maps are large-sized maps (max. 148-180 cm). They are suitable to retrace or discuss emigration issues, political borders or geological facts. To allow effective and interactive application during school lessons; the wall map is inscribable and washable. Also, teachers can hand out hand maps to the pupils (A3, inscribable and washable), which the children are able to use themselves. Additionally, a slide set for the overhead projector (A4, inscribable and washable) is offered. The map of the county is directly based on the map of the surrounding school area. Whereas this map shows the school and its nearby environment, the maps of the county broaden the concept by illustrating the whole locality. However, only a small number of these customized maps are produced. The maps of the county are particularly useful for social studies, because they often consider the geographical and political setting nearby. By launching the county maps in 2000, the Geo-Institut finally managed to compensate for the regressive sales of the school area maps. The country map is distributed in Germany and Austria, and has generated constant income since it was introduced to the market. Currently, the Geo-Institut is the only company offering county maps in Germany. This ensures a kind of exclusivity for the company.

Distribution. In order to distribute the products to schools, the Geo-Institut uses sales agents. Currently, 12 sales representatives are employed on a national and international level. Every representative works in a certain region. Contractually, the agents do not receive a fixed salary. Their wage depends on their generated performance. "A seller will only be paid if he generates revenues at the same time. That way I ensure motivation among the sellers", Hermann Muermann declares. The representatives can choose the products they would like to offer to their customers. In practice, it turns out that the best strategy is to focus on one or two products and try to distribute them successfully. A similar model is used by the four sales agents working abroad as well.

Of course, 12 agents are not enough to attend to all of Germany's primary schools. Traditionally, sales activities are limited to the states of North Rhine-Westphalia, Rhineland-Palatinate, Hesse, Bavaria, Saxony-Anhalt, Saxony and Baden-Wurttemberg. Due to this, a potentially relevant market is untapped. Against this background, the Geo-Institut is searching for reasonable options to widen its customer base. Lately, it tried to generate revenue by means of direct marketing with the help of active telemarketing. These first attempts at direct marketing have not yet been successful. It appears to be difficult to market products to conversational partners at the schools over the phone. At the moment, cooperation with retailers of teaching materials in and around Germany is proving to be another opportunity for widening the customer base. However, the results of this analysis are still inconclusive.

Exclusive Relief Products for Private and Corporate Clients

The sophisticated relief products of the Geo-Institut, in particular, are very much in demand from private and corporate clients. At the moment, 15 % of the revenues are generated this way.

Products. The relief globe is still the indisputable flagship of the Geo-Institut's offerings. After increasing budget cutbacks in the educational sector, the relief globe, originally designed for schools, has developed step-by-step into a product nearly exclusively bought by private and corporate clients. With the help of the globe, one can reconstruct the chain formation of massifs, the morphology of the ocean floor and the strata tectonics of the world both visually and plastically. The relief globe, which is up to 1.3 m tall, has a diameter of 64 cm. It consists of 14 single parts, map extracts which are produced individually and digitally, and are afterwards deep-drawn with the help of a special mechanical technique, whereupon the unique relief structure finally materializes. In the next step, the single parts are put together manually. The result of this complicated and personnel-intensive production is the relief globe. Its ingenious relief technique makes the difference between this globe and the competition. Nationally and internationally, the company sells about 120 relief globes per year, and the turnover has stayed at a constant level over the years.

In order to get a foothold in the private and corporate customer market, besides the relief globe, in 2008 the Geo-Institut decided to launch a high-quality relief map, the Silver Line. This product can be traced back to the relief map, which was sold to schools until the 1990s. The Silver Line combines the original relief map with an appealingly designed silver frame. Thus, the 1.5 m² map should find better acceptance in the living rooms and children's bedrooms of geological enthusiasts than in the offices of business clients. The Silver Line has only been sold as a map of the whole world so far. However, the Geo-Institut is coming up with variations: a map of Germany and a map of Europe, which will be available soon. In contrast to the relief globe, the Silver Line relief map is produced in one part, so that the production is significantly cheaper.

Distribution. As in the school segment, the Geo-Institut distributes the products, which are specially designed for the private and corporate customers, predominantly via the Internet. Nevertheless, this marketing policy turns out to be tricky because there are only a few sales agents who show real interest in selling relief globes and maps. Therefore, because of the passionate representative and geography fan Magnus Globufsen, 80 of the 120 relief globes sold per year are shipped to Denmark. This example shows the market potentials of other countries. However, not every representative manages to generate the sales of Mr Globufsen. For this reason, Hermann Muermann is continuously looking for new, talented sales agents for his company.

The first steps aim at increasing the volume of online sales. Those sales are exclusively realized via the corporate homepage and online retailers. With the help of this web presence, private and corporate clients can look up the entire product range and place their orders as well. In search of new distributive channels, Hermann Muermann approaches big German catalogue firms too. However, a listing of his products has not yet taken place due to the comparatively high prices and relatively low sales of the relief globes and maps.

THE WAY AHEAD

On Monday morning, Hermann Muermann is sitting in his office in Porta Westfalica again. He is still thinking about the question of where to direct his company. He has not found the solution yet.

"Schools have been our central buyers and will be even in the future", Muermann knows for sure. "How can we manage to grow in this segment despite the tense financial situation of the public providers? What is it possible to achieve with the existing resources?" The Geo-Institut needs inimitable products, which ease teaching for teachers, enhance the learning success of pupils and are not offered by any competitors. "The most untapped potential can actually be found in sales", Hermann Muermann thinks. It is getting more difficult to find adequate sales people, and this bottleneck hinders him from accessing additional attractive national and international markets.

Muermann needs a break to arrange his thoughts. While flicking through the daily newspaper and drinking a cup of coffee, this headline attracts his attention: "Google Street View, a resounding success". Since 2010, users have had the opportunity to follow road systems in a picture perspective via Google Street View. The article Muermann is reading illustrates the constantly expansion of the geography-based Internet applications produced by Google, starting with Google Maps, via Google Earth and through to Earth Enterprises and Earth Pro. In addition, the authors show that lately Google has even offered advice for the use of Google tools in school lessons. Hermann Muermann asks: "Are they going to be a real competitor for us?" For some time now, competitors like Klett, Westermann and Stiefel have been jumping on the multimedia bandwagon and expanding their know-how in this area. Hermann Muermann is hopeful that in the short term, physical maps are not going to be replaced by laptops and projectors in the primary school sector. This estimation is supported by the fact that the majority of teachers are sceptical regarding the use of computer-based tools in class. Currently, an all-encompassing increase of technology intensity in primary schools is considered improbable. Nevertheless, the mid- to long-term trend towards technologically intensive teaching methods is obvious. Is the Geo-Institut missing the connection in this case?

Besides schools, private and corporate customers must not be neglected. The sales agent Magnus Globufsen managed to sell 80 relief globes in Denmark. Hence, the product has significant potential. But the rest of the world only buys 40 relief globes. "There is still music playing", says Hermann Muermann confidently. "But how can we tap our additional sales potential?"

"However", Hermann Muermann restrains himself, "we cannot accomplish everything at once. Maybe it is necessary to focus our strengths and efforts in the market. Should we focus on the relief technique, which had once been the root of our success, and extend our strong position? Or should we concentrate on the schools, which made us successful during recent years? Perhaps we should show a stronger interest in their needs, even beyond the relief technique - it seems that we are good at this!"

•••

Setting of the case: 2011; last revision: 2014.

2

Geo-Institut Columbus GmbH (B) – Extending the Market Position

Bastian Schweiger, Roberto González Amor and Sascha Albers

The last few weeks have been less than relaxing but extremely interesting for Hermann Muermann, CEO of the Geo-Institut Columbus GmbH. The bustling manager is on the search for new directions for his company, which has built up a reputation for dealing in geographic, political and physical relief maps and globes.

During recent days, Muermann has once more travelled all over Germany. While talking to customers, sales agents and industry insiders, he has gained a profound impression of market developments and trends. His findings will help to perpetuate the Geo-Institut's success story in the future.

The competition in the core market of educational materials for schools is steadily increasing. The market volume decreases continuously, especially due to the stressed financial status of the communities and the federal states, fostering cut-throat competition among challengers. "The tone is becoming harsher, but we are ready to meet the challenge", Hermann Muermann says. The second pillar of GEO-Institut, the business with private customers and companies, requires active support as well. Just as in the market for teaching aids, growth potential exists but is very hard to realize.

TWO MARKETS, ONE TASK: THE RIGHT POSITIONING

Exploratory research and talks confirmed Hermann Muermann's perception of the competitive landscape: intensity of competition in educational materials as well as in the segments of private and business customers is increasingly rising. Product life cycles speed up and customers expect better and better products at lower and lower prices. As the preparation of Hermann Muermann's data indicates, this development affects both markets of the Geo-Institut, educational material as well as exclusive relief products, yet in different areas and with different characteristics.

Geographical Educational Materials: A Contested Market

Customers. Since the founding of the company, schools have represented the most important customer segment of the Geo-Institut. Accordingly, primary and secondary schools generate about 85 % of the overall turnover, of which 75 % is attributed to primary schools. That concentration on primary schools is motivated by two factors: firstly, primary education emphasizes geographic basics and local studies, so the Geo-Institut's products become more relevant. Secondly, the sales negotiations are much simpler when it comes to primary schools, although the decision making process is regulated by laws that are identical for primary and secondary schools. Sales negotiations within primary schools are held directly with the decision makers, i.e., the school principal and the teachers. An impression of the quality and functionality of the company's products can be conveyed to them in direct conversations with the Geo-Institut. In contrast, in secondary schools, geographical specialists and educational materials agents, as well as parents and governors, are involved in the negotiating process; this leads to a more exhausting and opaque decision making process for the suppliers.

Market. The Geo-Institut sells its cartographical materials mainly to primary schools. They represent the so-called primary segment in the German educational system, i.e., each pupil spends his first four or six years, depending on the particular federal state, at a primary school. The school life that follows in the "Haupt-", "Real-", "Gesamtschule" or "Gymnasium" school is called the secondary segment. With the completion of the secondary segment, the student's school career traditionally ends. Thus, "tertiary education" describes study at universities or other academies.

In school year 2009/2010, nearly half of the 34,600 schools in Germany were primary schools (more than 16,000)[1]. As measured by the number of pupils, three million out of 8.9 million pupils - about a third - were attending primary school. However, changes in the curricula caused a decrease in the emphasis on geography in primary schools. In contrast to the past, when local studies and geography were taught as separate subjects, nowadays both are integrated in the subject of social studies, which also has to cover topics including physics, social behaviour, hygiene and sex education, according to the curriculum. Hence, the thematic handling of local studies and geography has been heavily reduced in terms of time. This circumstance makes it harder for the Geo-Institut to convince principals to buy its products.

At the same time, it is necessary to consider that the expenses per pupil in the primary segment are below those in the secondary segment (see **Figure 2.1**). While in 2007 the average expenditures per pupil amounted to €5,000 across all segments, this figure was significantly lower at primary schools, with €4,200 per pupil. Taking into account the fact that only 12 % of these expenses per pupil are used for office or non-personnel expenses, the Geo-Institut competes with other providers of educational materials for a yearly budget of around €500 per pupil. For comparison: the yearly office or non-personnel expenses in "Hauptschulen" run to €720 per pupil. In view of these limited resources, the Geo-Institut needs to pay attention to the communication of the additional benefits of its products compared to other educatinal material.

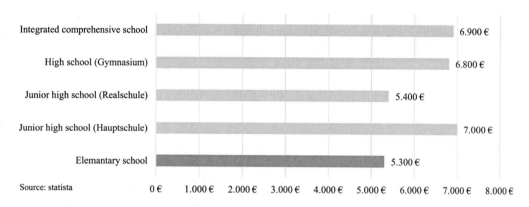

Figure 2.1: Expenditures per student by public school type in 2011 (in EUR)

Additionally, the financial scope of schools is substantially restricted by the reduction of financial power of the communities and federal states. The German school system is almost exclusively financed by the state; the federal states absorb about 80 % and the communities about 19 %. As opposed to other countries, private schools play only a minor role (see **Figure 2.2**). From 2000 to 2009, the public expenses for schools increased from €46.7 billion to €55.8 billion, an increase of 19.5 %. At the same time, though, the public debt of the federal states increased by 56 % and that of the communities by 16 % (as of 12/2009). At present, public providers are announcing a rigorous austerity programme for the coming years. Hence, schools will consider the purchase of maps or other new geographical materials even more critically. "The precarious situation of the public budgets has already induced the first sales declines", Hermann Muermann states, disenchanted.

Despite the above risks, both short- and medium-term opportunities for the Geo-Institut are ahead. Due to present local government reforms in Saxony-Anhalt, Lower Saxony, Rhineland-Palatinate and Mecklenburg-Western Pomerania, recently used geographical materials, such as maps of counties, have become unfeasible. Therefore, schools have short- to medium-term replacement needs.

Moreover, further national and international sales opportunities are unfolding. Present sales activities are only focused on schools in the federal states of North Rhine-Westphalia, Rhineland-Palatinate, Hesse, Bavaria, Saxony, Saxony-Anhalt and Baden-Wuerttemberg. Yet, by placing the central sales emphasis on the amount of public expenditure per pupil, it becomes obvious that the federal states previously served by the Geo-Institut are mostly below the overall German average (see **Figure 2.3**). In contrast, public expenditures per pupil of the eastern German states of Saxony, Saxony-Anhalt and Thuringia, as well as the city states of Berlin and Hamburg, are above the nationwide average. Consequently, relatively attractive sales regions with growth opportunities for the Geo-Institut are opening up. This also applies for international growth prospects: annual German expenditures per pupil in the primary education sector are far below the OECD and EU19 average (see **Figure 2.4**). Correspondingly, expanding the proportion of international sales is considered a realistic option for further development.

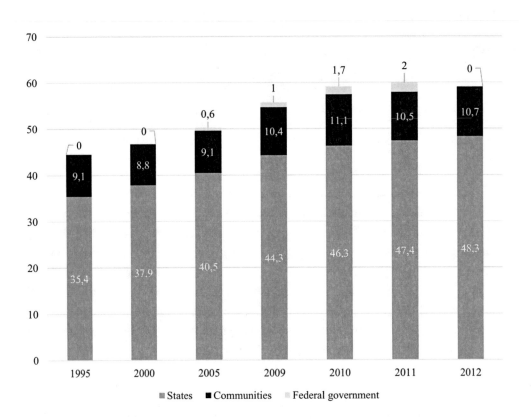

Figure 2.2: Public expenditure for schools by government body (in bn. EUR)

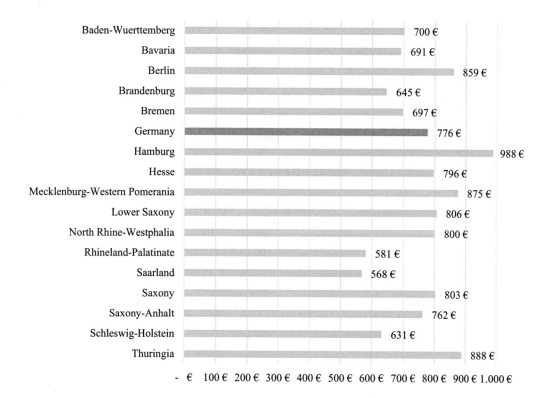

Figure 2.3: Operating expenditures for public schools per student and per federal state in 2007 (in €)[1]

Designer Objects for Private Customers and Corporate Clients

Customers. Currently, 15 % of Geo-Institut sales are achieved from selling relief maps to private customers and corporate clients interested in geography. The main share of these sales is generated by sales to private customers. Mainly, these buyers are interested in geography: enthusiasts, professionals or laypeople who buy relief maps as a designer product. The remaining part of the aforementioned sales is generated by corporate clients. Companies usually utilize the Geo-Institut's high-quality design products for display in their lobbies or offices. Furthermore, ocean carriers, naval museums and observatories are also important customers.

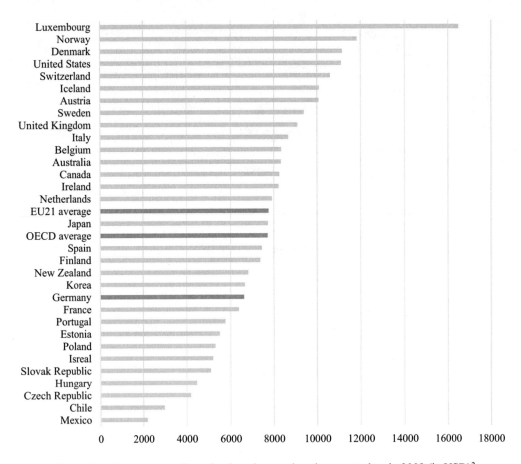

Figure 2.4: Annual expenditure for the primary education per student in 2009 (in USD)[2]

As in the learning materials sector, the distribution of the Geo-Institut's products to private and corporate customers is conducted by sales agents. However, since these agents specialize in selling one or two products, they do not offer the entire product portfolio to private and corporate customers. This leads to the situation where not all groups of buyers are addressed by these sales agents. In order to increase sales, the Geo-Institut has recently started to use its corporate website. On this website, private and corporate customers can find information about all the products offered and place orders online. But neither this measure nor the Geo-Institut's presence at trade fairs has increased sales significantly so far. Despite the satisfactory sales of relief globes at some tourism trade fairs, the cost of the exhibition presence was greater than the sales generated.

Searching for new distribution channels, Hermann Muermann started contacting large German catalogue firms. Eventually, the listing of his products failed due to the relatively high prices and low availability numbers of his relief globes and maps.

Competitors. The exploitation of the market for private and corporate customers can only be based on internal data from the Geo-Institut and an analysis of the main competitors. Those companies are more often found in the globe production sector - their number being manageable - than in the aforementioned group of competitors in the teaching materials market. Some companies from China and Italy that produce globes are acting in the lower-price segment, whereas one US company and the German Columbus Verlag Paul Oestergaard GmbH cover the entire market product range[4]. In addition to the Geo-Institut, several companies are located in the niche segment, especially in the higher-price segment. Before dealing with the lower-price segment, in the following, the self-declared market leader Columbus Verlag Paul Oestergaard GmbH will be considered.

Columbus Verlag Paul Oestergaard GmbH. Columbus Verlag was founded in 1909 in Berlin by Paul Oestergaard. It is the oldest globe manufacturer worldwide. Today, the company, with 60 employees, is located in Krauchenwies, where all Columbus globes are manufactured. Prices range from €39.95 to €8,995, due to the company's product portfolio ranging from plastic globes and globes for children to designer products, as well as mouth-blown glass globes. In particular, the demand for top-of-the-range globes starting at €3,000 has been increasing lately; customers use them as home accessories[6]. In this product segment, Columbus's mappers are cooperating with designers.

In order to strengthen its position as market leader, Columbus Verlag cooperates with prestigious partners. Among those partners are WDR (Mausglobus), Coppenrath Verlag (Hase-Felix-Globus) and Ravensburger (Ravensburger Kinderglobus). Furthermore, they founded the CartoDirect GmbH joint venture together with the US geography publisher Spherical Concepts Inc. in 2002, thereby improving the distribution and service performance in Europe. Currently, CartoDirect conducts the distribution of 21 well-known geography publishers all over Europe, among them Klett Perthes, National Geographic and Planet Observer. In order to stabilize its standing, in 2008 Columbus founded its own online shop, maptrade24, through which it distribute its own products as well as those of other publishers.

Lower-price segment. In addition to the challenging design and relief globes in the premium segment of the Geo-Institut or of Columbus, a wide range of globes in the lower-price segment are offered, from a starting price of €30 upwards. Although obviously of lower quality, customers prefer them to Geo-Institut's more expensive globes.

One has to consider that the competitors in the lower-price segment source their maps from the same external sources - mapping agencies and publishers - as the Geo-Institut. If, then, the lower-price segment offers the relief map at a price 50 % lower than that of the Geo-Institut, at least some of the customers seem to be willing to make compromises regarding quality.

Furthermore, the Internet is a very suitable distribution channel for globes, as the commercial enterprise Geosmile shows. The company sells geography-related products via the Internet (www.geosmile.de), addressing itself to different consumer groups, among others Geo-Institut's core segments: schools, private customers and corporate customers. Geosmile is a subsidiary of the German corporation s.mile Direkt AG. This collective of shops is a logistics service provider for geographical products. Despite its short company history, Geosmile has been able to position itself very quickly as one of the leading online shops for geography products by an aggressive pricing strategy. National and international partnerships give the company access to a wide variety of products. Geosmile acts only as a trader and offers Geo-Institut products as well.

THE INFLUENCE OF NEW TECHNOLOGIES

New technological opportunities, especially those created by the Internet, influence the Geo-Institut's business significantly. Two developments should be particularly considered in this context. Firstly, it is possible that innovative, Internet-based products may replace the use of physical teaching materials in geography. Secondly, however, the Internet provides a completely new distribution channel for globes and maps.

Competitors have already developed digital teaching materials in recent years. These developments were made under the assumption that a more extensive use of digital media will signify obsolescence for such products as wall maps. Furthermore, free Internet applications could influence geography as a school subject significantly. Thus, in 2005 Google started its map service, Google Maps, which enables users to view maps, to plan routes, or to locate positions via mobile/PDA. Only one year later, Google Earth was launched, providing users with the opportunity to explore our planet. For a fee, customers can also use the extended versions, such as Google Earth Pro or Google Earth Enterprise, which extras such as the generation of maps or the three-dimensional measurement of distances. Since 2010, Google Street View has even allowed customers to view the course of entire roads - on the basis of photos - via the Internet. Google also offers its services to teachers, giving advice regarding the use of its products in the classroom.

Besides Google's products, OpenStreetMap (OSM) - the Wikipedia of geography - is of considerable importance. This project was founded in 2004 and aims to supply users with free geographical materials, for example, relating to electoral districts, since normally this is very expensive. Everyone can join OSM and feed geographical data into the system. In contrast to Google, where the user cannot alter the existing maps, in OSM the underlying geographical data can be modified, so that the user is given the opportunity to create personalized maps.

However, Hermann Muermann believes that in the near future the Geo-Institut's physical products will not be replaced, but complemented by digital ones in the primary school sector. The long preparation times for technical devices, such as the time for acquiring and booting up the computers, make their daily use in class difficult.

QUO VADIS GEO-INSTITUT?

The latest data regarding the development of the market and the competitors' positioning are now on Hermann Muermann's desk. "The countless discussions in the past weeks were very fruitful. Now we have to work up, analyse, and evaluate the data carefully in order to choose a path for the future of the Geo-Institut".

During the revision of his notes, Muermann thinks about several questions which are of vital importance for further proceedings. "Should we focus on one market and only a few products? Which actions would strengthen our position in the market? How can we maximize our benefits from the private customer segment?" These three questions are only a small part of the reflections occupying the passionate leader of the Geo-Institut. Clearly, the main goal is to find a successful strategy orientation for the two main markets.

Hermann Muermann knows that there is a lot of work to be done! He is also aware of the fact that the solution will have to cover more than one dimension. It is past midnight when the director of the Geo-Institut leaves his office. The coming weeks will decide which strategy the company will choose in order to stay competitive.

•••

Setting of the case: 2011; last revision: 2014.

NOTES

[1] Calculations based on the Bundesfinanzberichtes (2010) and on publications of the German Federal Statistical Office, Fachserie 11 Reihe 1.

[2] Calculations based on OECD (2010): *Education at a Glance*, S. 202.

3

Going Up or Going Down? - A Case Study of the German Lift Market[1]

Markus Raueiser and Gereon Schumacher

"Is this how it is going to end?", Walter Kruger, owner and manager of Kruger Systems, a lift[1] installation and maintenance company founded in 1953, thought, lighting up a cigarette and leaning against his car. Turning his head, Kruger saw the massive steel and glass building in front of him that hosts the European headquarters of Schrader & Partners, an internationally renowned investment bank. Exhaling slowly, Kruger reflected on the industry convention in Augsburg, where he had met the bank's vice-president for mergers and acquisitions in Germany, Daniel Nolan.

"Now is the time to sell", Nolan had said during Interlift, the world's largest lift trade fair hosted by the German association, Verband für Aufzugstechnik (VFA). "Our bank represents one of the global market leaders in the lift industry, and our client is very interested in acquiring your business at a highly competitive price." What had stuck with Kruger was not the proposal itself. Since he had taken over the business his grandfather had founded, the large competitors had tried to acquire his company many times. It was the fact that he found himself to be open to the idea for the first time. "The lift market has changed", Nolan had argued, "and you should get out while the company is still worth something". Ever the engineer, Kruger never cared too much about profit margins, turnover numbers or strategic positioning. But even he had noticed how the lift market had changed in recent years. When he initially started to sell lifts, he used to calculate his costs, add a 20 % margin on top, and would still sell enough to grow his family's business from 10 to 80 employees. It never mattered to him if the lift was carrying people, freight or had to be designed for a special purpose. Architects and constructors alike had always appreciated his firm's high-quality vertical transportation installations.

---

[1] All figures, facts and assessments of the German lift market are real and dated as of April 2012. Market data cited applies to the relevant year, based on the provided source. Divergently, all characters in this case study are fictional and do not represent any members of the lift market, their views, values or opinions but rather aim to illustrate the characteristics and dynamics of participants within the market.

But recently, the world that Kruger had come to know had changed. The four large firms within the market, OTIS, Schindler, KONE and ThyssenKrupp, referred to as the "Big Four" of the industry (see **Table 3.1**), had become even more aggressive in acquiring market share, trying to adhere to their shareholders' desires. Prices for new installations had fallen. Long gone were the days of 20 % margins. Kruger was happy nowadays when the prices of lifts sold could cover his costs. Succumbing to the pressure, he had been forced to reduce his production staff, only producing special contracts in-house and procuring entire systems from a Chinese supplier to compete for "standard" lift systems.

	KONE	OTIS	Schindler	ThyssenKrupp Elevator
Founded, Headquarter	1910, Espoo, Finland	1853, Farmington, U.S.	1874, Ebikon, Switzerland	1999, Essen, Germany
Global Market Share New Constructions	11%	27%	18%	13%
German Market Share New Constructions	12%	19%	24%	15%
Employees	37,542	61,000	44,387	42,992
Revenue (in €)	4,986	8,816	6,537	4,930
Second Brand	-	DAT: Deutsche Aufzugstechnik	Haushahn	Tepper
Service Strategy	"VISION" - Excellence through Customer Service	"Be the Number One in Service"	"Leadership Through Service"	"Global Service Strategy"
Cartel Fine by ECC in 2007 (Total; Germany)	€ 142,120,000; € 62,370,000	€ 224,932,950; € 159,043,500	€ 143,748,000; € 21,458,250	€ 479,669,850; € 374,220,000

Table 3.1: The Big-4 of the German lift market

At the same time, one- to three-employee firms without production offered even lower prices for the servicing of the systems, making the once very lucrative subscription-based contracts less valuable and harder to come by. This increased competition from both sides had thinned out the market. When Kruger had taken over the company, there had been six other medium-sized producers in his region. Now, he felt like the last man standing, after his last such rival had sold his firm last autumn. Kruger Systems was now one of only 60 to 70 firms left that installed lift systems in Germany, down from over 200 in 1980[2] (see **Figure 3.1**). After it had become harder and harder to pay his bills, generate contracts for new installations, let alone profitable ones, and having laid off even more staff, Kruger had agreed to meet Nolan.

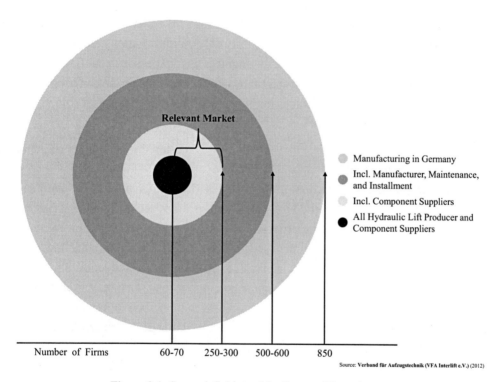

Figure 3.1: Scope definition of the German lift market

Lifts had always fascinated him, and he took great pride in finding technical solutions for vertical transportation where others saw no way to go up. But the past months had shown Kruger that it might be his time to get out. Get out, before the decline would ultimately make the decision for him. Putting out his cigarette, Kruger slowly started to walk towards the building.

THE LIFT AS AN IMPORTANT MEANS OF VERTICAL MOBILITY

While a number of mechanical solutions for vertical transportation exist, lifts have established themselves as a separate industry from other products such as hoists, temporary construction site lifts and theatre lifts. In its definition of the product and the relevant market, the European Parliament defined lifts, in their vertical transportation function, through three distinctive features: their permanent installation in or at a building, the closed car (referred to as a cabin) and the fact that they are inclined no more than 15 degrees.[3] According to the different legal and technical definitions and sets of rules, lifts can be distinguished into three different types: lifts transporting solely persons, solely goods, or both. While some larger lift producers also offer other vertical transportation and mobility solutions such as escalators, the majority of the firms offering lifts are specialized producers. These specialized suppliers are often met by experienced buyers, as in the purchase and construction process the majority of new installations are supported by a specialist consultant, usually an architect or engineer with expertise in the field of lifts. The specialist consultant draws up the requirements of the new lift and supervises the tender process. Thereby, the product becomes highly standardized, meaning that competition for new installations is largely on the subject of price.

Lift systems are produced, either by the firm installing the lift itself or its suppliers, and only assembled at the final site, generating both, large logistical challenges and difficulties in standardizing production processes. Due to a number of national and European norms, rules and specified regulations enforced by technical control boards such as the German TÜV, the planning process can often span several weeks or even months. After the installation and launch of the system, these rules further imply that the lift has to be maintained and serviced at regular intervals, depending on the frequency of its use. After a number of major components have become outdated or have lost their usefulness, often after 12 to 25 years, the lift can either be replaced by a new model or modernized. The life cycle of a lift is illustrated in **Figure 3.2**. The serving interval is determined by domestic or European laws, ranging from once a month to once a year. In addition, lifts are subject to audits through independent supervisory institutes such as TÜV or DEKRA, which ensure the functioning of the lift system and have the authority to demand the replacement or repair of specific components. The authorities thereby ensure safety for consumers and might also offer a source of additional income for lift suppliers.

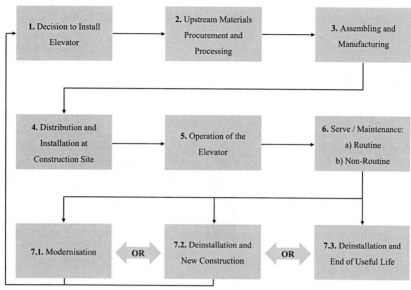

Figure 3.2: Product life cycle of a lift[4]

MARKET DESCRIPTION OF THE GERMAN LIFT INDUSTRY

As of 2010, the total market volume of the German lift market amounts to ca. €1.313 million. This market is separated into two major revenue drivers and market segments in which firms operate. Firstly, about €603 million (ca. 46 % of total market revenue) is generated through the installation of new lift systems. Due to the higher requirements for technical expertise, logistics and higher incurred risks and costs associated with the upfront financing of components and parts, this installation is mostly done through the four large international corporations and some well-established SMEs present in the market: Schindler, OTIS, ThyssenKrupp and KONE. As of 2012, no more than 60 to 70 companies manufacture in Germany.

The remaining 54 % of market revenue is generated through the servicing of lifts, both through regular contractual maintenance and the overhaul (Modernization) and repair of non-functioning lifts (Repairs). Here, there is an additional number of small enterprises of no more than two or three employees, often servicing only 200 to 300 lifts per year (see **Figure 3.3**).

The lack of reporting of such micro-service enterprises makes it difficult to assess the historical development of the service revenue in the market. New installations, on the other hand, have seen a moderate growth in overall market size since 2003, increasing within a compound annual growth rate (CAGR) of +1.95 %. The overall demand has been relatively stable, with a recent growth of 10.7 % from 2009 to 2010. This increase in growth is mostly accounted for by an increase in economic activity in the German construction industry. On a global scale, the industry has steadily grown into a €39 billion industry as of 2010[5], in which China has become the single largest sales market, accounting for 40 % of total new constructions.

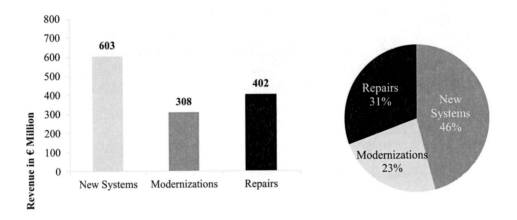

Figure 3.3: German lift market by types of revenue 2010 (in €)[6]

THE MARKET PARTICIPANTS

The "Big Four" in the German Lift Industry

The German lift market has been the centre of public attention following the fining of the industry's "Big Four" at a combined amount of €617,091,750 (KONE: €62,370,000; OTIS: €159,043,500; Schindler: €21,458,250; ThyssenKrupp: €374,220,000 (fine increased by 50 % for repeated offences)), as between at least 1994 and 2004, these companies rigged bids for procurement contracts, fixed prices and allocated projects to each other, shared markets and exchanged commercially important and confidential information, according to the European Union. As of the sanctioning in 2007, these were the largest fines imposed by the Commission for Cartel Violations.[7]

Together, the "Big Four" hold a combined market share in new constructions of 70 %. This has led German antitrust regulators to express antitrust concerns for a number of acquisitions in the past, among others KONE's acquisition of Hages in 1998 and Schindler/Haushahn (1998).

In recent years, the "Big Four" applied four manoeuvres that influence the competitive environment of the German lift market. Firstly, mergers and acquisitions play a key role in the attempt to consolidate the industry and grow the firms' overall market share. Through the acquisitions, the corporations acquire new technologies and know-how, an established brand, a customer base and most importantly numerous service contracts. In addition, the four corporations continue to increase their economies of scale by reducing redundant operational functions (often production and administration) and rationalize these in the acquired target companies. An example is Schindler's acquisition of Haushahn in 1999. To date, the renowned company from southern Germany has rationalized over 1,000 positions. Targets of the "Big Four" are often regional market players.

Secondly, with the exception of KONE that fully integrates acquired enterprises, the "Big Four" employ a dual brand strategy. The dual brands are: OTIS/DAT, Schindler/Haushahn and ThyssenKrupp/Tepper. The brand proliferation often aims to allow long-established regional companies that have been acquired to keep their brand name, which decreases the lack of identification of loyal customers towards a corporation name. In addition to economies of scale and increased bargaining power with suppliers, the dual brand strategy also leads to an increase in internal competition, whereby the two faces offered to the customer engage in increased competition, to a point where the parent company and the second brand compete for the same projects. The acquired firms retain a relatively high degree of post-acquisition independence, only switching to the corporation's product portfolio, and the approach is thus mostly utilized to increase total sales and market share, even at the expense of in-house competition.

Thirdly, the firms aim to improve their position within the service segment through a positioning of their core brand as a high-quality provider:

- Schindler's principle is "Leadership through Service" (Schindler, 2011).
- OTIS's vision is to be number one in service (United Technologies, 2011).
- ThyssenKrupp employs a "Global Service Strategy", centred on the concept of the "service technician of the future" (ThyssenKrupp, 2011).
- KONE's "VISION" strategy is centred on applied CRM to generate new maintenance contracts (KONE, 2011).

This indicates the importance of service contracts, which are often closed over 10 to 15 years and paid and carried out on a subscription-like basis, as a source of continuous cash flow and profitable sources of income.

Lastly, the market has seen an increase in the application of patents and proprietary technologies. The innovations within the German lift market can generally be grouped into three categories: product innovation (e.g., MRL lifts, gearless lifts, ThyssenKrupp's twin system, KONE's counterweightless lift), process and operational innovation (e.g., internal application of new production systems, globalization of manufacturing, certification and QM of employees, especially in SMEs), and service innovation (e.g., demand-oriented maintenance, introduction of remote diagnosis of lift interferences).

The corporations often use these intellectually protected technologies in their installations of new lifts, which do not allow competitors to service them. Spare parts are often intellectually protected and only sold to competitors with a large premium, allowing the "Big Four" to participate in the repairing and servicing of lifts they built in the past, even if they no longer hold the relevant service contract.

Small- and Medium-Sized Players

The competitive pressure through the "Big Four" has created a very difficult competitive environment for SMEs in the German lift industry. This has led to a strategic repositioning of SMEs from mostly standardized products towards market sub-segments: either product or regional niches. Fifteen to 20 years ago, most firms offered a full product portfolio; today they become specialized providers. Market experts forecast that specialization will become even more important for SMEs in the future.

The two largest independent SMEs, OSMA (3 % of new installations market share, ca. 550 employees, headquartered in Osnabrück, 16 branches in Germany) and Schmitt+Sohn (5 %, ca. 900 employees, headquartered in Nuremberg, 18 branches in Germany, also active in Austria, Portugal and the Czech Republic), are clearly distinguished from other SMEs present in the market due to their size, number of sites and large vertical manufacturing range.[8]

The other SMEs that compete considerably outside their domestic core region are Brobeil Aufzüge, Eggert Aufzüge, ELT, HIRO Lift, Lutz, Riedl Aufzugbau, Vestner Aufzüge and Windscheid & Wendel. These rather large SMEs typically employ 100 to 200 employees and still in-source a considerable part of their supply chain, mostly in the form of metal and steel processing.

The remaining SMEs focus on selected product market niches and/or primarily focus on a regional market. Common characteristics of such SMEs include typically 20 to 80 employees, and an often low degree of in-sourced value chain activities. These SMEs typically assemble components of different suppliers, with no or only a low degree of production participation, making them classical assembling firms. SMEs focusing on such strategies often procure the entire lift system - either in its entirety or in single components - from suppliers. Suppliers such as LiftEquip, LM, Wittur and GMW have specialized in the production of such preassembled lifts and thereby allow SMEs to compete for standardized lifts at prices similar to the price level of the "Big Four".

The last group of SMEs in the industry are microenterprises that are specialized in the installation of lifts as sub-contractors, and focus on repairs or service at very low prices due to almost non-existent overhead costs.

LEVEL OF COMPETITION IN THE TWO MARKET SEGMENTS

The high level of competition in the German new construction segment is indicated by comparing the actual unit growth rate to the monetary growth rate. While the total number of new units installed grew by a CAGR of 1.95 %, the new installations market has declined monetarily since 2003 with a CAGR of -0.52 %. Similarly, the growth rate of 10.7 % from 2009 to 2010 was only reflected in a monetary increase in the segment size of 7.2 %, from ca. €563 million to €603 million (see **Figure 3.4a** and **3.4b**). In total, the CAGR of the German lift industry is lower than the quantitative reference growth rate. Compared to the global lift market, the German market is also lagging behind. The estimated annual growth rate of the global market is between 15 % and 17 %, driven by the sharp increase in demand in emerging economies.

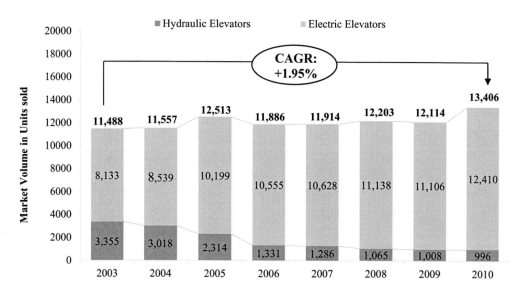

Figure 3.4a: Market size German lift market for new constructions 2003-2010 (in units sold)[9]

This shows the severe price competition in the industry, following the standardization process of the "Big Four" that enables the corporations to achieve high economies of scale for standardized lifts, which has in turn led to even tougher price competition in the standardized new installation market, where margins have declined by 10-12 % over the last decade. In particular, SMEs struggle to supply their products at competitive prices. The "Big Four" aggressively pursue sales through a low price level, having shifted the focus of their strategic actions to achieve two goals: firstly, consolidating the industry, and secondly, translating their new installation market shares into market share in the higher-margin service segment.

While margins, and consequently revenues, compared to unit sales of new installations have declined, both percentage contribution and margins of after-sales services have increased over the past decade. While only accounting for 36 % in 2002, services already accounted for 48 % of total market revenue in 2006, and currently make up 54 % of industry revenue. The increased importance of this segment is reflected in the value proposition of the "Big Four" in their active pursuit of service contracts. Currently, SMEs hold a total estimated market share of ca. 40 % in the service segment, which is caused by the traditionally higher number of micro- to smaller enterprises.

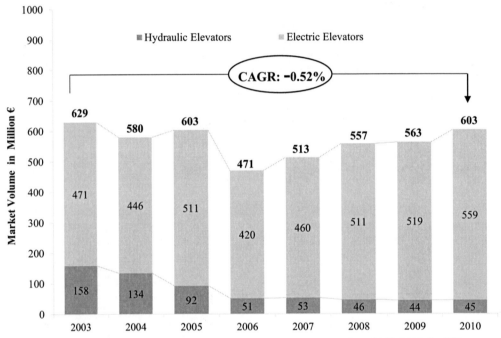

Figure 3.4b: Market size German lift market for new constructions 2003-2010 (in €)[10]

The market consolidation through M&A activities of the "Big Four" in the service segment is being slowed down by spin-offs, whereby a few mechanics go into business for themselves, spawning a one- or two-employee enterprise that is often able to take 100 to 200 maintenance contracts from the old employer. The concentration process, however, outweighs the spin-off effect, leading to an increasingly concentrated market segment. This concentration process has also steadily decreased the number of employees in the German lift market, as the efficiency-creating process of the "Big Four" has seen the rationalization of production sites of the acquired enterprises, which are often seen as a means to enter a market niche - sometimes a specialized product niche, but more often a local niche - in order to acquire the lucrative margin contracts. This has reduced the number of employees in the German lift industry from ca. 19,000 in 1998 to ca. 12,500 in 2009.[11]

ANTICIPATING FUTURE DEVELOPMENTS OF THE GERMAN LIFT MARKET

The current uptake in demand from 2009 to 2010 is explained by the short-term effects of the economic recovery of the real-estate industry following the 2008 financial crisis, legal changes in terms of environmental protection (revision of the VDI Guideline 2566) and safety concerns (EN 81, Parts 1 and 2), as well as speculation concerning the socio-demographic development of Germany.

Demand for lifts in Germany in terms of new installations was further increased by the shortened product life cycle as a result of a reduction in durability of standardized lifts. This reduction of lifetime due to the increased usage of wear-and-tear components allows the "Big Four" to firstly produce cheaper products, secondly to increase constant demand, and thirdly to reduce the importance of the service and after-sales segment; together, these changes enable the achievement of greater economies of scale. The reduced life cycle is often in accordance with the demand for the lowest possible price levels of general constructors facing severe price pressures; these constructors are only liable for cost and maintenance of newly constructed real estate for five years, and consequently have little to no concern for long-term costs.

The global lift market is dominated by six corporations, the "Big Four" present in Germany, and Mitsubishi (8 % of global new constructions) and Hitachi (6 %).[12] The two Asian global players continue to focus on their domestic growth markets as the margins and, implicitly, the profitability of the German lift market has continuously decreased over recent years. This makes a market entry for a completely new company very difficult. It is, therefore, doubtful that any new global players would enter the market, further supporting the ongoing consolidation process.

KRUGER SYSTEMS: EXITING THE INDUSTRY OR RESTRUCTURING THE BUSINESS MODEL

After an intense round of discussions, Walter Kruger left the conference room more indecisive than before. Sitting down in his office with Kruger Systems' head of engineering, Martin Schenker, and his accountant, Alexandra Geller, two long-time colleagues he had been working with for over 20 years, Walter recapitulated the two proposals Nolan had made on behalf of the bank's client.

"He pushed strongly to fully acquire and integrate our firm", Walter said, before adding that, "He did not give me a precise figure, but indicated that they would pay us a basic fee for the production site and the lifetime value of all service contracts we currently hold." Alexandra replied that, "This is usually the discounted cash flow of the service contracts, so about €2,750 per contract on average". "But what would that mean for us?" Martin asked. "He said that they would try to keep most of our technical staff on, but let's be honest, a year after the sale most of our staff would be gone - both technical and administrative", Walter said, thinking that, while this was the most lucrative offer, seeing his grandfather's company disappear after all these years would feel a lot like defeat.

"Did he not offer anything else?" Martin asked, giving Alexandra a concerned look. "After he got the feeling that I did not take kindly to the idea of giving up the company name, he offered something else", Walter replied. "They offered to make us part of their second brand network, so we would be able to keep the name for at least 25 more years and most of our staff, all the mechanics, actually." "Would they pay the same amount?" Alexandra inquired. "They would pay the same for the service contracts, but the fee for the site would be significantly lower." "So, to summarize, you would get less money, we would have to use their materials that none of our guys have ever worked with because they hardly ever sold them to us in the past when we needed them to repair one of their lifts, and you would have to report to some manager in a suit who had never touched a screwdriver in his life?", Martin asked sarcastically; "Your grandfather's name might still be on the door, but what would actually be inside?" "Look Martin, I never said I wanted to sell, but things are not looking good", Walter responded.

"Is there nothing else we could do?" Alexandra asked, "The association suggested getting in contact with the supplier from India. They offer low prices, which could make us competitive again!" But Martin immediately intervened by saying that, "Their lifts are basically made from plastic. This would be even worse than working with the material from the 'Big Four'. Our guys already dislike our current systems from China that we use for standardized projects. Remember the days when the two of us would produce the cabin ourselves, Walter? Those were real lifts that lasted for 30 years, not for 10 like these cheap ones."

"You are right, Martin", Walter said, nodding, "but do you know what it costs to produce them in our workshop? We are too expensive anyway; there is not a chance we could compete with our old methods. Times have changed and we need to make a decision before it is made for us." "But what about that inclined lift for the museum last month? That one you guys made yourselves in the workshop, and it made a huge profit", Alexandra said, pointing towards the assembly timeline hanging behind Walter's desk. "The profit was so high because we were the only ones that could do it. The 'Big Four' only want to sell their standardized lifts and the small ones do not have the expertise or staff that we have, but those contracts are few and far between. When was the last time we ever did a project like that? I am afraid that those would not be enough to keep us going", Walter mused.

"Well, there is always one last option", Martin said to their surprise. "I would hate to see the guys leave, but if we closed the new installation segment and only serviced our contracts, we should be fine." "I also thought about that," Walter agreed, "but it would mean that 80 % of our staff would be expendable overnight, and how long would it last before we are out of service contracts if we don't add any from the new installation segment? Five, 10, maybe 15 years if we are lucky?" "Is there nothing else we could do?" Alexandra wanted to know. Wearily, Walter looked from Martin to Alexandra before replying: "Nothing that I can think of. But Nolan wants an answer by the end of the week.

•••

Setting of the case: 2014; last revision: 2014.

NOTES

[1] We consider the terms 'lift' and 'elevator' as synonyms. For this case study, the term 'lift' has been chosen.

[2] IMU-Institut Stuttgart, (IMU) (2007): *Aufzüge und Fahrtreppen - Branche im Wandel*. Untersuchung zur Situation und Entwicklung der Branche Aufzüge und Fahrtreppen. Frankfurt: IG Metall Vorstand.

[3] European Commission, (EC) (1995): European Parliament and Council Directive 95/16/EC of 29 June 1995 on the Approximation of the Laws of the Member States Relating to Lifts. Retrieved [14/04/2012] from [http://eur-lex.europa.eu/LexUriServ/LexUriServ.do?uri=CELEX:31995L0016:EN:HTML].

[4] IMU-Institut Stuttgart, (IMU) (2007): *Aufzüge und Fahrtreppen - Branche im Wandel*. Untersuchung zur Situation und Entwicklung der Branche Aufzüge und Fahrtreppen. Frankfurt: IG Metall Vorstand.

[5] Credit Suisse, (2012): Elevators & Escalators. Retrieved [07/09/2014], from [https://doc.research-and-analytics.csfb.com/docView?language=ENG&source=emfromsendlink&format=PDF&document_id=962627281&extdocid=962627281_1_eng_pdf&serialid=irkdP8eoVZINsrKeYGDHCXYVx3eYo7pmfvq7CV5VmR0%3D].

[6] Verband Deutscher Maschinen- und Anlagenbau e.V., (VDMA) (2011): *Konjunkturticker Juli 2011*. Frankfurt: VDMA Verlag.

[7] European Union, (EU) (2007): Competition: Commission Fines Members of Lifts and Escalators Cartels Over €990 Million. Retrieved [13/04/2012], from [http://europa.eu/rapid/pressReleasesAction.do?reference=IP/07/209].

[8] Dresdner Bank, (2007): *Branchen-Report Hebezeuge und Fördermittel*.

[9] Verband Deutscher Maschinen- und Anlagenbau e.V., (VDMA) (2004-2011). *Konjunkturticker and Daten und Fakten 2004-2011*. Frankfurt: VDMA Verlag.

[10] Verband Deutscher Maschinen- und Anlagenbau e.V., (VDMA) (2004-2011). *Konjunkturticker and Daten und Fakten 2004-2011*. Frankfurt: VDMA Verlag.

[11] Verband Deutscher Maschinen- und Anlagenbau e.V. (VDMA), (2010): *Daten und Fakten 2010*. Frankfurt: VDMA Verlag; IMU-Institut Stuttgart, (IMU) (2007): Aufzüge und Fahrtreppen - Branche im Wandel. Untersuchung zur Situation und Entwicklung der Branche Aufzüge und Fahrtreppen. Frankfurt: IG Metall Vorstand.

[12] Credit Suisse (2012). Elevators & Escalators. Retrieved [07/09/2014], from [https://doc.research-and-analytics.csfb.com/docView?language=ENG&source=emfromsendlink&format=PDF&document_id=962627281&extdocid=962627281_1_eng_pdf&serialid=irkdP8eoVZINsrKeYGDHCXYVx3eYo7pmfvq7CV5VmR0%3D].

4

Modomoto vs. Outfittery - A Fierce Fight to free Men from their Shopping Pains

Svenja Clever and Roberto González Amor

On a nice and sunny Friday morning in Berlin, Kai Kruse, a business consultant currently analysing the market for curated shopping in Germany, is walking to his office alongside the picturesque Landwehr Kanal, and is absorbed in his thoughts. During today's breakfast he browsed through some interviews of Corinna Powalla, the founder of MODOMOTO, an e-commerce venture which delivers curated outfits to men who wish to avoid the stress of shopping for new styles. Impressively enough, she and her team of what is now more than 150 employees have managed to clothe more than 150,000 men in the last two and a half years.

Powalla has managed to establish MODOMOTO as an innovative player in the growing online fashion market. Simultaneously, however, a competitor by the name of OUTFITTERY has equalled if not outperformed MODOMOTO's track record over the past two years. Both players are competing fiercely to dominate the market for curated shopping. Over the last few months, MODOMOTO has fallen behind OUTFITTERY's commercial performance. Thus, Kai wonders what MODOMOTO's next moves will be in order to regain a competitive edge over its arch-competitor as quickly as possible.

THE EMERGENCE OF CURATED ONLINE SHOPPING

The Rise of Fashion E-commerce

The year 2014 marks the 20th anniversary of Amazon's founding. Over these years, e-commerce has developed from a marginal phenomenon into a massive market. The fashion industry has participated in e-commerce development since the early days. For example, first-class online fashion players like ASOS, Net-a-Porter and Yoox were all launched in 2000. In Germany, however, online fashion remained more or less on the fringes until Zalando revolutionized the market from 2009 onwards. Through aggressive TV placements, Zalando encouraged Germans to shop for fashion online, offering them a wide range of top brands, comfortable invoice payment, as well as free delivery and return policies. This offer turned into a huge commercial success. In 2012, only four years after being founded, Zalando exceeded one billion euros in revenue, marking a one-of-a-kind growth story.

While many customers appeared to appreciate the new experience of shopping online, the shortcomings of Zalando and other mass-market fashion e-tailers became apparent:

> "[…] consumers are frustrated with the process of discovering products. It's easy [to] browse through a physical store, but searching millions of items online is overwhelming. Even if you know you want to buy a black pair of shoes, you still end up with thousands of options. Discovering products that are right for you remains challenging." Elizabeth Knopf, former investment associate and co-founder of Sorced (The Business of Fashion, 2012).[1]

To address this need and simplify the shopping experience for overwhelmed customers, curated shopping ventures have emerged. Simply put, these firms arrange personalized outfits for their online customers, hence connecting online shopping with classic brick-and-mortar retailing. Both MODOMOTO and OUTFITTERY have spearheaded this curated shopping approach.

The Curated Shopping Business Model

Men are at the core of both MODOMOTO's and OUTFITTERY's business. As Corinna puts it, "[a]lmost everyone can relate to the fact that men do not like to go shopping". Similarly, OUTFITTERY's co-founder Anna claims to "take the pain out of shopping for men". Both firms aim to clothe their male-only customers, while sparing them the hassle of having to visit offline stores or searching for clothes online.

To this end, customers pass through a three-step process: (1) determining their style, (2) having style-appropriate outfits delivered and (3) returning unwanted items (see **Figure 4.1**).

Source: OUTFITTERY, 2014

Figure 4.1: The process of curated shopping from a customer's perspective

First, customers start by creating their own profile on a provider's website. They state their clothing size, favourite colours, brands and preferred styles (e.g., casual or chic).

Next, customers are contacted by a designated personal stylist (via telephone or mail), who creates a customized clothing selection for each customer. Then, the stylist sends a personally curated box of up to three outfits to the customer by mail. At home, customers try on the items they have had delivered and keep the ones they like. Finally, customers return the items they do not wish to buy (at no charge) and pay for the items they have kept.

As such, customers do not have to devote much time to shopping, but are still offered up-to-date and customized styles. Additionally, customers will benefit from sticking over time with their provider, as their stylist grasps the customer's taste increasingly well. In particular, returns help to understand customers' tastes and preferences. Simultaneously, stylists and buyers continuously develop the outfit stock to maximize customer satisfaction.

> "Our purchasing department is anxious to continuously spot new brands and maintains a personal contact with the manufacturers. This direct collaboration and our own stock […] provide many advantages for the customer: Our stylists work closely with the merchandise which enables them to harmoniously combine clothes with respect to fabric quality, colors and the cut of the garment." Corinna Powalla, founder of MODOMOTO (Für Gründer, 2014).[2]

Contrary to what one might think, women are far from irrelevant in the curated shopping process. On the contrary, seeking a well-dressed partner, they register their boyfriends or spouses online to be properly outfitted. Additionally, women play a key role in finally deciding which items to keep and which ones to return.

Financially, curated shopping providers benefit from attractive order economics. Customers receive packages worth up to €600-800. Although returns are a calculated component of the business, customers keep on average €250-300 worth of clothing, compensating for return costs. Additionally, both the curated shopping businesses offer mostly upmarket brands like Tiger of Sweden, Tommy Hilfiger or Scotch & Soda, which are not discounted and thus offer lucrative profit margins in return for curated services. On the other hand, service providers have to finance a considerable amount of working capital, important for getting access to and stocking clothing. These inventories face the imminent risk of having to be depreciated if they are not sold during their current season. Moreover, offering customers the option to pay via invoice entails substantial burdens in terms of accounts receivable (see **Table 4.1**).

	FY 2012			
	OUTFITTERY		MODOMOTO	
ASSETS	in k EUR	(in % of total assets)	in k EUR	(in % of total assets)
Non-current assets	10	1%	7	1%
Intangible assets	2	0%		
Property, plant and equipment	8	1%	7	1%
Current assets	1.000	99%	514	98%
Inventories	360	36%	216	41%
Accounts receivable and other assets	586	58%	112	21%
Cash and cash equivalents	54	5%	186	36%
Accruals and deferrals	2	0%	1	0%
TOTAL ASSETS	1.012	100%	523	100%

EQUITY AND LIABILITIES	in k EUR	(in % of total equity & liabilities)	in k EUR	(in % of total equity & liabilities)
Equity	433	43%	272	52%
Subscribed capital	52	5%	25	5%
Capital reserves	1.002	99%	400	76%
Profit/loss carried forward			-7	-1%
Net income/loss of the year	-620	-61%	-146	-28%
Special reserve item			8	2%
Provisions	318	31%	22	4%
Liabilities	261	26%	220	42%
TOTAL EQUITY AND LIABILITIES	1.012	100%	523	100%

Source: Unternehmensregister, 2014

Table 4.1: The protagonists' balance sheets

THE COMPETITIVE HISTORY: MODOMOTO vs. OUTFITTERY

Q4/2011-Q2/2012: Launch

In October 2011, Corinna founded MODOMOTO, the first German curated shopping venture. Being founder, CEO and stylist all in one, she ran MODOMOTO from her kitchen table in Berlin Kreuzberg. The idea for her start-up emerged out of her relationship. At that time, she found herself regularly doing the shopping for her shopping-reluctant boyfriend - buying clothes, delivering them to him, advising him on the styles and returning undesired items. Noticing that her boyfriend's traits were not uncommon for men, she decided to relieve a wider range of men of their shopping troubles.

In December 2011, her vision of clothing Germany's grouchy shoppers finally materialized with the launch of the MODOMOTO website. To build the business, the now 34-year-old entrepreneur relied on her studies in business administration and prior work experience in e-commerce. In particular, she spent one and a half years at Mister Spex, a German eyewear e-tailer, where she gained insights into online marketing and business intelligence. Having moved to Berlin during her studies, Corinna has become

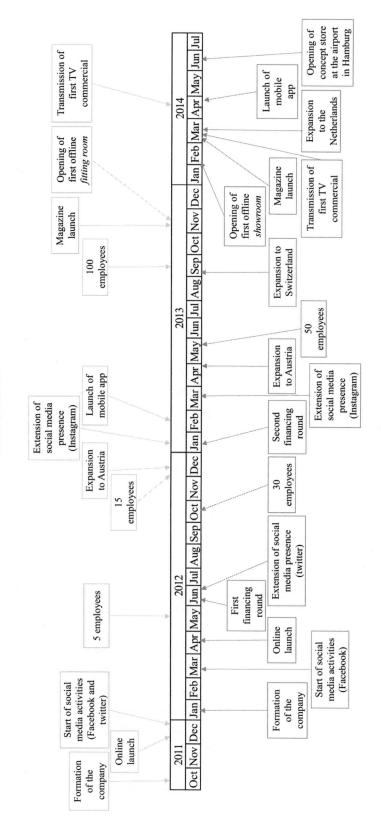

Figure 4.2: Timeline of the protagonists' competitive moves

fascinated by the Berlin start-up scene, and is convinced that there is no better place for MODOMOTO to be based.

> "[I]n Berlin you can find an interesting blend of tradition and innovations. Also, Berlin is the perfect place to launch a start-up. The structures are open and the scene is ambitious, dynamic and creative. [...] [I]t is inspiring and helpful to compare and share experiences with each other. It has been easy for me as a woman to become an entrepreneur and I appreciate how founders are willing to support each other. The capacity for innovation and the entrepreneurial enthusiasm in Berlin never cease to fascinate me." Corinna Powalla, (Webmagazin, 2014)[3]

In January 2012, one month after the launch of MODOMOTO, Anna Alex and Julia Bösch co-founded OUTFITTERY, located like MODOMOTO in Berlin Kreuzberg. The two female entrepreneurs both studied business and economics and met afterwards in Berlin, where they started their professional careers. Anna and Julia, both currently aged around 30, joined Rocket Internet, an aggressively ambitious e-commerce-focused venture capital firm and start-up incubator. Subsequently, Julia assisted in creating Zalando's growth story as head of international business development (Zalando was initially launched by Rocket Internet). Nonetheless, both Anna and Julia felt the imminent urge to build a venture of their own, lacking, however, a compelling idea. Finally, Julia became inspired by her boyfriend's excitement over a personal shopping assistant whose services he tried out while holidaying in New York. This led subsequently to the formation of OUTFITTERY. In April 2012, the website went live, five months after MODOMOTO's launch. Like Corinna, Anna and Julia purposefully chose to locate their start-up in Berlin, though highlighting more pragmatic reasons. They see Berlin as the perfect place for their start-up since such a cultural metropolis provides many opportunities for talent acquisition, especially when it comes to finding skilful fashion stylists.

Q2/2012-Q1/2013: Proof of Concept

MODOMOTO was, on the one hand, eager to increase awareness of its service by stressing its unique selling proposition. For this purpose, Corinna decided to rely heavily on inexpensive viral marketing through MODOMOTO's Facebook and Twitter channels. She recognized that MODOMOTO offered a service that men apparently liked to talk about with their friends, acquaintances and colleagues. This contributed to the advantage that the customers took care of the marketing themselves by sharing their experiences and prompting others to try the service for themselves. Additionally, the concept received huge media attention, boosting the awareness of MODOMOTO's brand. This strategy, combined with a very lean structure of the business operations, spurred the company's growth, which was financially backed by business angels, two affluent German businessmen. Operationally, however, MODOMOTO kept all its processes in-house so as to be in full control of an efficient process design. In times of rapid growth, these in-house logistical processes proved to be difficult to scale, requiring Corinna and her team to cope with bottlenecks to satisfy the ever-increasing demand. Corinna disclosed in an interview that her focus does not lie in the number but rather the quality of acquired customers, namely those who consume larger amounts of goods at a time and who return with a high frequency (i.e., existing customers receive a box every three to four months).

OUTFITTERY, on the other hand, made an effort to scale up its business rapidly by collecting more than a million euros in funding from several e-commerce-focused venture capital firms, among them Holtzbrinck Ventures (an early investor in Zalando) in June 2012. By the end of 2012, OUTFITTERY's capital reserves stood at a million euros, 150% north of MODOMOTO's €400,000 (see **Table 4.1**). In turn, a large number of employees were hired to accomplish future growth plans. Operationally, OUTFITTERY put considerable focus on scalability and outsourced the box packaging and part of its stock-keeping. In order to compete with MODOMOTO's image and reputation advantages, OUTFITTERY continued to call attention to its distinctive service via social media activities. For example, all OUTFITTERY stylists will add their customers on Facebook in order to get additional insights and be better able to assess their preferences. With provocative and bold slogans like "Dear gentlemen of BCG, we are your quick win when it comes to fashion", OUTFITTERY not only approaches potential customers within certain corporations but also demonstrates what kind of customers it values the most: a target group of well-off men with time-consuming professional lives.

Over the course of their first year, both MODOMOTO and OUTFITTERY were able to prove the soundness of their businesses. Meanwhile, a third rival by the name of Modemeister went out of business early 2013, only one year after being founded. However, this did not come as much of a surprise, given its lack of customer focus and process quality. For example, Modemeister performed miserably in a test by the renowned German *Manager Magazin*, not delivering an order even after three customer follow-ups. In contrast, MODOMOTO and OUTFITTERY acquired thousands of customers and were in turn able to attract external funding for future growth. As a further sign of their early success, both companies were named "Start-up of the Year 2012". While the E-Star trading congress chose to acknowledge MODOMOTO's achievement, OUTFITTERY was honoured by the leading online start-up magazine *Gründerszene*. Hence, both companies knew they had done well so far, but they also recognized that they were not the only player setting out to dominate curated shopping.

Q1/2013-Today: Battle for Market Leadership

To spur further growth, MODOMOTO took a range of initiatives. Primarily, it chose to expand into Austria in December 2012, adding a new source of potential customers. One month later, in January 2013, MODOMOTO established new social media channels (e.g., Instagram) to enhance picture-based and thus emotional communication with customers. In February 2013, MODOMOTO launched its own app to capitalize on the rising mobile commerce market. Broadening the service to mobile devices turned out to be imperative, as more and more customers began to prefer to get things done on the move and make efficient use of idle time.

MODOMOTO's growth initiatives, however, did not go unnoticed, that is, it did not take long for OUTFITTERY to follow: by March 2013, it had occupied the same social media channels as MODOMOTO, and by April 2013, OUTFITTERY's website was live in Austria as well. Within three to four months, OUTFITTERY had retightened on two major MODOMOTO initiatives. By then, OUTFITTERY served a customer base of approximately 50,000 with a workforce of 50 employees. On top, a second financing round provided OUTFITTERY with a (rumoured) additional four million Euros in January 2013. By gaining Mangrove Capital Partners as a lead investor, OUTFITTERY added a further Internet and e-commerce-affine venture capital firm to its portfolio of investors and stakeholders, contributing its online expertise from prior engagements including Skype and Brands4Friends. OUTFITTERY utilized these additional funds to take its European expansion to the next level. In September 2013, it launched its Swiss website, and later, in March 2014, its Dutch presence took off. Its next targets on the map are Scandinavia, Italy, Latvia and Belgium; markets for which OUTFITTERY is now heavily recruiting talent. As such, OUTFITTERY not only met MODOMOTO's initial internationalization initiative, but also aggressively expanded its own European footprint.

Meanwhile, MODOMOTO deployed its resources to grow further in its home market, Germany. In November 2013, Corinna and her team decided to add a brick-and-mortar component to their online business and presented the first MODOMOTO offline store, called *Fitting Room*, located in Berlin Mitte. This business extension has been well-received among its customers, allowing them to physically experience the curated shopping service on request in an exclusive environment.

> "[Fitting Room] opens up solely for individual customers that have arranged an appointment and is not accessible for walk-in customers during that time. The stylist then has the extra time to cater for the distinct customer's needs. And the customer experiences the calmness to try everything on while enjoying a coffee or a cold beer." Corinna Powalla (Für Gründer, 2014).[4]

Another means to retain customers was established via the *MODOMOTO Letter* in November 2013. This in-house magazine informs existing customers not only about the latest fashion and styling trends, but also provides behind-the-scenes reports about the curated shopping provider itself. By December 2013, MODOMOTO had acquired more than 50,000 customers with a workforce of by then more than 100 people.

However, once again, MODOMOTO's attempts to outcompete its main rival did not go unnoticed. In early 2014, OUTFITTERY managed to acquire an additional record sum of €13 million from its investors that were joined by US-based Highland Capital Partners, which has further stakes in French fashion e-tailer Spartoo and successful fashion businesses like Lululemon. Consequently, the well-funded OUTFITTERY first equalled MODOMOTO's earlier initiatives, launching an offline shop, S*howroom*, in early 2014, only three months after MODOMOTO's. In March 2014, it sent out its first magazine, *OUTFITTERY Magazin*, developed by its in-house editorial team, similar to the one MODOMOTO had initiated for its customers five months before. Far from being a competitive response, it is argued that:

> "The idea for the magazine was provided by a good friend of mine. He expressed how he would love to browse through and get inspired by a magazine on Sunday afternoons, while recovering from last night's hangover. He made clear that he would be induced to shop based on the magazine; hence, we tried it out." Julia Bösch, co-founder of OUTFITTERY (Gründerszene, 2014)[5]

Similar to MODOMOTO, the showroom offers customers the chance to drop in and receive styling advice on the spot, while the magazine is intended to inspire existing customers, featuring photo series of current fashion highlights and editorials on how-to and celebrity styles. Taking its offline approach further, OUTFITTERY opened a concept store at the airport in Hamburg in June 2014. Thus, business travellers are able to be comfortably outfitted by fashion experts at the airport shop before checking in, and so efficiently make the most of their waiting time. The selected clothes are subsequently sent to the customer's home address, ensuring the greatest possible comfort.

To further push new customer acquisition, OUTFITTERY chose to boost its brand awareness by broadcasting its first TV advertisement in 2014. Throughout these advertisements, OUTFITTERY claims that, "Real men wouldn't go shopping, even if they had the time to", and, "Real men let others do the shopping". Provocatively, a wider audience is encouraged to go for curated shopping (see **Figure 4.3**). The human resource intensive business model (especially in the form of style experts) made it necessary for OUTFITTERY to invest in mass communications in order to extend its customer reach. Shortly afterwards, OUTFITTERY proclaimed that it had reached the mark of 100,000 customers. Apart from all these measures to grow its business, OUTFITTERY's substantial resource endowment further allows the company to implement customer friendly policies, such as giving its customers 21 days to pay their invoices. MODOMOTO's invoices, on the contrary, are due for payment only five days after its customers receive them.

> (https://www.youtube.com/watch?v=DO_hi8vywkI)
>
> The TV commercial stars actor Simon Böer, known from his appearances in for example "Polizeiruf 110", "Elementarteilchen" or "Agnes und seine Brüder".
>
> "If I had a whole day free to myself, I would love to just go shopping…" the actor says and breaks out in laughter afterwards. "Forget to go shopping. The OUTFITTERY style experts consult you free of charge and send you exactly the clothes that suit you the most." is OUTFITTERY's reply. Briefly speaking, the commercial features a testimonial that highlights the fact that men don't want to sacrifice their free time to take care of necessary shopping and presents OUTFITTERY as the ultimate solution to this problem.
>
> (Source: Youtube, 2014a)

Figure 4.3: OUTFITTERY's TV commercial

In April 2014, one month after OUTFITTERY's TV spot went on air, MODOMOTO answered with its own TV campaign, under the title, "The agony of choice" (see **Figure 4.4**). In the 20-second advertisement, MODOMOTO presents itself as the solution for men to the problem of failing to pick the perfect outfit. Television was thought to be the most appropriate communication channel as it allows for the reaching of an audience that is not online-affine, or that has not yet gained experience of the service of curated shopping. Up to this point, MODOMOTO had more than 100,000 customers.

> (https://www.youtube.com/watch?v=JrwEGxKWrBw)
>
> "Out there are millions of pants, shirts and shoes but only some that really look good on you. That is why there is MODOMOTO now. Style experts put together your individual perfect outfits – free of charge and non-committally. You only keep what you like." is the content that MODOMOTO advertises.
>
> In contrast to OUTFITTERY, MODOMOTO's commercial emphasizes how men tend to choose the wrong clothing items out of the massive offerings available and presents MODOMOTO as the ultimate solution to this problem.
>
> (Source: Youtube, 2014b)

Figure 4.4: MODOMOTO's TV commercial

Both companies expended huge efforts to increase awareness of their own services and thus to extend the market, or to lure customers away from their rivals. This enthusiasm fostered the formation of creative service developments like OUTFITTERY's offer, as of April 2014, to spontaneously provide expert styling advice as a response to someone adding a "selfie" on twitter with the addition of @outfittery #styleme. Furthermore, OUTFITTERY launched its own iOS app for portable devices in April 2014, facilitating the communication between customers and their personal stylists through, e.g., shared wish lists. By contrast, MODOMOTO engaged in offline cooperation with consumer goods companies. For instance, every MODOMOTO box sent out in April 2014 contained a limited edition set of shaving supplies from Gillette.

OUTLOOK: WHAT HORSE SHOULD MODOMOTO BET ON?

Up until April 2014, both curated shopping providers were at eye level when it came to acquired customers (see **Figure 4.5**). Nevertheless, comparing their search traffic on Google and their follower bases on the various social media channels indicates that OUTFITTERY has recently outpaced MODOMOTO in its efforts to build an outstanding brand (see **Figures 4.6** and **4.7**).

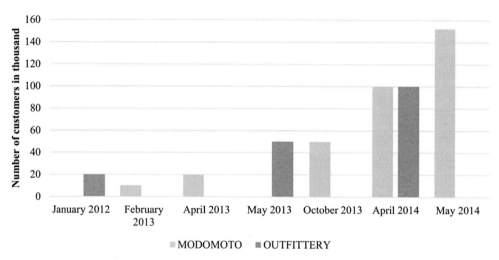

Source: Own illustration compiled from Berliner Morgenpost (2014), Carpathia (2013), Crinox (2013), Deutsche Apps (2013), Für-Gründer (2014), Gründerszene (2013), High-Tech Gründerfonds (2013), Manager Magazin (2014), Webmagazin (2014)

Figure 4.5: Customer accounts acquired and/or served (missing bars: no information disclosed)

Kai is certain that such a niche market cannot be occupied by many players at a time which will most likely result in market consolidation and a continuing battle for market dominance among surviving firms. Therefore, he is eager to find the recipe for success in this young branch of the fashion industry and initially focuses on past and potential future developments of the largest competitors. In order to be well-prepared for the kick-off meeting with his client in a few days, Kai thinks it would be best to discuss some of his thoughts with Susanne Drillich, a senior consultant working in his team. Still having Powalla's words in mind, Kai reflects upon possible reasons leading to MODOMOTO's current market position. "I believe that the realization of MODOMOTO's innovative ideas during the last year largely contributed to making the service and its brand more visible.

So maybe they have just been too passive this year?" He suggests while sipping his coffee. "My opinion is that OUTFITTERY simply ran MODOMOTO down. It has been extremely fast in imitating MODOMOTO's strategic moves and simultaneously introduced its own innovations. So far, MODOMOTO has just not been able to keep up with the scope, amount and speed of OUTFITTERY's competitive initiatives," replies Susanne.

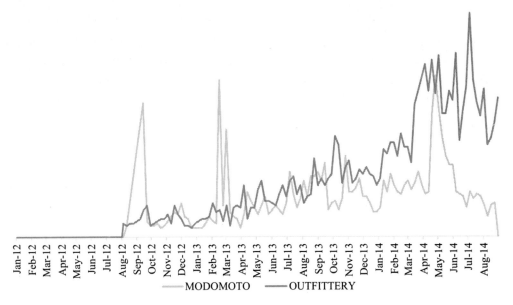

Source: Google trends, as of 26/08/2014

Figure 4.6: Interest over time - index of search traffic on Google

"I am right there with you", agrees Kai, "but we have to keep in mind that OUTFITTERY hugely benefits from its size and resources at hand. The fact that its attacks against MODOMOTO were strongest right after the completion of its financing rounds shows how dependent it is on external funding to continue its escalating approach to competing with them. I am sure that MODOMOTO can beat OUTFITTERY if it manages to create brand awareness for its service in the mass market." Susanne quietly ponders over what Kai has just said. „What would be the consequences of this?", she thinks, and subsequently discloses her thoughts to Kai. "Don't you think that this attention would also attract indirect competitors like Zalando, Amazon or offline retailers, make them enter the market and offer curated shopping solutions in addition to their existing services? The larger MODOMOTO gets, the more they lose the added value of personalized consultation in the eyes of the customer. Although these large-scale enterprises would have to set up the necessary processes from scratch, I think they are seriously worth to be considered in our analyses."

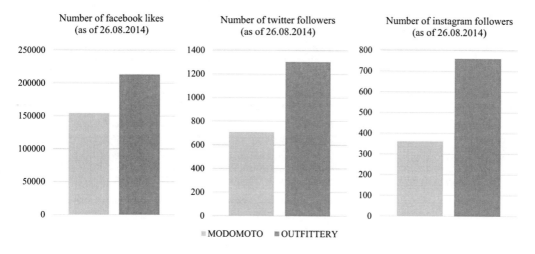

Figure 4.7: Social media attention

"You have a point", Kai answers; "these big players definitely represent a threat, and they will be more dangerous the more the market grows. They have a reputation, capital resources and lots of know-how, but MODOMOTO and the like are much more flexible and still have the chance to impede the market entry for them." After a short pause, he continues: "And what do you think about potential competitors like Kisura, the curated shopping service for women? Or other direct competitors like 8select, who have targeted men with curated services since early 2013? Are these players worthy of being included in in-depth analyses too?" asks Kai. "No, I don't think so" is Susanne's response, "they are too small to harm the existing and successful providers at the moment. I believe that crucial rivalry can mainly be expected between MODOMOTO and OUTFITTERY. I saw this morning that OUTFITTERY is heavily recruiting marketing personnel as well as people for its ongoing international expansion. What do you think could be MODOMOTO's response to these hints and in the light of all we know right now?"

Over the next two hours, Kai and Susanne comment on various options. Among other things, they ask themselves whether some players will pin their hopes on cooperation with offline retailers. In this manner, for instance, the US-curated shopping service Trunk Club was just acquired by American retail behemoth Nordstrom. Would such cooperation with an offline retailer provide MODOMOTO with the resources necessary to keep OUTFITTERY at bay for good?

•••

Setting of the case: 2014; last revision: 2014.

NOTES

1. The Business of Fashion, (2012): *E-commerce week – The stage is set for an e-commerce explosion*, URL: http://www.businessoffashion.com/2012/01/e-commerce-week-the-stage-is-set-for-an-e-commerce-explosion.html, 09.08.2014.

2. Für-Gründer, (2014): *Modomoto zieht an und kleidet Shoppingmuffel ein*, URL: http://www.fuer-gruender.de/blog/2014/05/modomoto-curated-shopping/, 27.06.2014.

3. Webmagazin, (2014): *Curated shopping in Berlin: An interview with Modomoto founder Corinna Powalla*, URL: http://webmagazin.de/en/Curated-shopping-in-Berlin-An-interview-with-Modomoto-founder-Corinna-Powalla-173745, 09.08.2014.

4. Gründerszene, (2014): *Wir haben schon absolut den Nerv der Zeit getroffen*, URL: http://www.gruenderszene.de/allgemein/outfittery-julia-boesch, accessed 22 July, 2014.5

5. Für-Gründer, (2014): *Modomoto zieht an und kleidet Shoppingmuffel ein*, URL: http://www.fuer-gruender.de/blog/2014/05/modomoto-curated-shopping, accessed 27 June, 2014.

5

Bringing Henkel Shared Services to the next Level – The Contribution of Shared Services to the Company Target Achievement 2012

Andreas Fries

HENKEL'S CHALLENGES IN 2008

November 2008. Mark Jennings, Global Head of Financial Operations at Henkel, played around with the numbers in his head. They made him feel excited, anxious and, at times, a little bit dizzy. "How on earth are we going to achieve this?" he muttered to himself. Just a few days ago, Kasper Rorsted, the company's fresh CEO, together with Lothar Steinebach, CFO, had announced new four-year Henkel company targets for 2012. At an analyst meeting in London, following a mediocre business year, the two board members were expected to justify the firm's failure to achieve their announced targets. The company stakeholders were disappointed. With the stock price in a slump, the analyst community was already compiling some sarcastic comments on the weak performance of the company.

However, it turned out to be a turnaround moment for Henkel. Rather than looking back and talking about missed achievements, Rorsted and Steinebach focused on the way ahead. With natural confidence, they laid out an ambitious plan for Henkel for the next four years. The path was summarized in new strategic priorities, which were quantified through three financial targets for 2012 (see **Figure 5.1**):

1. Organic sales growth of 3-5 % per year
2. Adjusted EBIT-margin of 14 % by the end of 2012
3. Earnings per share growth of more than 10 % per year

HENKEL UNTIL 2008

At the beginning of the company's history, we meet a 28-year-old merchant who was interested in science: Fritz Henkel. On 26th September, 1876, he and two partners founded the company Henkel & Cie in Aachen and marketed their first product, a universal detergent based on silicate. During the following years, this German family of entrepreneurs and thousands of their employees built Henkel into a global company.

Figure 5.1: Kasper Rorsted announced targets 2012

By the 1920s, Henkel, based in Düsseldorf, Germany, had become a leading German detergent producer, expanding its portfolio into adhesives. Following Fritz Henkel's death in 1930, the company shares were equally distributed to his three children. Even today, the family holds the majority of company shares. After the Second World War, with many of the company locations and resources destroyed, Henkel reopened several plants and started selling personal and beauty care products in addition to detergents and adhesives. In the subsequent years, Henkel professionalized its business and launched the first ever German TV advertisement for its flagship brand, Persil.

By 2008, global sales had grown to more than €14 billion: the majority coming from the EMEA region (63 %), followed by North America (19 %), Asia Pacific (11 %), Latin America (5 %) and Corporate Sales (2 %). Henkel was organized in three business units: (1) Laundry and Home Care (30 % of sales) sold detergents and related home care products, with brands such as Persil, Purex and Pril; (2) Beauty Care (21 % of sales) produced and marketed personal care products such as shampoos, hair colouring, skin creams, deodorants and toothpaste, both in the retail sector as well as for professional hair salons; and (3) Adhesives Technologies (47 % of overall sales in 2008) sold sealants and industrial adhesives to, e.g., the automotive, electronics, transportation and construction industries. The portfolio also covered consumer adhesives, such as the famous Pritt Stick or Loctite superglue (see **Figure 5.2**).

Although all three business units operated in a highly competitive environment, the positioning of Henkel in the respective industry and the business models differed greatly. For adhesives, Henkel was a global market leader with the highest share in a mostly B2B-structured and highly fragmented market. The only comparable player acting with a large diversified adhesives portfolio was American-based 3M, famous for its Post-it products, and renowned for high-end quality solutions (industrial and consumer adhesives, operating in 60 countries, sales of €18.1 billion, operating/EBIT margin at 20.7 %). Other peers in the adhesive market included Beiersdorf (Tesa), Sika and PPG, acting more as specialists in their own field. However, Henkel was a smaller player on the global consolidated detergents and cosmetics B2C market. Here, the company competed with their brands Schwarzkopf and Persil against some heavyweight players such as Procter & Gamble (Laundry and Home Care, Beauty Care, operating in 180 countries, sales of €50.4 billion, operating/EBIT margin at 20.4 %), Unilever (Laundry and Home Care, Beauty Care, operating in 150 countries, sales of €40.5 billion, operating/EBIT margin at 14.3 %), L'Oréal (Beauty Care, operating in 130 countries, sales of €17.5 billion, operating/EBIT margin at 15.5 %) or Reckitt Benckiser (Laundry and Home Care, operating in 60 countries, sales of €6.7 billion, operating/EBIT margin at 23.4 %).

Figure 5.2: The Henkel portfolio

Looking at the financial performance compared to its industry peers, it was evident that Henkel was performing below its potential (see **Table 5.1**). The main competitors, such as P&G and Unilever, either outperformed Henkel based on sheer size and financial firepower, or they outran Henkel based on their strong focus on a single business field, such as L'Oréal in cosmetics or Reckitt Benckiser in the Laundry and Home Care market. This led to a situation where Henkel lagged behind the competition both in terms of total sales and sales growth in mature and, specifically, emerging markets. Furthermore, with a

10.3 % EBIT margin in 2008, Henkel's gap compared to the industry leaders was huge. P&G, Reckitt Benckiser and 3M performed consistently above 20 %, and the remaining peers around 15 %. Less EBIT means less financial power and resources to invest into growing markets. The future looked bleak.

	2000	2001	2002	2003	2004	2005	2006	2007	2008
Total Revenue (€ millions)									
P&G	41,733	46,312	40,749	37,764	42,215	46,845	53,650	55,387	50,364
Unilever	47,582	51,514	48,270	42,693	38,566	38,401	39,642	40,187	40,523
3M	17,778	18,027	15,573	14,465	14,780	17,869	17,372	16,751	18,084
L'Oreal	12,671	13,740	14,288	14,029	13,641	14,533	15,790	17,063	17,542
Henkel	12,779	9,410[a]	9,656	9,436	10,592	11,974	12,740	13,074	14,131
Sales Growth (%)									
P&G	4.8	-1.8	2.5	7.8	18.5	10.4	20.2[c]	12.1	6.9
Unilever	16.1	8.3	-6.3	-11.6	-9.7	-0.4	3.2	1.4	0.8
3M	6.2	-4.0	1.7	11.6	9.8	5.8	8.3	6.7	3.3
L'Oreal	17.9	8.4	4.0	-1.8	-2.8	6.5	8.7	8.1	2.8
Henkel	12.5	2.2	2.6[a]	-2.3	12.3[b]	13.0	6.4	2.6	8.1
EBIT Margin (%)									
P&G	14.9	12.1	16.6	18.1	19.1	18.5	19.4	20.2	20.4
Unilever	11.1	11.2	11.8	13.1	14.9	13.2	13.6	14.5	14.3
3M	17.2	13.6	18.7	20.9	22.9	22.9	20.2	21.8	20.7
L'Oreal	12.0	11.5	12.1	12.6	15.0	15.9	16.1	16.5	15.5
Henkel	7.4	6.4	6.9	7.5	9.4	9.7	10.2	10.3	10.3

Table 5.1: Financial performance of Henkel and its competitors (2000-2008)

THE NEW STRATEGIC PRIORITIES AT HENKEL

Mark remembered the sarcastic comments of analysts and the media the days after the London analyst meeting. Specifically, the setting of the 14 % EBIT/operating profit margin made the community shake, since it was an ambitious improvement of four percentage points. This would lead to an all-time high and start closing the gap on industry peers. Hence, the most ambitious target definition came from the most fragile area, since Henkel had missed its EBIT targets regularly in the past.

Along with the financial targets, the company defined new strategic priorities which were to contribute to top-line sales and bottom-line operating profit improvements (see **Figure 5.3**). First and foremost, the company was to focus more on its customers, initiate one-to-one top management meetings between Henkel and the A-customers and establish a professional customer relationship management policy. The top managers at Henkel had realized that much time was spent internally in discussions with colleagues, rather than concentrating on the essential element: the market customer. Second, a strengthening of the global Henkel team was needed with a stronger focus on professional development and diversity, specifically in the strongly growing emerging markets. Also, a more robust performance culture was to be established. Third, an effort was needed to improve Henkel's processes and structures through achieving the full business potential of the company. This area includes a focus on portfolio optimization measures, strengthening top brands and incentivizing product and process innovations. Another contribution came from the area called operational excellence. Here lay the great hope of the company leaders that the EBIT gap of between 10 % and 14 % could be closed. Operational excellence looks at raising the internal efficiency through implementing new purchasing strategies and cost-saving projects, streamlining the global manufacturing footprint and reducing the general sales and administrative costs through the usage of outsourcing partners and an extension of shared services. With Kasper Rorsted's IT industry background prior to joining Henkel, his experience with the use of shared services and outsourcing partners had been a positive attribute. These opportunities he also saw for Henkel.

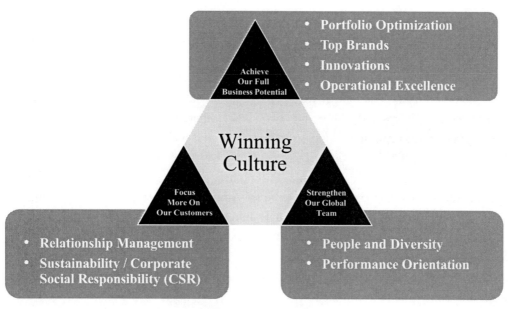

Figure 5.3: 2012 Strategic Priorities

Shared Services at Henkel until 2008

Shared services can be viewed as the provision of valuable services from a central entity, the Shared Service Centre (SSC), to different clients within a company. Its typical scope covers corporate functions such as finance and accounting, human resources, procurement, information technology, facilities and estates management. Furthermore, services can be delivered on a business unit level, such as in customer support and helplines, sales reporting, master data management or material planning. These activities are usually not highly visible at the front customer-end, but they have a major impact on the quality and efficiency of processes which the customer might perceive. As a result, the use of shared services ensures that key business processes are efficient and globally harmonized to achieve a high process quality. A seamless communication and working environment between the SSCs and local organizations is guaranteed through a common set of tools and IT applications.

The main benefits of implementing a shared services concept include the following:

- Consistent quality
- Higher flexibility and speed
- Enabling better decision making
- Simplified and standardized solutions
- Improved transparency and better compliance
- Reduced costs

In 2008, the sub-business unit of financial operations within Henkel, for which Mark Jennings was globally responsible, was organized one level below the CFO, Lothar Steinbach, who was responsible for several corporate functions such as purchasing, IT and the legal department. The unit of financial operations included the responsibility for the area of shared services and, at the time, two Henkel Shared Service Centres. It was still a rather young organization seeking to gain acceptance within the large Henkel world. Looking back at the foundations, the first Henkel-captive Shared Service Centre was established in 2003, located in Manila, Philippines, providing financial services first to Asia Pacific and later, as of 2007, also to North America. The communication was mainly based in English with some specialized resources covering the Korean and Japanese languages. In 2007, another Henkel-owned SSC was added in Bratislava, Slovakia, concentrating on providing finance activities for Western and Eastern Europe. In this market, language competencies in German, Romanic and Eastern European languages were commonly found.

The processes covered by the SSCs included:

- Purchase-to-pay: Handling accounts payables, e.g., through the receipt of supplier invoices and processing them until ready-for-payment status
- Order-to-cash: Managing accounts receivables, e.g., by allocating customer payments to the correct internal customer ledgers
- General accounting and controlling: supporting the local finance organization, e.g., through standard financial reporting

- Selected IT services: Providing IT helpdesk support to Henkel employees
- Selected HR services: HR data management or global short incentive/bonus payment calculation for the Henkel management circles

Looking at one of the abovementioned processes in more detail, one service provided by the SSC Manila to the North America region included invoice verification and payment proposal. This activity is part of the purchase-to-pay process. The overall purchase-to-pay activity is part of the purchasing process and, hence, based upon a Henkel purchase of a material or service from a third party. Upon receiving a scanned or printed invoice, the SSC processor indexed the main information into an SAP frame (e.g., supplier name, invoice amount, payment terms and local VAT/tax codes). Later, this information was compared to the data on the original purchase order, which could also be viewed within the SAP application. In the case of inconsistencies, an internal communication process was initiated by the SSC employee contacting the responsible purchasing or supply chain manager via an IT based communication tool to identify the reasons. Once clarified, the processor in the SSC signalled a ready-for-payment status to the local country treasury department in Rocky Hill or Scottsdale. Next, the local American finance organization picked up the information from the shared SAP system and concluded the purchase-to-pay process by initiating the payment to the supplier according to the payment terms agreed. As a complementary activity, an accounts-payable management was executed on a local basis. This included searching for the missing goods receipts where a supplier invoice was received, but the goods could not be found. Based upon the overall purchase-to-pay activities, an operational reporting was prepared to inform relevant agencies of the status of executed payments, the average payment terms and improvements of cash net working capital.

By the end of 2008, about 300 employees were working in the two SSCs, providing almost exclusively services in the finance area, mainly to Western Europe, North America and Asia Pacific, with a smaller share to Central Eastern Europe. The depth of the process coverage in the SSCs was far from 100 %. The finance activities were split in close cooperation between the SSC employees, selected central headquarter entities and the local country organizations in countries such as France, Italy and Spain. Moreover, the shared services coverage of other corporate functions, such as HR services or operative purchasing services, was still rather limited, to say nothing of activities coming from the three business units of Laundry and Home Care, Beauty Care and Adhesives Technologies. Such areas as business controlling, supply chain planning or customer back-end activities were not yet touched at all (see **Figure 5.4**).

Mark Jennings sat back in his office chair. He looked at the results of an industry benchmark report he had just received from a specialized consulting firm. It compared Henkel's use of shared services with that of its main industry competitors, such as Procter

& Gamble, Unilever, Beiersdorf and L'Oréal. Compared to the Anglo-American community, Henkel and most other European companies showed little shared services process coverage. Specifically, Procter & Gamble stood out with its established Global Business Services (GBS) unit. P&G GBS had been formed as an individual legal entity in 1999 through a CEO initiative, and brought together internal services such as finance, accounting, employee services, customer logistics and information technology. These were bundled into a single, global organization providing these services to all P&G business units, ranging from Global Beauty, Global Baby, Feminine and Family Care, Global Fabric and Home Care to Global Health and Grooming. P&G GBS also offered its services to the external market, competing with business process outsourcing (BPO) specialists such as Accenture, IBM, Cap Gemini and Wipro. Already in 2001, a comprehensive review revealed that P&G GBS had reached a decent market value as a standalone business unit that could compete within the BPO market.

Bratislava
- 31.12.2008: ~150 employees
- Geographical coverage: Western Europe, Eastern Europe
- Process coverage: Purchase-to-Pay, Order-to-Cash, General Accounting/ Controlling (all Finance), some IT

Manila
- 31.12.2008: ~150 employees
- Process coverage: Purchase-to-Pay, Order-to-Cash, General Accounting/Controlling (all Finance), some global HR-functions
- Geographical coverage: North America, Asia-Pacific

❱ **300 employees by the end of 2008 almost all from the Finance area**

Figure 5.4: Henkel shared services at the end of 2008

Mark Jennings sighed. The report revealed how much more potential there was in the field of shared services. He picked up the phone and called his assistant in. "Jenny, could you please set up a meeting with the heads of HR, purchasing and IT. We need to discuss the future potential of shared services within the corporate functions at Henkel. And, yes, please also include Jim, Eric and Thomas, the financial directors from our three business units. I am sure they will have some constructive ideas as well". So, one day in December 2008, the eight corporate senior vice-presidents came together to discuss new ways to extend shared services.

The Henkel Shared Services Journey From 2009-2012

Coming out of the meeting in December 2008, Mark Jennings knew it was going to take some time and a lot of persuasion to bring all his fellow management members from across Henkel on board. On that very day, the team of top managers from the corporate functions and the financial directors from the three business units had collectively decided to establish a joint Service Optimization Program (SOP) to explore future efficiency potential. However, it was not the breakthrough decision he had hoped for. A focus regarding the identification of new offshoring potential was to be put on the corporate functions, namely finance, HR, IT and purchasing. This outcome was foreseeable since the business units had little to no experience of transferring parts of their work to SSCs. They still needed to gain confidence regarding the SSC environment and that way of working. Hence, one of the first actions Mark suggested was to invite all of the group members to hold the next group meeting at the Shared Service Centre in Bratislava. He and his shared services team had to invest a great deal of time in change management activities in order to overcome the reservations of the Henkel organization. This invitation marked merely the initial activity at the start of a process to make the business units more accustomed to the idea of shared services over the next few years. In 2009 and 2010, some small lighthouse projects were launched for the business units, while the functions continued on their path to shift more and more activities to the Shared Service Centres.

At the beginning of 2011, Mark looked back with pride. Shared services had become a hot topic within the company and was at the top of the agenda of many internal meetings. The entire Henkel organization seemed prepared to bring shared services to the next level. In the subsequent months, two areas of shared service expansion were proposed to the Henkel management board and shareholders' committee, a meeting body consisting of both Henkel family members and senior managers:

1. A Process Service Optimization (PSO) initiative to identify further shared services extension potential with a focus on the Henkel business units and a complementary share of the corporate functions
2. Suggestions for how to establish a professional shared services organization managing growth in the area

The process service optimization initiative. One of the first tasks Mark Jennings and his team were given was to support the business units gathering ideas for new offshoring potential. As the field of finance had gained extensive experience in the use of shared services, his team was asked to suggest evaluation criteria. He came up with a list of factors, the most important of which are as follows:

- Degree of process standardization/harmonization: In what way could a clear rule-based process be documented so that independent members of the organization could perform the task in a consistent way? In what way is it possible to further harmonize the process activities across several countries or regions?

- Language requirements: To what degree is the use of local languages (e.g., French, Spanish, Russian) mandatory in written or spoken word?

- Customer interaction: How much direct contact is made with the external market and internal customers in the retained organization?

- Business risk: What is the potential business damage in case of mistakes or a temporary shut-down in one of the SSC locations (e.g., because of typhoons in Manila)?

- Labour availability and cost advantage: Is the employee profile locally available, and what is the salary advantage, the so-called labour arbitrage, of the SSC location?

- Degree of automation/IT requirements: How much IT is used? Is it possible to use these tools globally from different locations to perform the task?

Based on this set of criteria, the heads of the corporate functions and the financial directors from the three business units were sent back to their respective organizations. Within the next few weeks, a very intensive process was begun in the BUs with regular points of contact with Mark's transformation management team to validate ideas. As a result, the different departments came back with concrete suggestions about how to enlarge the shared services coverage. The list ranged from new ideas from the corporate functions to completely new activities coming from the business units. Some of the ideas included:

- Finance: (1) intercompany/transfer pricing accounting, including all internal accounts' receivables and payables, and general accounting activities

- Purchasing: (1) transactional order management, (2) vendor enquiry management by email and phone, (3) sourcing support and regular reporting activities

- Human resources: (1) learning, life cycle and expat transfer, and HR data management, (2) recruitment support, (3) HR support helpline for Henkel employees

- IT: (1) global service delivery, (2) reporting and Service-Level-Agreement (SLA) management and support

- Business controlling/reporting: (1) standard and ad hoc reports on the market development of Henkel brands, SBUs, regions/countries vs. main competitors

- Customer service: (1) sales order creation, invoicing, returns and commercial complaints management, (2) handling of incoming consumer requests

- Master data management: maintenance of (1) customer, (2) supplier and (3) material master data in the SAP systems

- Supply chain management: (1) coordination of the material, inventory and supply planning process, (2) support of the logistics execution and transportation planning, execution and controlling, (3) calculation of export prices

The Henkel management board was impressed. The ideas from the different departments were carefully selected, but ambitious in their implementation timelines and savings potential. To implement the suggestions, a process and service optimization (PSO) initiative was launched which was to be coordinated by Mark's shared services team. It included regular reporting to the management board regarding the status of implementation. In addition, a governance structure was formed with regular meetings between nominated representatives from the business units and corporate functions and the shared services/PSO team. It was essential to share common experiences, issues and risks, as well as best practices which arose during the implementation process.

The implementation of the planned initiative was to change the Shared Service Centre landscape drastically. From around 95 % finance-oriented process scope in 2008, the SSCs moved more and more to a multifunctional approach, providing services to very different departments within the company. By the end of 2012, finance still contributed the largest share of the overall scope, with 50 %, followed by the remaining corporate functions, such as HR, purchasing and IT, with an estimated 25 % share. However, the Henkel business units of Laundry and Home Care, Beauty Care and Adhesive Technologies had gained a very high momentum. Already, 25 % of the SSC employees were dedicated to working for the business units, performing not only purely transactional tasks, but also more value-adding, judgement-based activities (see **Figure 5.5**). One often-mentioned shared services success story came from the area of master data management for the Adhesive Technologies area, a service provided by the SSC in Bratislava. In the past, the set-up of new materials in the SAP system as part of new product introductions was sequentially performed by up to 10 different departments, such as marketing, research and development, packaging development, supply chain management or purchasing. In the process of compiling the necessary article information on formula, costs and packaging details, nobody felt overall responsibility for driving the process. This led to an often lengthy procedure with an average process time of 40 days, too long for some customers to wait. In the new set-up, the master data department located in the SSC was given the responsibility to collect the necessary data and steer the process in a central manner with a newly implemented tool. Within a few months, this brought down the number of necessary process steps from 20 to eight, linked with the requirement to finish the new material creation process within 14 days, hence contributing to a much better cycle time performance.

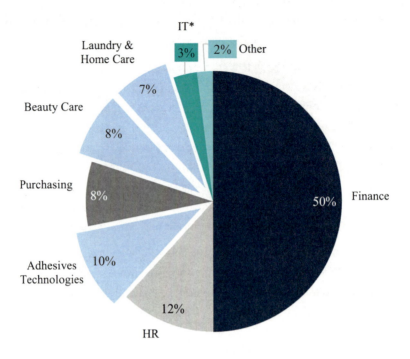

▸ 25% of SSC employees are working for the BUs (7% as of January 1st, 2012)

*excluding existing outsourcing ACN / IBM

Figure 5.5: Henkel shared services as of January 1st, 2013

Establishing a professional shared services organization. After the formation of the PSO initiative, it became evident that the lean shared services organization in the headquarters in Düsseldorf had to be extended. Mark and his team, overseeing not only shared services, but also the global financial operations world, would run short of capacities to effectively manage the planned growth initiatives.

Hence, at the beginning of 2012, a dedicated shared services organization was established in Düsseldorf, consisting of the following three pillars (see **Figure 5.6**):

- Transformation management
- Service delivery
- Shared Service Centres in Bratislava, Manila and Mexico

To lead the shared services transformation management team, a corporate vice-president was nominated who had gained deep knowledge of the Henkel business units in the past. He was to stand at the forefront of the PSO initiative, and use his experience to support the business units in their implementation path. The CVP was supported by a small team responsible for tracking the status of improvement, coordinating the meetings and supporting the business units in the migration of planned activities or the evaluation of new shared services potential. Furthermore, the team was responsible for identifying new feasible SSC locations to enlarge the regional coverage and manage growth. In 2011, a new captive Henkel-owned location was opened in Mexico City to provide finance services for the Latin American continent. In this region, it was essential to cover the local languages, such as Spanish and Portuguese, since only a few local employees were qualified to use professional business English. One team resource was entirely dedicated to communications initiatives around shared services. This included such tasks as setting up an intranet presence with an opportunity for employees to ask questions, and preparing change management workshops. Very importantly, the shared services communications manager was responsible for coordinating an ambassador programme. This was aimed at supporting the transitions within the Henkel organization and consisted of selected members from the different departments. The members were given a unified information deck covering the background, targets and project timelines of the PSO initiative. They were asked to serve as local contact partners within their units for any arising questions regarding development in the area of shared services. This local communication proved to be a much more effective measure than limiting the information flow to some central entities which were expected to inform the rest of the organization.

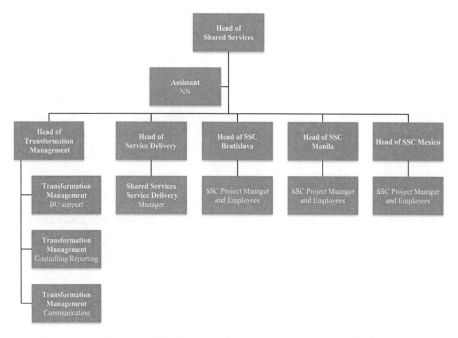

Figure 5.6: Henkel shared services organization in 2012

With the envisioned growth of the shared services area within Henkel, it became evident that the Shared Service Centres in Bratislava and Manila, as well as the newly planned locations, needed to be coordinated more professionally. Hence, a shared services service delivery team with members from Düsseldorf and the local SSCs was set up to steer the operations within the shared services area and develop more professional structures. One field to be enhanced included joint quality management with regard to service level agreements and KPIs with the business partners in the retained organization to measure the quality of the delivered services. In conjunction with measuring the performance, the business partners were looking for proactive suggestions from the SSCs to enhance the existing processes. Therefore, a continuous improvement team was formed, which was to collect improvement ideas from within the organization and coordinate them in a structured way. Furthermore, a clear governance model defining roles and responsibilities between the SSCs, the central headquarter entities and the local country organizations was needed. The service delivery team was also nominated to implement the first ever business process outsourcing project within the field of shared services. In 2012, the decision was taken to move selected standardized and substantially harmonized finance and HR activities from the existing SSC locations to an external partner located in Bangalore, India. The main drivers of the decision were the quick support of the growth path coupled with the desire to enhance processes further and identify industry best practices which could help the Henkel-owned Shared Service Centres. The transition of services was carefully prepared and executed through cooperation between the local SSC organizations and the external BPO partner. This proved to be essential to the success of the migration.

The importance of managing the upcoming growth was reflected within the local Shared Service Centre organizations as well. To support the heads of the SSCs in the upcoming tasks related to managing the SSC extension, a dedicated project manager position was established. This resource manager was responsible for coordinating the new incoming transitions from the local Henkel entities in the frame of the PSO initiative. They also gave support in recruitment questions, enlarging capacities and establishing best practices within the SSCs in close alignment with the process managers overseeing the operating teams.

By the end of 2012, the shared services organization was fully integrated into the Henkel world and working at full speed. Compared to 300 in 2008, the SSCs engaged 1500 full-time equivalent employees (FTE) by the end of 2012. This growth resulted mainly from the ideas implemented in the course of the SOP and PSO initiatives. From a purely transactional activity profile, the SSCs had moved to provide more and more value-adding services to all Henkel regions, all corporate functions and selected activities for all major business units in the areas of marketing, supply chain or R&D. The first initiatives to leverage cross-BU synergies and best practice exchange in the SSCs were launched, further strengthening the high-quality profile of the provided services (see **Figure 5.7**).

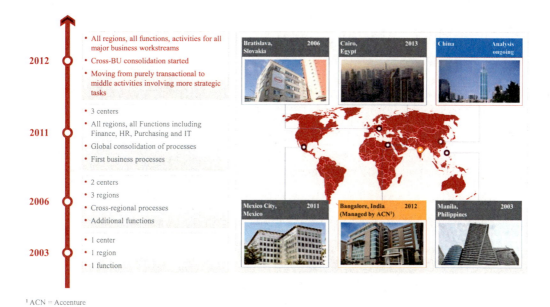

[1] ACN = Accenture

Figure 5.7: The Henkel shared services journey until 2012

In February 2013, Mark was given a slot during a management board meeting to report on the shared services status. Following his presentation to the board, Kasper Rorsted rose. "Mark", the CEO began, "in the name of the entire Henkel organization, I would like to thank you and your team for your outstanding achievement in the area of shared services. This development was one of the key contributors to the successful achievement of all three of our 2012 financial targets. Through establishing faster and more agile processes while at the same time closing the EBIT gap with some of our competitors, Henkel is well prepared for the future" (see **Figure 5.8**).

The CEO paused for a second. "However, as you know, our competition does not sleep. I heard Unilever is about to acquire further targets in the emerging markets, driving both their growth and profit goals. They also have a world class shared services organization, which they aim to further strengthen by integrating the new firms. Our journey at Henkel has only just started. Let us use the existing momentum. I have just released the latest organizational chart which can serve as a guideline for you to come up with further activities to move to our Shared Services Centres (see **Figure 5.9**). We are very happy with the regional coverage of our Western European and to some extent our North American region. However, we are sure the emerging markets show further potential. Please come up with some new shared services opportunities, which we invite you to present at the strategic board meeting in May. Thank you."

> # Henkel's sales and earnings reaching record levels
>
> - Sales rise 5.8 percent to 16,510 million euros (organic: +3.8%)
> - Adjusted* operating profit: +15.1 percent to 2,335 million euros
> - Adjusted* EBIT margin: +1.1 percentage points to 14.1%
> - Adjusted* earnings per preferred share (EPS): +17.8% to 3.70 euros
> - Strong performance in the emerging markets (organic: +7.8%)
> - Proposed dividend: +18.8 percent to 0.95 euros per preferred share
> - 2013 set to be another year of growth
>
> 2012 was the most successful year for Henkel so far: we achieved excellent results in a highly volatile and competitive market environment and met or exceeded all financial targets," said Henkel CEO, Kasper Rorsted. "All three Henkel business sectors showed profitable growth with expansion of market shares in their relevant markets. We also delivered on the ambitious financial targets we set in 2008 for the period up to 2012. We have substantially strengthened Henkel's competitiveness, establishing a strong foundation for our future growth."
>
> Looking at fiscal year 2013, Rorsted said: "The strong dynamics and high volatility in our markets will persist. Although Henkel is well positioned, we will continue to further simplify and improve our processes in order to respond to changes faster than our competition.
>
> We expect organic sales growth for the full fiscal year to be between 3 and 5 percent. We also expect to increase our adjusted EBIT margin to around 14.5 percent, and improve adjusted earnings per preferred share by around 10 percent."
>
> Sales and earnings 2012

Figure 5.8: Henkel results 2012 – press release

Mark left the room with mixed feelings. Obviously, there was a strong recognition of what his team had achieved in recent years. However, the board's demand for the next step was only natural. The journey was to continue, and he had to go back to his team and identify new ideas on how to further extend and professionalize shared services. Not only was it important to think about the enlargement of the coverage of shared services. With an ever-growing scale and wider coverage of shared services in the organization, a more professional shared services organization was needed. Until this point, the area of customer service performance and quality control through valid key performance indicators and measurable SLAs had been underdeveloped. Further, it was necessary to think about such topics as risk management in the case of business or IT outages through the installation of solid business continuity plans. Moreover, how could his organization ensure continuous employment of high-quality workers in such overheated markets as Bratislava and Manila? Could Henkel learn from business process outsourcing partners such as Accenture, IBM or Genpact, or from industry leaders such as Procter & Gamble or Unilever, which served as role models in terms of professional organizations? He noted his thoughts down on a napkin on the table, and left the restaurant full of optimism about taking Henkel's shared services organization to the next level.

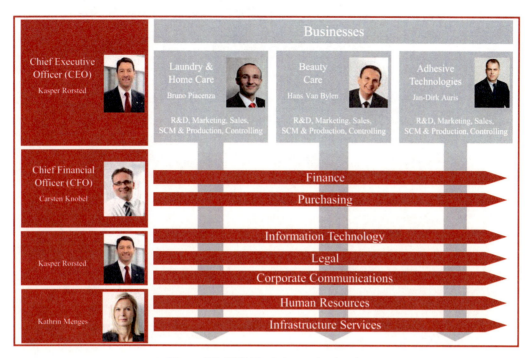

Figure 5.9: 2013 Henkel organizational set-up

•••

Setting of the case: 2014; last revision: 2014.

6

You'll Never Walk Alone: Stakeholder Management and Corporate Strategy at Borussia Dortmund

Jan-Philipp Büchler and Thilo Heyer

After publishing preliminary figures for the fiscal year 2007/08, Thomas Treß felt relieved – but only for a moment. Borussia Dortmund GmbH & Co. KGaA had just reported revenues to be up by +10.7%, amounting to a total of € 107.6m, but as Chief Financial Officer (CFO) of the only publicly listed football club in Germany his work had just begun. Thomas Treß had been appointed CFO three years ago, when the club was facing a severe financial crisis that almost forced it into bankruptcy. Within these three years, Treß and his management team were able to stop the financial bleeding, caused by high losses in the previous two years, and start a financial restructuring process. Additionally, the team saw that Borussia Dortmund needed to change several aspects of the company's operations, and establish a new, long-term orientation and a corporate strategy.

As Treß walked back to his office after the press conference at which he informed the public about the improvement in the club's finances, he thought about the next steps. Bearing in mind that the centennial of the traditional football club was less than two years ahead and that the club was on its way to regaining financial stability, he thought it could be the right time for more significant strategic changes to be made in order to prepare the club for a brighter future. For the next strategy talks with the management team he planned to discuss possible approaches to reduce the dependency of financial performance on the league performance of Borussia Dortmund. In order to prepare this discussion, he commissioned a detailed report on the sources, development, and composition of the sales revenues from his division heads and managers (see **Appendixes 6A and 6B**). From this information he expected to gain a better understanding of the key success factors at Borussia Dortmund.

FINANCIAL PERFORMANCE AND REVENUE STREAMS OF BORUSSIA DORTMUND – AN OVERVIEW

After the initial public offering (IPO) in 1999 the former management board had made huge investments to sign famous international players for the club and to extend the existing stadium capacity to become no. 1 in Germany in every way. Initial success in national and international competitions contributed to a significant increase in sales revenues, but when the club missed out on the international qualifications in 2003/04 it suffered a dramatic decrease in sales revenues and earnings (-23.7% compared to FY 2002/03). Within only two years, Borussia Dortmund became unable to finance its operating expenses and interest payments, and almost needed to file for bankruptcy. As one of Germany's most popular football clubs, located in a densely populated area of Germany, North-Rhine Westphalia, this scenario would have had wide-ranging negative consequences not only for the club's home town of Dortmund. Fortunately, the new management took action and, after many discussions and arrangements with several stakeholders, notably investors, Borussia Dortmund was able to solve the crisis.

In the fiscal year 2007/08, Borussia Dortmund accumulated sales revenues of € 107.6m (see **Table 6.1**). Growth in sales compared to the previous year added up to € 10.4m (+10.8%), partially due to a successful run in the national DFB Cup, which also had an influence on the increase in income from ticketing (+23.7%), TV rights (+23.5%) and sponsoring (+10.9%). Borussia Dortmund thus managed to solve the severe financial situation, leaving some room to focus on long-term strategic change. Revenues in recent years were generated as follows:

BVB GmbH&Co. KGaA	1999/00	2000/01	2001/02	2002/03	2003/04	2004/05	2005/06	2006/07	2007/08
Sales Revenues (€m)	91.4	77.0	102.4	124.4	94.9	73.9	88.7	97.2	107.6
Sponsoring (€m)	26.0	13.2	28.0	44.9	25.7	26.4	32.6	30.5	33.9
Ticketing (€m)	17.6	13.8	17.8	17.9	20.3	17.5	17.2	18.3	22.6
TV Rights (€m)	35.0	19.3	46.0	49.9	19.3	14.9	14.8	21.3	26.0
Merchandise & Catering (€m)	9.7	5.3	9.4	11.4	16.6	14.4	11.7	20.3	19.7
Transfers (€m)	3.0	25.3	1.2	0.3	13.1	0.7	12.4	6.8	5.4

Table 6.1: Financial performance 1999–2008

Sponsoring: This main pillar of revenue generation contributed almost one third to sales revenues (for revenue streams of other European football clubs see **Appendix 6E**). As sponsors have an essential impact on revenues, the club management looked for strategic sponsors and partners in order to establish long-term relationships to help guarantee the long-term financial stability of the club. But during a time of low sporting success, it is difficult to acquire new sponsors.

The sponsorship strategy differentiated several arrangements and marketing rights for sponsors (see **Figure 6.1**). In 2005 the Dortmund-based insurance company Signal Iduna signed a long-term contract for premium sponsorship that included the naming rights of the stadium until 2016. In addition to this strategic partnership, Borussia Dortmund continued contracts with their main sponsor Evonik Industries AG, with headquarters in Essen. The *regional champion* partnerships with Sparda-Bank West and AWD were continued on a mid-term basis. The regional champion partner Warsteiner was exchanged for a long-term contract with Dortmund-based brewery Brinkhoffs No.1.

Figure 6.1: Sponsors of Borussia Dortmund in 2008

Ticketing: In the 2007/08 season ticketing revenues rose to a total of € 22.6m (+ € 4.3m vs. PY) thanks to additional matches. The team qualified for the final round of the DFB Cup (+ € 3.9m) and played several friendly matches at home. These additional revenues compensated for the negative development in ticketing revenues in the Bundesliga (-0.2m vs. PY). In 2007/08 the club registered another decrease in spectators (see **Table 6.2**). Though Borussia Dortmund still reported the highest number of spectators among German clubs, compared to an average attendance of 41,802 in the German Bundesliga, capacity utilization in the biggest football stadium in Germany decreased to an all-time low of 88%. New approaches for filling the capacity of the stadium needed to be found.

Borussia Dortmund	1999/00	2000/01	2001/02	2002/03	2003/04	2004/05	2005/06	2006/07	2007/08
Ticketing (mill. €)	17.6	13.8	17.8	17.9	20.3	17.5	17.2	18.3	22.6
Spectators (ø / Play)	64,600	63,729	66,206	67,859	79,647	77,235	72,643	72,164	71,650
Capacity filled (%)	94%	93%	97%	99%	98%	95%	89%	89%	88%

Table 6.2: Number of spectators and capacity utilization (1999–2008)

Merchandising. The sales revenues from merchandising in the season 2007/08 increased by +€ 2.7m (+51.9% vs. PY) up to € 7.9m. The merchandising assortment included around 300 items, consisting of typical fan articles such as apparel and flags as well as a broad portfolio of duvets, towels, glassware, dishes, watches and jewelry. The merchandising items targeted diverse groups of supporters, and the designs were just as diverse as the company sought to offer something for every taste (see **Figure 6.2**).

Figure 6.2: Examples from the merchandising collection in 2008

A remarkable example of using the power of branding in order to boost sales revenues independently of sporting success is provided by the marketing and merchandising strategy of St. Pauli FC. In contrast to other club brands, St. Pauli FC positions itself as a differentiated lifestyle brand, and has more than 11 million fans around the world. Perhaps a direct result of the club's fandom and brand positioning, FC St. Pauli claims an impressive € 6–8m worth of merchandise sales per year. As a result, the club ranks around the top positions in terms of merchandising, even while remaining at the lower end of the achievement scale in terms of sporting performance.

Best-Practice Merchandising: St. Pauli FC

The club's anti-establishment brand identity as likeable rebels has apparently triggered a certain gentrification and commercialization of the club itself, which is particularly visible in its core visual – the Jolly Roger. The reason why the skull and crossbones became a symbol for FC St. Pauli fans to display was the club's resilience in winning three promotions in a row, eventually reaching the Bundesliga. The symbol has been widely used and during the season 2000/01 it was displayed on the club's football shirts. Based on a strong brand image rooted in the club's home territory, an alternative left-wing district in Hamburg, several branded fashion lines have been developed that reach out to different target groups (see **Figure 6.3**).

Fig. 6.3 Branded fashion product lines, St. Pauli FC

The fashion line 'FC St. Pauli' offers vintage and retro-lifestyle fashion items (e.g., caps, shirts, training jackets) in the official club colors of brown and white; the focus is on tradition and heritage. The product line 'Jolly Roger St. Pauli' consists of around 60 articles in black colors only and displays the Jolly Roger prominently. The brand communication is bold and concentrates on attributes such as 'being rebellious'. The fashion line '20359' targets a young, lifestyle-oriented, urban group of people favoring an alternative open-minded Hamburg lifestyle; the fashion articles are co-designed with local designers in trendy colors and cuts for each season. The brand 'Viva St. Pauli' makes use of a Latin-American left-wing revolutionary image; the product line offers army jackets and military caps in olive and jungle colors.

Transfer revenues. After the financial crisis in 2004/05 the team needed to be completely rebuilt, and transfer revenues decreased significantly. Sports director Michael Zorc made the best of a difficult situation by systematically promoting and developing local players who were making a name for themselves within the club. The result was a young and talented team with remarkable passion and ambition. This also gave the club the opportunity to create extra value and sell promising young players to generate additional cash.

TV rights. Television rights in the football industry are a phenomenon in their own right. In 2003 the revenue of Borussia Dortmund generated via TV rights amounted to more than 40% (€ 49.9m) of the overall revenues, illustrating the high importance of the revenue stream. In the German Bundesliga the TV rights are sold centrally via the Deutsche Fußball Liga (DFL), and each club in the first and second division gets paid relative to its ranking over the past five years. Thus, the better the league performance, the higher the TV-rights revenues. The high figures generated by Borussia Dortmund were mainly driven by a well-paying contract between the Kirch group (a football broadcaster) and the DFL, as well as participation in the first round of the UEFA Champions League, which created significant international television-broadcasting revenues. In 2008 the revenue from TV rights was only half that of 2003, and only accounted for less than 25% of Borussia Dortmund's revenue. This was partially due to a new contract between a football broadcaster and the DFL, as well as the fact that Borussia Dortmund did not qualify for any international competitions in 2007.

REVENUE DRIVERS FOR BORUSSIA DORTMUND

After analyzing the existent revenue streams of the club, Treß was confident he could steer Borussia Dortmund in the right direction. Nevertheless, he needed to dig deeper into potential drivers for the identified revenue streams. He asked himself which of the revenue drivers was the most important, and whether there might be other opportunities besides the existing revenue streams to generate sales and growth for the club.

Borussia Dortmund – League Performance

The fact that the financial performance of a football club is still directly dependent on league performance becomes obvious when the league finish one year is seen in the context of the next year's financial performance (see **Table 6.3**). The delayed effect of revenue increase is mostly a result of participation in international competitions, for which a club has to qualify the previous year. The revenue increase is mostly visible through additional income from TV rights and ticketing in international competitions. Especially qualification for, e.g., the UEFA Cup (now called the UEFA Europa League) or the UEFA Champions League (CL) drives sales revenues in the subsequent year. Thus, when Borussia Dortmund finished 13th in the German league (the Bundesliga) at the end of the 2007/08 season one could already forecast that the next season would not be easy, financially speaking. Therefore the club management stated a top-five position as the minimum objective for all future seasons, in order to put the club on a sustainable financial basis through regular participation in international competitions generating additional revenues from television rights, ticketing and merchandising. A slight decoupling of financial performance from league performance could be targeted through revenues generated away from the playing field – but this seems to be rather difficult for a football club, as mentioned.

Borussia Dortmund	1999/00	2000/01	2001/02	2002/03	2003/04	2004/05	2005/06	2006/07	2007/08
German Bundesliga Ranking	11th	3rd	1st	3rd	6th	7th	7th	9th	13th
International Qualification	-	UEFA-Cup	CL	UEFA-Cup	-	-	-	-	-
German Football Federation Cup (DFB Cup)	3rd Round	4th Round	1st Round	2nd Round	2nd Round	4th Round	1st Round	2nd Round	Final
Sales Revenues (€m)	91.4	77.0	102.4	124.4	94.9	73.9	88.7	97.2	107.6

Table 6.3: League performance 1999–2008

Marketing Strategy

When Thomas Treß became CFO of Borussia Dortmund, the club did not have a clear marketing strategy and many fans were unsure what the club stood for, especially given the financial crisis and the misbehavior of some of the players. The brand communication of the club had focused on universal traditional values for more than 10 years, based on the claim 'Tradition · Leidenschaft · Erfolg' (Tradition – Passion – Success). This claim had been used, for example, on the cover of the club's annual reports since the IPO in 1999. A number of additional claims had also been used in the club's communications, such as 'Wir sind Schwarz-gelb' ('We are the black-and-yellows') and 'Unser ganzes Leben. Unser ganzer Stolz' ('Our life. Our pride'). These claims varied depending on the communication channel and the target group, but all of them had a strong regional focus (see **Figure 6.4** and also **Appendix 6E**).

Figure 6.4: Marketing claims 1999–2008

As Joachim Watzke stated during his first shareholders' meeting as the new CEO of Borussia Dortmund, "We are a medium-sized enterprise, with the appeal and awareness of a German blue chip". Yet this potential needed to be developed, and, more importantly, captured, which would require a well-defined marketing strategy and professional customer-relationship management. The marketing strategy would have a significant impact on the fans of the club, one of the major stakeholder groups. The fans regard themselves literally as the 12th player and a part of the team. Borussia Dortmund's stadium has the largest standing terrace in Europe, which the fans affectionately call the 'Yellow Wall'. It is the epitome of fan culture and pure passion, creating an atmosphere in the Signal Iduna Park (as the stadium is known) that provides a famously intense football experience for all spectators, even those watching it on TV (see **Appendix 6C**).

In recent management discussions, Treß became more and more convinced that a sharp-edged positioning of the club's brand could lay the foundations for a new corporate strategy that could help secure sales revenues even without (or with low) sporting success. Looking at the historical timeline of Borussia Dortmund, he felt that the upcoming centennial might provide a wonderful opportunity. First, the club needed to review his national and international brand positioning and strategy, as well as several distribution channels and respective slogans. Nevertheless, other drivers such as the cost structure of the club were also important aspects to focus on.

Cost structure and a new financial mantra

A severe driver of the financial crisis that Borussia Dortmund was facing in 2005 was the cost structure of the club. One key element was that players' wages accounted for a high share of the costs. In 2003, for instance, Borussia Dortmund paid € 67.9m on its professional squad. To reduce these costs the club had three options: sell players, negotiate salary cuts with the players due to the severe financial situation, or introduce a flexible payment plan. Since the management knew that an earlier renegotiation with the current players had failed in 2003, the other two options seemed more appropriate. The club introduced flexible payment, meaning that the players were paid relative to the points gained during the Bundesliga season. This flexibility in the players' wages served as another cornerstone helping to make the club's financial situation more independent of club performance in the league. After a while, almost 50% of the players' salaries were performance-driven, making it possible to reduce wage costs to € 34.3m in 2007. Furthermore, the club sold several players to increase transfer revenues and lower the total wage costs further.

Another key element was the debt structure at Borussia Dortmund. At the peak of the crisis the club had around € 200m in liabilities, compared to less than € 75m in revenues, as well as high rents to pay due to the sale-and-lease-back agreement that had been arranged regarding the stadium. Through a new loan issued by Morgan Stanley in 2006, Borussia Dortmund was able to buy back the stadium, which it had sold in December 2002, and bundle many liabilities. This approach reduced the company's financial distress significantly. Furthermore, it gave the management time to invest in other projects, as it was easier to negotiate liability agreements with only one major partner. With the appointment of Thomas Treß as the CFO the club entered a new financial era, heralded by Treß's commitment that Borussia Dortmund would never again spend more than it earned. This commitment was undertaken partly in order to rebuild lost trust with certain stakeholders.

In order to profit from the potential revenue drivers and increase the identified revenue streams the club would need to align several, sometimes conflicting views of stakeholders. Therefore, it is crucial to gain a clear picture on the characteristics of the most important stakeholders of Borussia Dortmund.

IMPORTANT STAKEHOLDERS FOR BORUSSIA DORTMUND AND THE MANAGEMENT TEAM

Fans. For a long time, Borussia Dortmund had been perceived as a likeable 'second team' by supporters and other interested parties. Borussia Dortmund was one of the few football clubs with supporters all over Germany. In 2004, right before the financial crisis, about 20 million people in Germany found the club 'likeable', 63% of the fans from all over Germany. This national basis meant Borussia Dortmund stood out from most other Bundesliga clubs, which only had local or regional fans (see **Figure 6.5**).

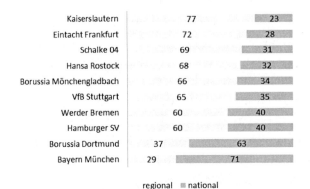

Figure 6.5: Fan base of Bundesliga clubs 2008 in % (Source: Sportfive 2004)

In the 2004/05 season Borussia Dortmund lost much of this sympathy and suffered a loss of image due to the financial crisis. The club management at the time proposed several measures to raise cash, including the sale of the Borussia Dortmund brand rights; at the same time, certain expensive players neither scored goals nor respected the fans.

Supporters dissociated themselves from the club and their protagonists, with loud protests. They accused the management and the players of being arrogant, megalomaniacal and detached from the club's values, culminating in a demonstration involving several thousand fans, who marched through the city of Dortmund to the Borsigplatz (the place the club was founded). It was the first time in history that a club had polarized football fans in Germany in this way. As a result, Borussia Dortmund lost about 30% of its national fans and suffered a decline in interest and support within the Ruhr region. Thomas Treß reflected on the expectations and interests of the stakeholders of Borussia Dortmund as follows: while followers in the Ruhr region could be targeted with honest and authentic communication because of their emotional relationship based on brand heritage, attractive new sponsors and investors would base their support on clear facts and figures regarding the perception and reputation of the club's brand on a regional and national level (see **Appendix 6D**).

Financial Stakeholders. Banks exercise a legitimate influence by offering financing instruments to football clubs such as bonds and loans. A bank's financing of football clubs is highly dependent on the performance of the club, as it will significantly impact the club's ability to pay back interest and loans. After 2005, the relationship of Borussia Dortmund to its banks was improved significantly, as the club was able to satisfy its creditors again, and thus creating trust among their relationships again.

As the only public listed club in Germany, Borussia Dortmund is required to manage the expectations of its shareholders. The club has been listed on the Frankfurt Stock Exchange since it was floated with much fanfare in October 2000. The initial euphoria, however, was gone within a few years. The value of shares started at 11 € and dropped to an all-time low of 1 € in the 2004/05 season, when Borussia Dortmund faced its sporting and financial crisis. The initial inflow of cash was quickly absorbed to pay for high-profile and highly-paid stars, and the management faced € 200m in liabilities. Hopes of an attractive return on investments were dashed. In the following years Borussia Dortmund finished in no-man's land in the league, and a recovery of the share price seemed wishful thinking. Over the years the club's shareholder structure changed fundamentally. Most of the initial large institutional investors were gone by 2007/08, and over 80% of the shares came to be owned by diverse minority shareholders – mostly fans buying shares of their beloved club in order to feel a part of it.

Sponsors. Sponsors are individuals or companies who make payments to a club in exchange for agreed goods (e.g., tickets) or services (e.g., VIP lounges, catering). Company sponsors often get involved for charitable reasons, e.g., to show support for the local community or gain trade advantages, for example by selling more goods or services through links to a certain club. Most sponsors prefer to associate themselves with a reputable club that fits with the company's brand image, and look for positive image transfer. Sponsors can be differentiated into several categories depending on the financial commitment and agreed goods and services (see **Figure 6.1**). Whereas simple sponsors usually have a limited relationship with a club, champion sponsors or champion partners are more intensively tied with the club management, and closely monitor sporting performance and the club's image. Due to their financial impact and visibility, champion sponsors might even exert some power over the club management.

Sponsorships usually last only for one or two seasons. Establishing a sponsorship agreement can take some time, and financially solid and strategic sponsors are hard to find. Treß knew it is much easier to keep a sponsor than to find a new one. Looking at the sponsoring pyramid, he saw the advantages of long-term relationships with Brinkhoff's No. 1, Evonik and Signal Iduna – these companies were all based in Dortmund or the Ruhr region, and could be considered as strategic partners. The exclusive contract with the supplier Nike, on the other hand, would expire at the end of the 2008/09 season, leaving room for an early start to the search for a new supplier or long-term negotiations regarding a prolongation of the relationship with Nike. Treß was not afraid of such negotiations, because the prolongation of the club's deal with the sports marketing agency Sportfive until 2020 had taken some risk out of the acquisition of new sponsors, thanks to the huge international network and vast experience of the agency.

DFL. The DFL is the governing body that sets the administrative and sporting rules common to all German football clubs. Besides management of all operations of club competitions, the DFL also audits clubs' financial stability, checking their balance sheets and accounts. Healthy financial conditions are a precondition for getting a license after qualifying for one of the top leagues. These measures aim at financial fair play. The DFL will never engage actively in club management. This governing function results from experiences of financial disasters such as the case of Borussia Dortmund in 2004/05. Without healthy accounts, a football club in Germany will not get a license. In addition, the DFL manages and negotiates the media and broadcasting rights for all clubs in the league. According to an allocation key that is based on league performance, all clubs benefit from these revenues.

City of Dortmund. Football is a local spectacle with few direct competitors. Matches attract supporters from all over Germany and the city benefits from the positive spill-over effects for local retail, hotel and catering industry; generating demand and tax revenues. Dortmund has a well-established trade fair that has similar importance for tax revenues and jobs as the football club. However, Borussia Dortmund offers more opportunities to unite the city around a team, establishing a source of local pride and identification. Derbies are highly popular events, for example when Borussia Dortmund plays against Schalke 04 or VfL Bochum. Football is perceived as a source of fame that transfers a positive image of dynamism onto the city and the local authorities. For all these reasons, local authorities can benefit from providing various forms of support for local teams, covering direct subsidies or loans, public equipment, e.g., training facilities, and infrastructure, helping create positive social effects through boosting local business and tourism.

Players. The team is the core of the club and provides the main source of identification for many stakeholders, especially fans and sponsors. It is often a problem that teams do not focus enough on homegrown talents, but instead prefer to transfer mercenaries into their ranks. Treß knew that the problem with such players is their tendency to move quickly from one club to the next; Borussia Dortmund might be used simply as a stepping-stone. In any case, the club's financial situation did not yet allow for expensive transfers. However, the training and development of young and hungry talents would yield rewards soon. Treß already dreamed of a new generation of players who adhered to the values of the club and would act as real ambassadors at national and international level.

Employees. After years of uncertainty and restructuring, the situation improved internally for employees. The club management reduced the organization from over 300 employees pre-crisis to 193 in 2005/06, and further to 175 employees in 2006/07, as part of the financial and organizational restructuring program. These cuts were painful, but there was no alternative in order to regain a solid financial basis. In the 2007/08 fiscal year the club reported an increase of employees to 195. The turn-around seemed to have been achieved.

Media. Apart from broadcasting the football matches, media companies report with high interest and intensity on the changing fortunes of Borussia Dortmund. The rebirth of the iconic club could reveal a potential for communication that might win back disillusioned fans and attract new sympathizers. Thus, the media companies could be partners in creating visibility for the club and reshaping the public opinion.

PREPARING THE STRATEGY TALKS

Under the stewardship of the new management team from 2005, the club had bought back the stadium, built a state-of-the-art training center, paid back interest and debt, and undergone a shift in focus towards developing young players instead of buying overpaid stars. Treß felt that they could now start reaping the rewards. However, he was convinced that their aim should always be to achieve the maximum possible sporting success without going into debt. He favored spending funds wisely and efficiently.

Thomas Treß looked at the agenda of the upcoming strategy talks. He would have to prepare and deliver presentations on the agenda items 'Financial Performance of Borussia Dortmund', 'Brand Positioning', and 'Borussia Dortmund 2020'. A reasonable beginning seemed to be a detailed analysis of the situation of the club with regard to the drivers of financial and league performance. A discussion with his management would probably center on potential levers for uncoupling financial and league performance.

He wondered which key success factors and levers would be most relevant to boost revenue sales independently of Borussia Dortmund's position in the league table. How could he make use of the traditional fan base in order to increase brand awareness beyond the Ruhr region? What brand positioning of Borussia Dortmund would be acceptable for the regional fan base and also attractive to national as well as international fans and sponsors? How could he ensure no stakeholder would be left behind? Treß took a pen and wrote down the focal questions he needed to answer in the following days:

- Analysis of levers for uncoupling financial and sporting success
- Analysis of the club's strengths and weaknesses

➔ What are the implications for the long-term strategy of Borussia Dortmund?

- Identification of relevant stakeholders
- Development of a change in management approach

➔ How could all internal and external stakeholders of Borussia Dortmund be aligned?

•••

Setting of the case: 2015; last revision: October 2015.

This case study was made possible through the generous cooperation of Borussia Dortmund GmbH & Co. KGaA, especially Thomas Treß (CFO – Borussia Dortmund GmbH & Co. KGaA). The authors also want to thank FC St. Pauli von 1910 e. V. for their friendly support regarding best practices for merchandising strategies, Julius Osthues (M.Sc., University of Cologne) for his valuable insights, and Jennifer Decker (M.Sc., CASEM / FH Dortmund) for her research assistance and proofreading.

Appendix

6A: Organizational structure, Borussia Dortmund Group (2008)

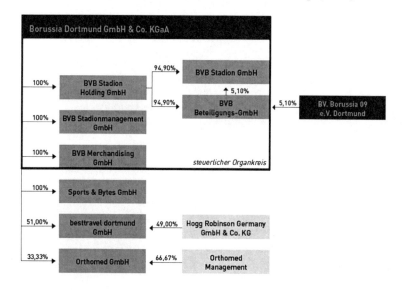

Source: Borussia Dortmund GmbH & Co. KGaA, Annual Report 2007/08

6B: Functional structure, Borussia Dortmund 2008

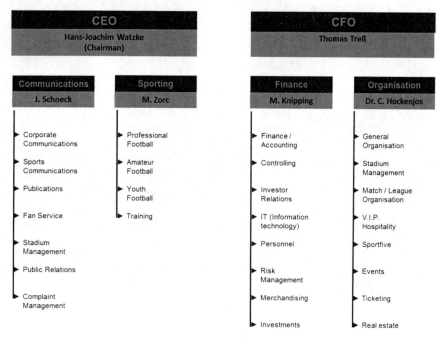

Source: Borussia Dortmund GmbH & Co. KGaA, Annual Report 2007/08

6C: Brand coverage of Bundesliga clubs

International Brands
Bayern München

National Brands
Schalke 04, Werder Bremen,
VfB Stuttgart, Bayer Leverkusen, Borussia Dortmund

Regional Brands
Borussia Mönchengladbach, 1. FC Köln, Hertha BSC,
Hannover 96, 1. FC Kaiserslautern, 1. FC Nürnberg, FC Hansa Rostock

Local Brands
Energie Cottbus, Karlsruher SC, Arminia Bielefeld, Mainz 05, Vfl Bochum

Source: Kind (2008)

6D: Stadium atmosphere: Grandstand ('YELLOW WALL')

Source: Advertisement, Frankfurter Allgemeine Zeitung

6E: Branding and communication channels

Source: Borussia Dortmund GmbH & Co. KGaA

6F: Revenue streams, Europe

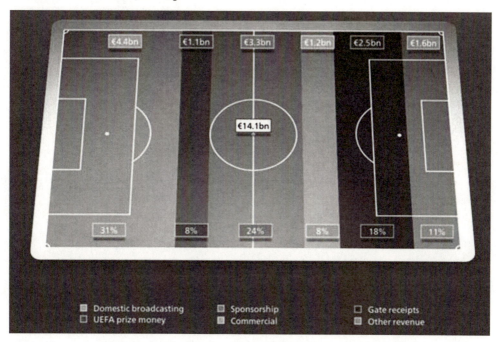

Source: UEFA Club Licensing Benchmarking Report FY 2012

7

The Takeover of Boxler – A Quantum Leap for Markus Schober?

Bastian Schweiger and Sascha Albers

The owners of Markus Schober Innenausbau und Bodendielen GmbH, Markus and Christine Schober, are sitting at their massive wooden dinner table in Point, Tegernsee (Bavaria), while reminiscing about their acquisition of Boxler, a parquet, cork and laminate manufacturer, 10 months ago. In the beginning, the deal seemed to be fairly easy. Taking over the insolvent Boxler suited the ambitious plans of Markus Schober: his intentions for Boxler were to produce the supplies needed to cover the increasing demand for Schober's interior construction products and, additionally, to tap the lucrative market for flooring material. The initial situation appeared to be ideal: a low purchase price, synergy effects and the opportunity for further growth of Schober GmbH.

Shortly after the acquisition, however, the Schobers realized that their plan had proved to be unsuccessful. Boxler was an extra burden. Markus especially had to regularly drive the 130 km distance between Miesbach (headquarters of Schober GmbH) and Rammingen (headquarters of Boxler) to solve post-acquisition problems. "Tomorrow morning I have to be in Rammingen. A potential customer is visiting and I have to ensure that we close the deal. Afterwards, I have to fly to Stockholm to negotiate the licences with the Swedes. We urgently need them to make progress with Boxler!" Markus told his wife during dinner. "But I thought we'd resolved the issue with Thomas and the new Vapiano in Brazil before you left", Christine replied. "Without me, something might go wrong and you know we need that customer for Boxler", answered Markus. "I know… but you are also needed here in Miesbach, Markus. It's time for Boxler to stand on its own feet. You can't run the business of both companies." Of course, his wife had a valid point, but what was the alternative? Watching Boxler fail? Not a chance! But doubts remained. Did we overestimate ourselves with the acquisition? What did we do wrong? Where can we improve? Exhausted and with a buzzing head, Markus Schober goes to bed. One short night of rest lies ahead of him before things get serious for Boxler.

SCHOBER GMBH BEFORE THE TAKEOVER OF BOXLER

The Company

The success story of the Schobers' company started with a small carpentry firm in Kreuth at Lake Tegernsee, founded in 1954 by Hans Schober. As the business thrived, the company was shifted to Gmund in order to build up larger production facilities. In 1998, a fire destroyed a huge part of the production site, so that the Schobers were forced to look for a new location. They chose a vacant 4000 m² building in Miesbach, approximately 20 km away from their place of foundation, Kreuth.

By choosing Miesbach, the Schobers set the course for the company's future. Since the capacity of the new facilities allowed for a larger production volume, the relocation offered the opportunity to grow the flourishing business by expanding the premium interior constructions and flooring materials market. Nevertheless, this move was impossible without outside support from investors. Thus, it was decided to change the ownership structure of the firm: today, Schober's operating company holds 53 % of Schober GmbH, while the remaining 47 % is controlled by two investors. This financial boost gave the family business enough room to realize new business ideas and to tackle the problems of in-house production. In particular, the local competition for the production of floorboards was very intense. Over 70 carpenters operate in close proximity, which results in a business-damaging price war. By further developing the company and its products and services, today Schober is playing in a different league. Additionally, in the past, the company struggled to stick to deadlines, as employees were lacking morale and effort in their work. Some employees just could not keep up with the rapid pace of the creative entrepreneur Markus Schober. Therefore, several long-term employees had to leave the company. With the new financial flexibility, the company could shift most of the production of flooring material to a sub-contractor, who had to cope with the risks of working to deadlines and employee motivation from then on.

Benefitting from several contacts and mutual projects, the Schobers were able to get an idea of their suppliers' work streams, capabilities and prices, which resulted in fixed contractual relationships. While reducing in-house production, the company's strategic focus changed. Today, Schober GmbH produces high-quality floorboards and designs customized interior fittings for customers all over the world. However, another core competency has developed over time. Schober has become a consultant for premium customers, and conducts the whole construction process, including the coordination and reconciliation of customer wishes, as well as planning, production and assembly, in order to guarantee an exclusive design experience. Every customer is provided with a 360 degree service package, guiding him or her through the planning and realization phase. To find an optimal solution for every customer's wishes, high-quality materials are needed as well as experienced, competent and particularly creative carpenters, wood technicians and interior designers. Over time, the company developed into a premium interior decorator, fulfilling the highest standards and expectations of solvent private and corporate customers, including Porsche Design, Hugo Boss, Feinkost Käfer, SAP and many more. Accordingly, Christine Schober formulates the company guidelines as follows: "Entrepreneurship, effort, fun at work, creativity and innovative skills". Besides hard work, recreation, creative breaks and togetherness are also promoted within the company through exciting company events such as rafting, visits to amusement parks and numerous parties throughout the year (see **Figure 7.1**).

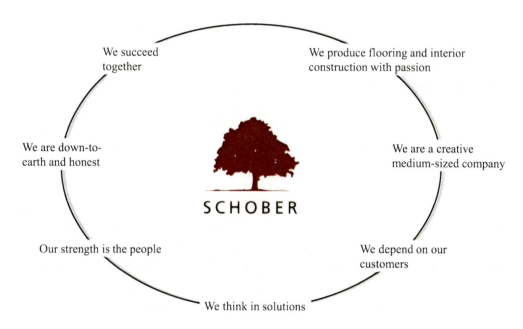

Figure 7.1: Mission statement of Markus Schober GmbH

Business Areas and Customers

The core product of Schober GmbH is high-quality floorboards, which are made out of regionally and globally sourced premium wood species such as oak, checker tree, American nut tree, Canadian maple and mahogany. Besides the wood species, the customer can also choose the width, length and surface texture of the boards. Through grinding, brushing and hand-scraping, different superior finishes can be offered. The manufactured floorboards are up to 14 m long and 400 mm wide. Every inquiry is given customized service, which guarantees premium performance for the customer. The customers for these floorboards can be divided into two groups: on the one hand, international private customers who want floorboards for their private houses or office facilities, and on the other hand, wholesalers from Spain, Austria, the UK, Russia and Switzerland, who will further distribute the floorboards. With a gross margin of roughly 40 %, the premium floorboard business is highly lucrative.

Besides floorboards, the company also offers individualized, customer-specific all-in-one premium solutions for exclusive interior construction of private homes, conference and office facilities, and yachts. The design of the rooms mostly consists of wood, while materials such as steel and glass are also incorporated. All materials and services are established in the higher-price segment. This results in a gross margin of 20-30 % for the company. By increasing international interconnectedness with suppliers and assembly companies, interior designs conceptualized in Miesbach can be realized all over the world. Among the customers of Schober GmbH are Real Madrid, Finca Vega-Sicilia in Valbuena, and IWC Boutique in Hong Kong, Seoul and Bangkok, as well as private homes in Europe, Russia and the United States.

As a third pillar, Schober GmbH gained a foothold in the interior design of restaurants. An exclusive cooperation with the catering chain Vapiano, in particular, really boosted the business. After the first cooperation in Hamburg in 2002, the ambitious Italian restaurant chain expanded rapidly, and is currently present in 120 locations in 27 countries. The Schobers specially designed an interior and exterior concept for Vapiano featuring workpieces of wood, glass, marble or slate, which is found globally in all Vapiano restaurants. The increase in demand through Vapiano caused the catering system to become an independent business field for the Schobers, and accounts for 40 % of the total revenue of the company. Because of the economic success of the cooperation with Vapiano, Markus Schober wants to expand the business in this segment. Therefore, Schober GmbH looks for and supports interesting business ideas in the field of system catering, such as the Kölsch bar concept Das Eigelstein, for which the company designed two pilot projects in Münster and Essen.

The Situation before the Takeover of Boxler

The Schobers want to continue their success story, but to do so they need larger production facilities. The already reduced in-house production at their headquarters in Miesbach is close to hitting its capacity limit. Thus, to succeed in dealing with all incoming orders, the company is forced to forward some of them to inexperienced and unknown sub-contractors. "This can't go on", Markus Schober says to himself. He wants to continue growing his company, but he needs reliable, high-quality and individualized fabrication with small batch sizes. No supplier is able to deliver that for acceptable prices. But how can these bottlenecks be overcome? Since an extension of the production facilities in Miesbach was impossible, the offer to take over the wood constructor Boxler in mid-2011, who had been insolvent since December 2010, came just at the right moment. After an initial company evaluation, Markus Schober immediately recognized that, "Boxler is a really good fit."

THE TAKEOVER OF BOXLER

The Boxler Company

Boxler, founded in 1924, is located in Rammingen, approximately 85 km west of Munich, close to the autobahn A96. With a production area of 10,000 m², Boxler produces floorboards in different designs. During peak times, over 160 people were employed at the company founded by Josef Boxler. Its client base consists of prestigious hoteliers, sheiks and yacht owners, who are seeking individual and extravagant floorboards which are put to use in bathing, sauna and pool areas. The brand Castellana is of particular interest to them. The company is well known for its industrial manufacturing, which until 2009 was conducted in a three-shift operation. A large customer base of industrial clients used Boxler to fabricate floors in serial production. This so-called contract production enabled a high utilization of the large, slightly outdated production facilities. The customers can choose between different types of surfaces such as lacquer or wax, different structures, qualities such as oil or fire resistance, as well as between materials such as wood, vinyl, cork, linoleum and leather. However, this market is very competitive and suppliers from low-wage countries exercise downward pressure on prices, which led to constant decrease in the total market turnover in the past, whereas the average sales volume increased from 2005 to 2011 (see **Figure 7.2**).

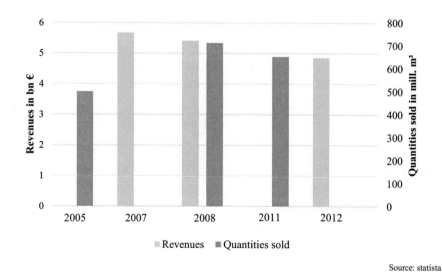

Source: statista

Figure 7.2: Flooring material segment in Germany

The good times of Boxler are long gone. Since a couple of years ago, the company has dragged itself from one crisis to the next. First, the headcount was reduced from 160 to 120 between 1988 and 2009. In addition, the debt level increased continuously. In 2008, for example, €800,000 was added to the already existing debt. As of December 31st, 2009, the debt level increased to a total of €9.2 million. This negative trend culminated in December 2010 when, instead of the company management or a cheated creditor, 19 employees of the company took the initiative and filed for insolvency at the district court of Memmingen.[1] The employees feared for their livelihoods, since, according to them, wages had not been paid for over three months. They were hoping for an investor to get the business up and running again, because employees and management agreed that their products were competitive, their order books filled and the staff motivated. But a lack of liquidity hindered the company in acquiring large clients, as it was unable to cover upfront expenses caused by advance deliveries.

In February 2011, insolvency proceedings against the troubled wood constructor, whose slogan, "Competency in wood", was still justifiable according to the liquidator and the workforce, were started. The business kept on going throughout the whole proceedings, while the headcount was further reduced. Back then, only 80 employees were still with Boxler. However, the liquidator stated that the order situation was still good and that all stakeholders of the company had agreed to take part in the restructuring process.

The Takeover

After the search for investors took more than half a year, at the end of July 2011, the takeover of Boxler by the Markus Schober Innenausbau und Bodendielen GmbH was announced. Schober took over the business with retroactive effect from 1st July, 2011.[2] In cooperation with an independent businessman, who financed the acquisition of the large compound, Markus Schober took over the wood constructor. By contrast, Schober GmbH funded the purchase of the machines, the warehouse and the licenses out of their own pockets. At the time of the acquisition, Boxler was financially stable, the liquidator claimed. In 2011, the company aimed to achieve a revenue of €10 million.

A couple of other potential buyers were also interested in Boxler, which was why the decision had to be taken quickly at the end of July. The Schobers perceived the acquisition as the optimal means to ramp up their production quantity, and thus did not hesitate to close the deal. As a consequence, they renounced in-depth due diligence. Instead, Markus Schober hired a second, independent liquidator to look into Boxler. The second audit revealed almost the same results as the first. Since the price was also acceptable, the parties reached an agreement fairly quickly. Markus Schober took over the company, including all employees who were willing to follow his new path for Boxler. Under the new name Boxler Innenausbau und Bodendielen GmbH, the company was to be revived again.

Schober's Motivation

From the moment of his appearance as saviour of Boxler, Markus Schober was introduced as a strategic investor. And that is exactly what he is. From a strategic perspective, the acquisition of Boxler is the logical consequence of the production bottlenecks at Schober GmbH at Miesbach. The floorboard production was completely shifted from Miesbach to Rammingen, including all machines, to serve the increase in demand for Schober's high-quality interior construction. Administration, sales and marketing remained in Miesbach. The long-term sub-contractor factory, previously based in Munich, moved its operations to Miesbach, which allowed the Schobers to make efficient use of the vacant production area. Schober now orders from Boxler, which results in a stable order situation and creates synergies. Additionally, shifting the production results in higher capacity, which solves another of Schober's problems. Because of the high demand, floorboards had to be purchased from suppliers, which further strengthened the market position. With this approach, the Schobers promoted competition in their core business of floorboards. The acquisition and integration of Boxler in the Schober Group put an end to this development (see **Figure 7.3**).

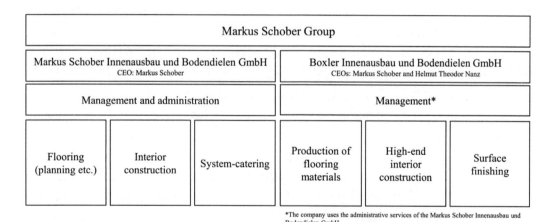

Figure 7.3: New organization chart of the Schober Group

Markus Schober has high hopes for Boxler. In 2012, he wants to increase revenues by 50 % and the net income margin to 3 %. The production should become more effective, the machinery extended and the operative processes streamlined. In addition to that, Boxler is able to benefit from Schober's marketing and distribution experience. Market shares in the serial production of floorboards should be captured from the competition, since this market segment seems to be highly attractive with its lucrative gross margins.

Integration Measures

Markus Schober initiated, together with Boxler's interim manager Georg Gemeiner and the rest of the management team, individual talks with employees and the works council as well as with several work assemblies. He anticipated that these measures might give Boxler new drive, and that the employees would understand and support his vision. However, he knows that the Boxler staff are frustrated because of the years of inertia in the company; therefore, each move Markus makes will be thoroughly observed and evaluated. Markus Schober wants to be a hands-on boss, somebody who is on an equal level in professional debates while still steering and guiding the company. He is in permanent discussions with Boxler's engineers and mechanics as to how to improve the production process. The combination of technical know-how, entrepreneurial thinking and willingness to change longstanding routines raises the scepticism of the Boxler staff. However, with his outstanding technical knowledge, Markus can make some points right at the beginning. For example, he requests the coating of two laminate boards on top of each other at the coating machine. Nobody, neither the engineers nor the workers who have operated this machine for 20 years, believes that this would work. Surprisingly for everyone, Markus Schober was right. From now on, the coating of laminate is done twice as fast as before. With this open communication approach, Markus Schober is sure that the employees of Boxler will understand and adapt the corporate culture promptly. To support this change process, 15 employees, among whom were several carpenters, were transferred from Miesbach to Rammingen. The idea was to bring Boxler up to speed as fast as possible.

The longstanding uncertainty and demotivation of the Boxler employees needed to come to an end. Revitalization was the key word. The set-up process was accompanied by the introduction of several traditions of Schober GmbH, such as rafting tours. However, a corporate feeling did not really arise. Despite his best intentions with Boxler, Markus could not fully banish the distrust of the Boxler staff. He tried to convince through technical innovations and process reconfiguration, but the employees wanted to know what his strategic plan for the new corporation was. The communication needs to be improved. Therefore, the Schobers decided to hire a communication coach to get rid of the atmospheric blockages. During team meetings, in which also some of Schober's employees participated, prejudices needed to be overcome and a sense of community established. "It can't be that difficult to align these two companies," Markus Schober thought at the beginning of the takeover. However, he was to be mistaken.

A ROUGH START FOR THE SCHOBER-BOXLER MARRIAGE

Despite all integrative efforts, post-acquisition business does not run smoothly at Boxler. In particular, the corporate cultures of Schober and Boxler differ more than was initially assumed. Boxler and its workforce are lacking in skills like creativity, entrepreneurial thinking and innovative capacity; skills that Schober GmbH has long cherished. In contrast to Schober, Boxler usually produced for the masses in large batch sizes, and was rarely hired for individual orders that require flexibility and swiftness of action. The open-minded, solution-based approach to satisfying every customer need fostered by Schober, with a team of experienced master carpenters, interior designers and material suppliers, is a world Boxler can barely access. Many of the retained employees are not able to keep pace with or even refuse to accept the changes and the speed of restructuring. It was originally planned that Boxler's CEO would supervise the restructuring. However, it became apparent quite fast that he was not capable of realizing the necessary change.[3] This display of inertia among the top management also impacted on the remaining personnel, which was why some of the most capable employees left the company shortly after its acquisition by Schober. The mood among the Boxler workforce is tense.

In the following period, Georg Gemeiner, a consultant and friend of the Schobers, steps in as the new CEO and takes over Boxler's business. This interim solution was thought to steady Boxler for the moment. Gemeiner is a renowned expert in business matters, but lacks technical know-how. Consequently, Markus Schober is still responsible for introducing, overseeing and ensuring the technical changes. It is up to him to convince the staff on the shop-floor of his vision.

Markus Schober had to realize that the integration of Boxler proved to be more difficult than expected. The years of mass production banished all innovative energy and moreover it seemed as if he was not able to persuade the workforce of the path he had envisioned for Boxler. In addition, the company experienced production-related issues: the current machinery turned out to be too error-prone on closer examination, and many of the machines did not follow the qualitative standards that the Schobers requested for the production of premium products. For instance, Boxler operates a laminate machine in three shifts so that the subsequent production steps can be performed by a single shift. If this machine breaks down, the whole production stands still. Nevertheless, this machine is one of the oldest currently being operated, liable to malfunctions and generally in a bad state. Furthermore, the changing of attachments of other machines sometimes takes up to half a day, an issue partially rooted in the fact that skilled workers left Boxler and it is difficult to find trained employees on the labour market. But since Schober mostly needs customized wood cuttings and coatings, the changing of attachments for different lengths, widths and coatings may be necessary at any time. All things considered, the current resource endowment does not allow for an economically efficient production process for small batch sizes and individual jobs.

Another thing that bothers Schober is the incoming order situation at Boxler. Many returning customers left the company after its insolvency and placed their orders elsewhere. Contrary to the positive predictions of the liquidator, Boxler currently counts only two solid customers. Important licences expired during the acquisition, which contributed to customers not being served. In order to regain these licences, lawsuits and hearings are ongoing, while at the same time a new customer base has to be set up by a newly hired sales department. The head of sales worked for Schober GmbH prior to the acquisition, and establishes customer relations with five sales representatives. For now, Schober GmbH is Boxler's largest client, but only to keep the production running. Boxler's cost structure does not permit the production of small batch sizes, like the ones of Schober. Thus, Schober currently pays considerably more than it would with other manufacturers.

ARE WE ON THE RIGHT TRACK?

Markus Schober doubts his decision to acquire Boxler from time to time, due to the numerous problems that have emerged. But the licence negotiations in Sweden went very well, and Boxler will obtain the licence shortly, improving the much-needed planning security. With these licences, the marketing and sales campaign to attract new and reclaim former customers can finally start. The brand of Boxler will be re-established to position the company in the market. But this does not solve all the problems in place. It is still unclear if and when Boxler will be able to fulfil the role of the profitable high-volume producer and make-to-order manufacturer of Schober.

Markus Schober need an action plan to tackle the problems one by one. But where should he start? Strengthening the sales team? He is sure that Boxler will be profitable once incoming orders pile up. But what if we cannot quantitatively and qualitatively keep up with an increasing demand, given our present-day workforce and machinery equipment? He discussed his thoughts with his wife, Christine. "Maybe we have to improve internal production processes or buy new machines first, before aggressively acquiring new customers," Markus explains. "Furthermore, we have to face the issue of training, as we need highly trained personnel for our products." Christine reminded him: "Before you buy anything or acquire new customers, the leadership issue has to be solved. Markus, you can't continue with the double burden of running Schober GmbH and Boxler at the same time". The question of who should become CEO and chief engineer at Boxler has also not been resolved. Georg Gemeiner will leave Boxler as soon as his one-year contract as interim manager ends. "Georg will leave soon. His job is done. It is extremely pressing to sort this out. There must be a permanent solution for Boxler; the staff are getting restless," Christine adds. "It's good that there is a potential candidate for the CEO position coming in next week. So, we are on the way to finding a solution. In the meantime, we can prepare for the future. I'm truly excited for Boxler!" Markus replied.

•••

Setting of the case: 2012; last revision: 2014.

NOTES

[1] Eisele, F. (2010): *Boxler ist insolvent*, Augsburger Allgemeine, URL: http://www.augsburger-allgemeine.de/mindelheim/Boxler-ist-insolvent-id9089701.html, 20.10.2010.

[2] Antosch, M., (2011): *Boxler ist gerettet*, Augsburger Allgemeine, URL: http://www.augsburger-allgemeine.de/mindelheim/Boxler-ist-gerettet-id15995626.html, 22.07.2011.

[3] Antosch, M., (2011): *Neuanfang bei Boxler*, Augsburger Allgemeine, URL: http://www.augsburger-allgemeine.de/mindelheim/Neuanfang-bei-Boxler-id17196506.html, 20.10.2011.

8

The WOW Air Cargo Alliance

Tobias Schmitz, Lisa Brekalo and Sascha Albers

In October 2013, it hit the news again: with the headline "Lufthansa Cargo takes the Star Alliance as a model", the German newspaper *FAZ* cited Lufthansa Cargo CEO Ulrich Garnadt announcing that Lufthansa Cargo is planning the launch of a new multilateral cargo alliance in 2014, "beginning with one partner" (*FAZ*, 18/10/2013). The alliance logic that has seen the rise of Star Alliance, Oneworld and SkyTeam, which together account for almost 67 % of the world's airline passenger revenues, has again unfolded its attractiveness for the cargo side of the industry. However, at least once the logic has failed to materialize into accountable profits: the failure of the WOW alliance is firmly imprinted on Lufthansa Cargo's recent history - and Garnadt undoubtedly knows about the failure of this alliance venture. So why should they try it again, and what is to be learned from WOW's failure?

THE WOW IDEA

At the very end of the 1990s, the market conditions in the air cargo business were about to change. The demand for air cargo services continued to increase due to shippers' preferences for global high-speed and high frequency transportation. However, concentration processes among cargo airlines' customers (mostly global forwarding companies) all but compensated for the positive demand effect. In this setting, Lufthansa Cargo, SAS Cargo (SASC) and Singapore Airlines Cargo (SIAC) announced to set up the global air cargo alliance WOW, which initially started with the working title "New Global Cargo (NGC). NGC aimed to establish a seamless global network of their air cargo products and services for their joint customer base. Thereby, LHC, SASC and SIAC expected to lower costs and offer value-added towards their customers, as well as to ensure a stronger market position for each member airline and the alliance in general.

THE AIR CARGO INDUSTRY

The air cargo industry grew up supported by different economic developments, such as an increasing globalization that requires a connection between places of production and places of consumption in a fast and reliable way all around the globe. Today, airfreight transportation has developed into a crucial and basic connector in global supply chains, carrying nearly a third of the value of the entire world trade per year.[1]

Industry Development. At its beginning, cargo only served as a generator of additional payload for passenger aircraft with overcapacities. Aircraft whose storage areas were not entirely filled with luggage started to carry mail, parcels and other smaller shipments. Over time, high growth rates of almost 20 % p.a. in the 1960s motivated the airlines to offer distinct air cargo services, which resulted in a dedicated air cargo market emerging over the years. Particularly since the late 1980s, the market has grown significantly, resulting in a doubling of the amount of annually transported revenue-tonne-kilometres (RTKs) by 1998. In general, air cargo is highly dependent on overall global economic development; it is often seen as an (early) indicator of economic up- or downswings. Traffic volumes drop sharply in times of economic or political crisis, as in the months after 11th September, 2001, or during the financial crisis in 2008. After the financial crisis worldwide, air cargo production (measured by FTKs) dropped by 11 %. The market for air cargo express shipments appeared to be much more robust during the crisis than the market for standard shipments, which started to recover in the second half of 2009, especially due to an increasing demand in Asia. As a result, the industry showed a growth of 22 %, accounting for 194.4 billion RTKs in 2010. By the end of 2010, the airfreight volumes even caught up with the pre-crisis peaks of 2007. For the forthcoming decades until 2032, industry forecasts estimate annual FTK growth rates of about 5 % (see **Figure 8.1**).

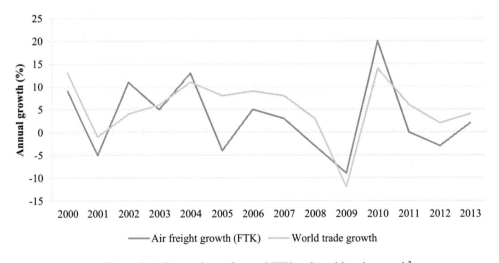

Figure 8.1: Comparison of annual FTK and world trade growth[2].

Since the air cargo market depends on the general development of domestic economies, some regions are expected to demand more cargo traffic than other. As such, the inter-Asian and domestic Chinese market will lead future expansions with above-average growth rates of 8-9 %. In addition, cargo volumes to and from Asia are expected to benefit from the local economies. On the other hand, volumes between South America and Europe or North America, as well as from Europe to Africa or the Middle East are forecasted to grow on average, whereas connections between Europe and North America are expected to develop below average (3-4 %) as illustrated in **Figure 8.2**.[3]

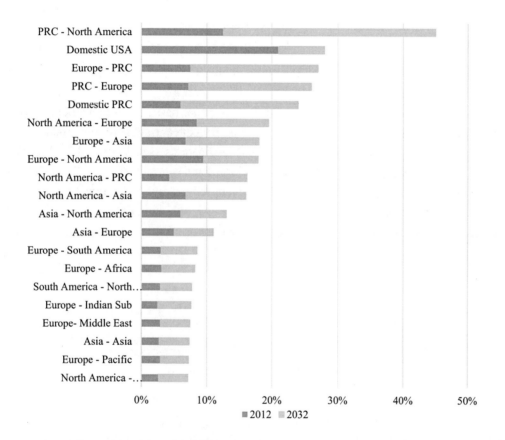

Figure 8.2: Airbus global market forecast – Top 20 largest flows in 2032[4].

According to these market developments, the number of aircraft in the freighter fleets will also increase by more than two-thirds to serve the growing market. Within their fleets, airlines primarily rely on the increasing importance of long-haul aircraft that will represent a third of all planes by 2025. To save costs, about 70 % of the future cargo planes will be converted into passenger machines, whereas the minority will be newly built aircraft. With these new aircraft, the cargo airlines try to address recent technical improvements, such as reduced fuel consumption or availability of wide-body planes that provide extended capacity.

The Air Cargo Business Model. Air cargo connects all continents of the world in the fastest means of transportation. It is also the most expensive transportation mode. It is mostly products with a high value-to-density ratio or with a need for fast transportation that are flown on the international routes. Commonly flown goods include, for instance, electronics, pharmaceuticals, machines and spare parts, perishables such as fresh food or flowers, as well as urgent express mail and parcels. Air cargo competes with ocean shipping and railway transportation. However, strongholds of these other transport modes are rather bulky goods that can afford longer delivery times and command lower prices.

To be able to fly goods around the globe in an efficient and effective way, air cargo carriers organize their flight network accordingly. Therefore, normally, the so-called hub-and-spoke networks are operated on a global or regional basis. Such networks consist of major hubs as well as several minor destinations. By concentrating flights around a hub, airlines are able to connect many origins and destinations (see **Figure 8.3**). Incoming flights from several different origins are consolidated at a central hub, to be flown either to a certain destination in one single outbound flight or to be redirected via the hub to another non-central destination. From a structural point of view, hub-and-spoke networks resemble star-shaped networks, in which all points are interconnected.

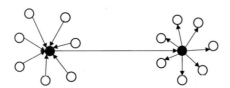

Figure 8.3: Hub-and-spoke network

While large cargo airlines operate their network globally, smaller airlines only cover a region or continent. To serve these routes, air cargo airlines can make use of two different kinds of aircraft. On the one hand, airlines use the so-called belly capacities of regular passenger flights, and thereby use the density and variety of the passenger flight network. On the other hand, airlines also use dedicated freighters, which are newly built or converted planes explicitly designed for carrying large amounts of palletized goods.

Actors. Three actor types serve the air cargo demand: *integrators, air cargo carriers* and *airlines*. *Integrators*, i.e., air express carriers, have their own air and ground assets to handle the entire shipment journey and provide a one-stop door-to-door service (e.g., UPS,

FedEx, DHL). *Air cargo carriers* exclusively operate cargo aircraft and use them for line and charter traffic (e.g., Cargolux). *Airlines* offer both passenger and air cargo transportation, while the passenger aircraft's belly capacities are used to support the cargo business. Although some airlines concentrate their air cargo activities in a separate subsidiary, others solely rely on belly transportation as a sub-product of the passenger business, which leads to differences in airfreight's strategic importance for the overall airline.

Rank	Airline	Scheduled FTKs in 2001 (in millions)	Rank	Airline	Scheduled FTKs in 2013 (in millions)
1	Federal Express	10,809	1	Emirates	10,459
2	Lufthansa	7,176	2	Cathay Pacific Airways	8,241
3	United Parcel Service	5,955	3	FedEx	7,691
4	Singapore Airlines	5,848	4	Korean Air	7,635
5	Korean Air Lines Co.Ltd.	5,424	5	Lufthansa	7,213
6	Air France	4,633	6	Singapore Airlines	6,24
7	Japan Airlines	4.050	7	UPS Airlines	5,545
8	British Airways	4.047	8	Cargolux	5,225
9	Cathay Pacific	3.709	9	Qatar Airways	4,972
10	KLM	3.422	10	China Airlines	4,813

Table 8.1: Airline ranking 2001 and 2013 (in FTKs).[5]

From a process perspective, airlines are dependent on further actors. In order to transport a shipment from the sender to the receiver, the sender gives its freight to a carrier. The carrier transports the shipment from the sender to the airport to hand it over to the air cargo operator flying the shipment to the destination airport. Here, another carrier picks up the shipment to deliver it to the receiver.

Customers. As described before, airlines cover only one part of the entire logistics chain from shipper to receiver. Since some airlines only connect airports, they are in the middle of the entire transportation chain. The customer side in particular is an important source for challenges to the cargo airlines. Here, the freight forwarders are a mixed blessing for cargo airlines: on the one hand, they are the airlines' most important customers. On the other hand, they consolidate and bundle freight volumes from many smaller carriers or manufacturers, and thus have high bargaining and negotiation power in relation to the cargo airlines, since these freight forwarders' customers usually leave the choice of the airline with the service provider. Lastly, some air cargo customers directly contact the airline to fly a shipment. In that case, the airline receives the shipment from a carrier and hands it over to another designated carrier at the point of destination.

When serving its customers, an airline needs to cover demands as well as the special characteristics and handling requirements it needs to manage. In order to meet these demands, the airlines offer distinct air cargo products, which can be differentiated into three main air cargo product types: express products, standard freight and specialties. Express products are time-definite services, promising to be delivered within a given time frame of usually one to two days all around the globe. On the other hand, standard freight consists of regular shipments that are flown according to a given schedule of the airline. Lastly, special transports are offered for sensitive freight, such as pharmaceuticals, chemicals, animals or temperature-controlled shipments.

WOW – LHC'S AIRFREIGHT ALLIANCE

Although the air cargo market was performing extremely well in the late 1990s, the customer demands on air cargo airlines were about to change. While most airlines served distinct routes and destinations, the customers more and more demanded a global, seamless cargo network, able to transport goods from any origin to any destination. Moreover, the air cargo airlines faced increased customer demands regarding the speed, cost, quality and security of transportation services. However, a single cargo airline, and LHC in particular, did not have sufficient resources or capacities to operate such networks and services on its own.

In addition to these customer requests and market potentials, traditional air cargo airlines increasingly faced competition from the growing integrator business. Integrators offer their customers seamless (one-stop shopping) and comprehensive (door-to-door) transportation services in a very efficient way, thus offering a viable alternative to the cargo airlines. Consolidation in the forwarding industry, e.g., among FedEx, UPS and TNT Post Group (TPG), further increased the competition in the cargo market. These changes in the industry left the cargo airlines with a shrinking customer base: as a result, fewer customers approached the cargo airlines with larger freight volumes, which weakened the airlines' negotiation base.

In order to address the challenges of changing customer demand and increased competitive pressure by freight forwarders, the cargo airlines needed to strengthen their market position. At the same time, in the late 1990s, the passenger airlines also experienced changing economic and regulatory conditions. In response, many airlines grouped together between 1997 and 2000, such as in the now well-known strategic multi-partner alliances Oneworld, SkyTeam and Star Alliance. This should support the airlines in exploiting synergies regarding the utilization of aircraft, ground operations, route networks and schedules. Thereby, a single airline was able to offer more destinations and a broader range of services, as well as a higher flight frequency to their customers. Following the example of their passenger equivalents, the cargo airlines attempted to address the customers' changing demands and to face the increased competition on the market by setting up strategic alliances. As such, Lufthansa Cargo, Singapore Airlines Cargo and SAS Cargo agreed upon a strategic alliance, as a measure for establishing a global seamless network and improved transportation services in April 2000.

Lufthansa Cargo. Lufthansa Cargo (LHC) is the cargo subsidiary of the Star Alliance member Lufthansa, and is considered a separate legal entity, headquartered in Frankfurt. When WOW started in 2000 (at that time called NGC), LHC operated 20 freighters, mainly based at Frankfurt airport. In addition, the cargo subsidiary had access to the belly capacities of more than 300 passenger aircraft. With this, LHC belonged to the world's largest freight carriers, transporting more than seven billion freight-tonne-kilometres (FTKs) in 2000. LHC mainly served the European markets, and provided connections to other continents, especially the US and Asia. Due to the use of belly capacities, LHC was also able to serve minor markets. By fostering the foundation of an alliance, LHC aimed to establish high-quality logistics services supported by its partners' capabilities and capacities. Thereby, an improved strategic position on the global cargo market, additional improvements in traffic volume and efficiencies, as well as higher overall profits have been expected. Highlighting NGC's important status for LHC, it became a separate business unit, which indicates its special meaning.

SAS Cargo. Since 2001, the Star Alliance member Scandinavian Airlines has operated the independent airfreight subsidiary, SAS Cargo (SASC). Mainly connecting the Scandinavian markets to Europe, SAS Cargo operated its three hubs in Copenhagen, Oslo and Solna (next to Stockholm) at the time the alliance was founded. As the cargo airline does not own any dedicated freighters, it entirely relied on the belly capacities of its passenger fleet. In 2001, the Swedish airline transported 610 million FTKs and planned to increase this number by entering NGC. Moreover, access to LHC's and SIAC's network represented a substantial extension of SASC's market reach.

SIA Cargo. SIA Cargo (SIAC) has existed in its legally separated form since 2001, and is a subsidiary of the passenger airline Singapore Airlines. In 2000, it served the intra-Asian market and operated on intercontinental routes between Asia and Europe, as well as Asia and Australia. Belonging to the world's top five cargo carriers, in 2001 SIAC transported nearly six billion FTKs with its eight dedicated freighters. Participating in NGC allowed SIA to extend the market reach of its customers to the inter-European routes. In turn, SIAC's participation gave access to Asian destinations for the German and Swedish partner firms.

WOW's Promise. By setting up the cargo alliance, the airlines reacted to the present market conditions. These were especially favourable since organic growth and merger and acquisition strategies were not relevant options due to cost and time issues, as well as legal restrictions. WOW's aims consisted of improvements for the individual partner airlines, the joint market position, and the cargo customers. For the airlines, the overall aim was to strengthen and enlarge their market position in competition with the integrators. Moreover, the partners aimed for an increase in freight volumes and higher average yields. The intended advantages for the customers were a higher service level on a global scale in connection with high-quality standards, reliable operations, and a single point of contact based on an innovative online booking system. In order to realize these targets, the partners emphasized the two key measures of a harmonization of products and operations, on the one hand, and a common market image, on the other. By realizing economies and efficiencies through the consolidation of joint resources, yielding sales and efficiency increases, the three airlines expected to perform better in the marketplace than they would on their own.

A POTENT COMPETITOR? SKYTEAM CARGO

SkyTeam Cargo was founded concurrently with the SkyTeam passenger alliance in September 2000 by the airlines Air France, Korean Air, Delta Airlines and Aeroméxico; it can be interpreted as a response to the foundation of WOW. The original membership from Europe, South and North America and Asia quickly grew, as Czech Airlines Cargo and Alitalia Cargo joined in April and August 2001, shortly after entering the SkyTeam passenger alliance.

Later in 2004, Air France would merge with KLM, the Dutch cargo division further enlarged the alliance as the seventh member. To close a perceived gap in the US market, the SkyTeam members convinced Northwest Airlines to join the alliance in September 2005, before they merged with Delta Airlines in 2008. Since SkyTeam also wanted to meet the potentials of the rising Chinese market, China Southern Airlines was also approached and welcomed in late 2010, as well as China Airlines (2012) and China Cargo Airlines (2013). Simultaneously, Russia's Aeroflot Cargo joined SkyTeam Cargo in 2011, and Aerolineas Argentinas Cargo in 2013. Today, the cargo alliance comprises 11 of the world's largest cargo carriers and accounted for nearly 34 billion FTKs in 2013. Of that amount, Korean Cargo and Air France/KLM Cargo each contributed roughly 40 %, as the two strongest members in the alliance[6].

RISE AND FALL: WOW'S ALLIANCE DEVELOPMENT

Aiming to improve customer value and, thus, the partners' market positions, LHC, SIAC and SASC decided on a stepwise integration of their air cargo activities in order to provide a seamless global network. Therefore, the partners focused primarily on the harmonization of their products and the promotion of a joint market presence. A harmonization of products and operations should (1) ensure synergies and a common market appearance and (2) communicate the cooperation and its advantages to the customers. Therefore, the partners strived for aligned IT systems, common handling processes and joint standards to secure a high level of quality and reliability in their joint cargo services. In doing so, WOW aspired to position itself as a premium provider in the market. After founding WOW, a dedicated alliance management team (consisting of four business integration teams: product, sales, handling and IT) headed by a central alliance manager was implemented and was responsible for the development and coordination of the alliance activities.

Harmonization of Products and Operations. After setting up WOW in spring 2000, the partners and especially the business integration teams focused primarily on the stepwise harmonization of the partners' products required to ensure joint premium quality and reliability standards. As such, the standardization of the members' different products, and their booking, registration and handling procedures were the major areas of activity. Since the aim of the alliance consisted primarily of the creation of customer value based on improved transportation processes and services within a seamless, global, and out-of-one-hand network, a joint IT system was seen as a crucial facilitator for the alliance's success.

Express services. In October 2001, the alliance members began to harmonize their express services by offering a joint network of nearly 500 destinations in over 100 countries worldwide. Express services, such as td.Flash (LHC), SAS Priority (SASC) and Swiftrider (SIAC), were those products that needed to be delivered to one of the alliance's 240 destinations by a given arrival time. In offering these products, WOW realized a milestone in its cooperation shortly after its foundation. As LHC's board member for marketing and sales, Dr Andreas Otto, stated, "[…] *all three partners have now reached the second big milestone in the alliance with the confirmation that al 'time-definite' offerings from the three carriers are now fully adjusted*". Summing up, he added, "*along with the first big milestone of harmonized express products introduced last October, over 80 % of the total cargo business of all three airlines is now harmonized*"[7]. In order to push the partnership forward and to provide sufficient capacity, the passenger divisions of Lufthansa, Singapore Airlines and JAL started to block 10 % of their belly capacities for exclusive use by WOW's express shipments in January 2002.[8] In doing so, WOW strived for a better exploitation of complementarities on their route network. The capacities were blocked until 48 hours before the respective flight, and were only offered to the external market in cases where they were not fully utilized. The top management of all members judged this agreement as a "*significant step and the most important innovation in the existence of the cargo alliance*." In the future, the booking procedures for the standard cargo products td.Pro (LHC) and General Cargo (SASC, SIAC) were expected to be aligned in April 2002. Furthermore, the alignment of the remaining product segments, premium express, standard cargo, and large and heavy express, were planned for the winter schedule in 2002.

Joint handling processes and standards. To support the harmonization plans, the partners agreed on standardized handling procedures for their joint products to provide the customers with the same services, information and transparency regardless of the airline flying a shipment. Furthermore, common security standards were set based on the IATA requirements. To facilitate the joint handling processes and realize efficiency gains, the partners agreed on a "one roof" policy, striving for the joint utilization of warehouses, terminals, and other facilities to leverage synergies. Thus, WOW started to operate the first freight terminal exclusively used by the alliance in autumn 2003 at the airport in Frankfurt. This unique facility was set up for WOW members in order to collectively load and unload dedicated WOW freighters.

IT systems. An important prerequisite for the realization of WOW's harmonization targets was a joint IT system for all members. This should support the operation of a global and seamless network across company borders, as well as one central booking gateway for the customers. Creating a common system required connecting the four existing IT systems of the partner airlines, in order to get access to data concerning bookings, routes or capacities. Furthermore, the system should be capable of combining the resources of the member firms to enable customers to book transportations across the entire network. However, the implication of such a system came with considerable costs for the airlines that previously relied on and invested into two different systems. While LHC used the Global Freight Exchange (GF-X) electronic system, JAL and SIA Cargo preferred a different one. Thus, the adaptation was not realized in the expected scope, since no carrier wanted to resign its system completely. However, this would have confused customers, since they would have to use different systems to book a single WOW shipment. Hence, discussions and negotiations among members caused a delay in the implementation. In summer 2003, the partners concluded that they could not agree on buying and implementing an entirely new system due to reasons of cost. Instead, several provisional solutions to connect the IT systems were preferred.

Promotion of Joint Market Presence (Branding). To leverage the alliance opportunities, the alliance partners promoted a joint market presence for the customers. In the course of a branding process, the alliance abandoned its initial project name of NGC and launched its new brand, WOW, officially in January 2002. The innovative brand name should capture attention at the customer side and stand for the reaction the alliance aspired to evoke with their performance. The new name accompanied the simultaneous harmonization of express products, and a "Member of WOW" sign was painted on the aircraft of LHC, SAS Cargo and SIA Cargo. But the customers did not understand the renaming, and found "NGC" to be more appropriate, because "WOW" did not seem to embody logistical activities. This might have been due to the delayed launch of the WOW marketing campaign that was planned for autumn 2001, but then postponed until 2002 because of the 11th September terrorist attacks. This time lag between the WOW launch and the corresponding marketing campaign caused the failure to bestow the name with strategic contents as well as the failure to make linkages with logistics services that should have been clarified in the following months.[9]

As well as the alliance brand, WOW also strived for a distinct naming of their products. In contrast to the harmonization of their express products on an operational level, these products were still offered and commercialized under their firm-specific product names (td.Flash (LHC), SAS Priority (SASC) and Swiftrider (SIAC)), as the airlines refused to give up their brand representation in the markets. *"We do not intend to change the brand names of any of our individual products,"* stated SAS Cargo CEO, Mr Grønlund, because *"they represent high-value and high-recognition names, which we do not want to change"*[10]. As a result, customers had four different product names for ordering express freight, one from each of the member airlines. Accordingly, customers claimed to miss the central contact persons, and simply went on contacting a single airline as usual.

Alliance Extension. Based on the idea of a globally operating air cargo alliance, WOW searched for potential and powerful partners that shared the same ideas of a global quality-oriented cargo alliance to enlarge the existing network. Since North America represented the most important cargo market, the alliance especially looked for a US airline: *"It is widely known that we need a strong North American partner and an equally strong South American partner for the future"*[11], noted Howard Jones, SASC's head in the US. The desired partner should constitute a strong counterpart on the North American continent for LHC and SIA Cargo and their main hubs in Europe and Asia. In March 2002, Lufthansa's Star Alliance partner United Airlines looked set to become the fourth WOW member. However, due to the dominance of UPS and FedEx on the American market, United saw its future not in the cargo business. It became clear to the WOW members that starting negotiations with United had poor prospects of success. Therefore, they did not initiate serious negotiations United's alliance entry. The second candidate, and a KLM partner in the passenger segment, Northwest Airlines, had a strong position in the US cargo market, though the collaboration failed during the negotiations. As a result, WOW faced a gap in North America, in contrast to its rival SkyTeam Cargo, already operating with Delta Air Logistics as a partner.

Instead of an American partner, WOW announced that Japanese Airlines Cargo (JAL) - based in Tokyo and a long-term LHC partner - would join the alliance in summer 2002. Since the merger with Japan Air System, JAL has been among the world's 10 largest airlines. The freight unit JAL Cargo serves the domestic Japanese market, connects it with intercontinental destinations, and transports goods on longer intra-Asian routes as well. The integration of JAL would substantially add capacity to the alliance. Adding in JAL's freighters and belly capacities, WOW's total fleet grew to more than 40 dedicated cargo craft and the belly capacities of a further 760 passenger craft in 2002, accounting for nearly 20 % of the worldwide air cargo traffic to more than 240 destinations. JAL Cargo's express service, JSPEED, was aligned with the WOW partners' express services, while also keeping its established product name. Later in 2007, the JAL group would join the Oneworld alliance in the passenger business.

After integrating JAL, media reports discussed several airlines with other bilateral LHC partnerships that might join the alliance. As LHC already served South America's east coast, LanChile was discussed as a potential WOW member. Further rumours brought up Air China or South African Airways, among others, but these rumours never turned out to be realistic options. Instead, WOW announced in August 2003 that its search for further members would stop. Since the integration of new partners turned out to be more complicated than expected, and incomparably difficult compared to passenger alliances, WOW announced to stick with its current size of four partners in the future. This was particularly due to the challenging integration of cargo operations in an alliance that appeared to be much more complex than in the passenger segment. WOW would rather focus on the further integration of the businesses of the four existing members.

External Partnerships. The decision to not foster an enlargement of WOW's member base appeared to be a major limitation, especially for SASC: Since the Scandinavian carrier completely relied on belly capacities for airfreight, and its passenger segment simultaneously reduced the number of flights to the US, SASC needed to search for another cargo partner with both adequate aircraft and connections between Scandinavia and the US. None of the WOW partners could serve this crucial route for SAS with a dedicated freighter and the desired capacity. Hence, only a few days after Hwang's announcement about not enlarging WOW, SAS Cargo signed a contract with Korean Air Cargo (KAC) in late 2003[12]. Both parties agreed on a three-year contract guaranteeing freight capacity for SASC on Korean's weekly flights between Copenhagen and New York. Already one of the world's largest cargo airlines, KAC was also a member of the competing SkyTeam Cargo alliance. Although SASC's WOW partners criticized the decision to cooperate with a member of a competing alliance, the agreement was commented as a rational decision that had to be accepted. SASC's CEO justified this step, pointing to LHC's cooperation with KAC on the Frankfurt-Seoul route that had already existed for many years.

In the following months, WOW members established further bilateral partnerships alongside their membership of the WOW alliance. Thus, LHC started to cooperate with the express service provider DHL in early 2004. This cooperation is today known as Aerologic, and consists of the shared use of a 777F aircraft fleet between Germany and the US. Both operators fly from Leipzig, mainly to the US, India and Asia. Commenting on their first impressions, LHC managers admitted that, "it is easier to work closely with an express operator that is not a direct competitor than with WOW partners that are."[13] Besides Aerologic, LHC set up two other partnerships with an American and an Asian airline. In September 2004, the airline agreed with their (at that time) Star Alliance affiliate, US Airways, on managing their cargo capacities for transatlantic flights, enabling LHC to add the volume of one and a half freighters per week to the US to its capacity. Furthermore, LHC arranged a new cooperation with Shenzhen Airlines, as the carriers founded JADE Cargo in October 2004 to connect the major European airports with Chinese and Korean destinations. JADE Cargo flies several times a week between the continents, using six dedicated freight aircraft.

Alliance Achievements. After two years of cooperation and intense efforts to implement the WOW alliance in the daily business of all alliance partners, a comprehensive assessment of the alliance activities showed that the tangible results remained below initial expectations. However, the partners agreed in 2002 to continue, and tried to improve their activities through the establishment of a fifth business integration team network. This team focused on the opportunities to smoothen the scheduling and capacity coordination among the partners within the legal frame (antitrust regulations). Despite these efforts, the alliance implementation seemed to reach over and above its limits. This was due to the lack of (1) an antitrust immunity, which impedes a stronger integration of partners' activities, e.g., in terms of joint price setting, (2) a joint cash box or adequate risk- and reward-sharing mechanisms which would balance the remaining competition between the alliance partners, and (3) a joint IT system ensuring the required speed and accuracy of the information and data exchange between the partners. In the following year, 2004, LHC underwent a substantial internal reorganizational process leading to a resolution of the dedicated WOW team into the respective line organizations and departments. Moreover, LHC called on the Asian WOW members in particular to intensify their efforts for the alliance by taking over more leadership positions. In the first four years of its existence, LHC performed the alliance manager role within WOW. Dr. Andreas Otto of LHC explained: *"When I joined the company five years ago, the idea was that sooner or later we would have one cash box, because that is what the market requires. But we have discovered that for various reasons - legal issues, traffic rights - it is very difficult to do that [...]. We feel that after three or four years it is time to leave it to someone else to take the initiative."* Asked for the future synergy potential of the alliance, he concludes: *"The long-term vision has to be a joint cash box. Anything less than that, and we don't see benefits."*[14] By the end of 2004, the WOW Air Cargo alliance managed to harmonize the operations of their express and cargo products across the company borders. In contrast to the market for express shipments, non-alliance-specific products, such as container- or pallet-based shipments, were excluded from the agreement. On these specific markets, the members still competed against each other. Furthermore, the commitment to blocking 10 % of the belly capacities on passenger flights demonstrates a second measure of cooperation. Despite the operational harmonization of their products, these still appeared under their airline-specific brand names. Also a common IT system could not be implemented. Moreover, the WOW network did not cover the US market intensively, and the alliance was unable to find an American partner. While the dedicated freight terminal in Frankfurt is the only shared resource among the partners, the members are engaged in several new bilateral partnerships alongside their WOW membership.

After 2004, media and annual reports about WOW, and about the engagements or investments of member firms, are scarcer. Sources about WOW and its performance disappear from 2004 onwards, although the cooperation still existed legally until 2009. In 2008, three years after the last official reports on WOW, LHC announced its official withdrawal from the cargo alliance, stating that WOW never worked out the way the Star

Alliance in the passenger segment did. The absence of customer loyalty programmes, as well as booking and IT systems, seemed to impede a closer cooperation or market appearance.

LHC'S WOW EXPERIENCES – LEARNING FROM THE PAST?

Considering the media reports about LHC's plan to start new alliance initiatives[15], the WOW alliance could serve as a template for future activities. However, this history shows that WOW came with some obvious deficiencies regarding design and conduct of the alliance. The somewhat less than perfect set of partners, as well as shortcomings in their joint operations and IT landscape, are only the most obvious areas for improvement. On the other hand, the air cargo market now looks different compared to the beginning of the 2000s. For instance, consolidation in the US airline industry leaves potential for alliances, with a smaller set of US partners to choose from compared to 2001. Furthermore, LHC's situation as reported in the abovementioned *FAZ* (18/10/2013) has also changed, and its customers' demands are not comparable to those of the time in which WOW was instituted. Therefore, simply addressing past mistakes would not be sufficient to succeed with an alliance in the marketplace. Furthermore, the industry now shows examples of standalone airlines acting successfully in the airfreight business today, raising the question of whether alliances are an appropriate concept at all. What has changed in the last decade? Which developments will the airfreight industry face in the upcoming years that one needs to take into account? Is an alliance still the correct measure to address the market? Most probably, interested airlines need to take a more holistic and comprehensive perspective: how do the market conditions look, and what is expected to arise the future? If an alliance is the right measure to go for, how would it need to be adapted in comparison to the WOW set-up? What is most important? How would these important aspects need to be arranged? These aspects certainly require more in-depth consideration in the future.

•••

Setting of the case: 2011; last revision: 2014.

NOTES

1. Airbus, (2013a): *Global market forecast 2012-2032.*

2. IATA, (2014): *Annual review 2014*, URL: http://www.iata.org/publications/Documents/iata-annual-review-2014-en.pdf, p.15.

3. Boeing, (2012): *World air cargo forecast 2012-2013.*

4. Airbus, (2013b): *Global market forecast – Top 20 flows in 2032.*

5. IATA, (2013): *Members' Rankings*, WATS 58th edition 2013.

6. Skyteam, (2013): *Skyteam Fact Sheet* as of June 5th, 2013.

7. Roger, T., (2002): *Wowing Cargo*, in: Air Cargo World, Vol. 93(5).

8. DVZ, (2003a): *Wow-Carrier schliessen Aufbau eines Expressnetzes ab*, Deutsche Verkehrszeitung DVZ, Nr. 097, 14.08.2003.

9. DVZ, (2002a): *New Global Cargo hat sehr bewegtes Jahr vor sich*, Deutsche Verkehrszeitung DVZ, Nr. 008, 19.01.2002.

10. Turney, R., (2002): *Wowing Cargo,* Air Cargo World, May2002, Vol. 93, Issue 5.

11. DVZ, (2002b): *Wow-Carrier sollten wie eine Einheit agieren Top-Spediteure aeusserten ihre Erwartungen an die Allianz*", Deutsche Verkehrszeitung DVZ, Nr. 142, 28.11.2002.

12. DVZ, (2003b): *Ja zu Korean ist kein Nein zu WOW*, Deutsche Verkehrszeitung DVZ, Nr. 321, 09.10.2003.

13. Conway, P., (2004): *Teamwork*, Airline Business, URL: http://www.flightglobal.com/news/articles/team-work-189139/, 1.11.2004.

14. Conway, P., (2005): *Pulling together*, Airline Business, Apr2005, Vol. 21, Issue 4.

15. Scherff, D., (2013): *Lufthansa Cargo nimmt sich Star Alliance zum Vorbild*, Frankfurter Allgemeine Zeitung, 18.10.2013.

9

Business Strategy in Russia: Market Entry and Development of Vaillant

Jan-Philipp Büchler, Markus Tandel and Carsten Voigtländer

NEED FOR GOOD GROWTH

Oliver Nehring was well prepared for his presentation to the management board of Vaillant Group, and looked forward to presenting the attractive sales growth in Eastern Europe for the fiscal year 2011. He was the regional director of the strongest emerging market region in the group's business portfolio, and meanwhile used to please the management board by generating double-digit growth and leading market positions in most country markets year over year. When Oliver Nehring commented on the business in Russia, the CEO of Vaillant Group, Dr Carsten Voigtländer, challenged the performance: "Double-digit growth is nice to have, but absolutely normal in an emerging market. When are we going to be in the black? What are your plans for making the business operations profitable? I feel that we need a strategy for profitable growth - only profitable growth is good growth!"

After a short discussion among the members of the management board, Oliver Nehring was asked to develop a strategy for profitable growth in Russia, and to present this strategy to the management board in the next meeting. Without further ado, Oliver Nehring arranged a management meeting with the board of directors of the affiliated company (AC) in Russia for the following week. In preparation of this meeting, he compiled a dossier of information on the market and business development of Vaillant Group in Russia since the time of market entry.

VAILLANT GROUP: DEVELOPMENT AND STRATEGY

The Vaillant Group is an international market leader in the field of heating and ventilation technology. The company was founded in 1874 and is still 100 % family owned. Vaillant Group generates annual sales revenues of €2.3 billion, on the basis of a global market presence operating from its headquarters in Remscheid. The company is known to be one of the "hidden champions" in German industry based on its expertise and market position as the second largest player in its industry and leader in the market segment of wall-hung boilers.

The company manages a portfolio of eight international brands in the heating and ventilation industry. Most of the brands were integrated into the portfolio by selective acquisitions and contribute significantly to the international growth strategy of Vaillant Group.

The brand Vaillant is positioned as premium brand in all markets around the world and covers a broad assortment of the most sophisticated product solutions in the field of heating and ventilation. The Vaillant brand is the most important driver of sales revenues and profit in the brand portfolio, and always provides the highest technological standards and quality to its customers. Products of the Vaillant brand are mostly ranked as winning products in their respective categories by independent product testers such as Stiftung Warentest. Vaillant is the highest priced brand in almost all markets in its relevant segments.

The brands Saunier Duval, Bulex and Glowworm were integrated in the brand portfolio in the context of the acquisition of the UK-based company Hepworth PLC in 2001, while maintaining the brands' regional positioning for their respective markets in Central and Northern Europe. The French brand Saunier Duval offers a universal product assortment in heating and ventilation with a long tradition dating back to 1907, and shows the highest levels of customer loyalty in France. The Belgian brand Bulex comprises a large assortment of qualitative heating products and even serves as a generic term for boilers in Belgium due to its long tradition, its high market penetration and high brand awareness. Glowworm recalls a similar brand history and image. The sales and distribution activities of the brands are managed separately.

This acquisition kicked off a phase of accelerated international expansion which was continued by the acquisitions of majority interest in Hermann - an Italian manufacturer of heating equipment - in order to establish a foothold in the South European market.

In the course of internationalization, Vaillant acquired the Slovakian company Protherm in 2005. The brand Protherm is well known in many Eastern European countries and provides an ideal platform for further sales growth and business development in Eastern Europe, as well as in Asia and the Middle East.

The Vaillant Group kept pushing its internationalization efforts and acquired a majority interest in the Turkish heating and air conditioning specialist Türk DemirDöküm Farbikalari A.S. in 2007. The acquired company was founded in 1954 and developed a leading market position in heating and ventilation in Turkey, and established a promising foothold in the North Africa region.

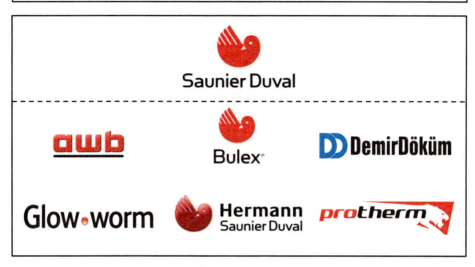

Figure 9.1: Brand portfolio, Vaillant Group

The Vaillant Group maintained the diversity of the acquired brands because of the high brand awareness and strong market positions in the regional markets. At the same time, the company combined the presentation and operations of the acquired brands under the umbrella brand Saunier Duval in order to realize synergies in purchasing, production and distribution activities. Therefore, the Saunier Duval brand group serves as platform for the international operations and encompasses the brands below the dotted line in **Figure 9.1**. These brands concentrate mainly on the middle- and high-volume price segments providing an attractive value-for-money offering targeted at the needs of price-conscious customers. The core brand Vaillant is the flagship brand of the Vaillant Group, and focuses on the highest demands of a discerning clientele in the premium segment. As a supplier of tailor-made systems and products for upmarket demand, a focus is put on environmentally friendly and energy-saving heating. The two brand groups Vaillant and Saunier Duval address different market segments and cover the most diverse customer demands; thus, they are sold separately.

Growth Momentum in Eastern Europe

The Eastern European market has generated important growth momentum for the Vaillant Group for more than two decades. The company started to establish its own legal entities in Poland and Slovakia, as well as in the Czech Republic and in Hungary as of 1992, while some of these markets had already been entered via an indirect export strategy in the sixties

(Hungary) and the seventies (Czech Republic). Due to the early market entry, Vaillant maintains market leadership in these country markets. As a next step, Vaillant established its own legal entities in Ukraine (1999) and Romania (2004) as illustrated in **Figure 9.2**.

Figure 9.2: Market presence, Vaillant Group

The business activities of Vaillant Group in Russia started with a cooperative arrangement between Vaillant and independent sales agents in Saint Petersburg in 1994, followed by a first sales office in Moscow in 1996 and a training centre for sales representatives in 1999, as illustrated in **Figure 9.3**. The after-sales business (i.e., servicing activities and maintenance) started in 2002 with external service partners in a cooperative arrangement. In the course of the stepwise acquisition of Protherm, Vaillant Group bundled all sales and distribution activities in Russia for both brand groups in one place in order to achieve synergies.

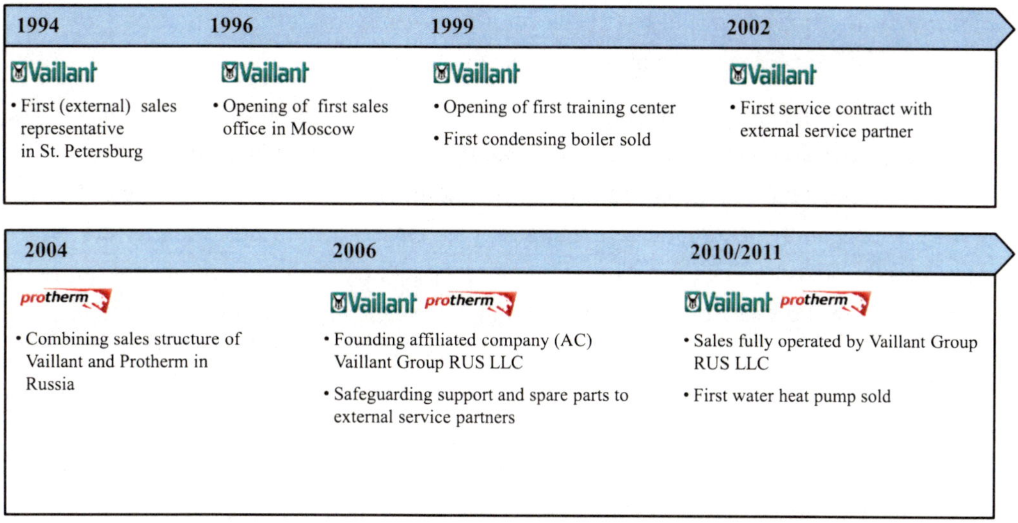

1994	1996	1999	2002
Vaillant	**Vaillant**	**Vaillant**	**Vaillant**
• First (external) sales representative in St. Petersburg	• Opening of first sales office in Moscow	• Opening of first training center • First condensing boiler sold	• First service contract with external service partner

2004	2006	2010/2011
protherm	**Vaillant** *protherm*	**Vaillant** *protherm*
• Combining sales structure of Vaillant and Protherm in Russia	• Founding affiliated company (AC) Vaillant Group RUS LLC • Safeguarding support and spare parts to external service partners	• Sales fully operated by Vaillant Group RUS LLC • First water heat pump sold

Figure 9.3: Market entry of Vaillant Group in Russia

The legal entity Vaillant Group RUS LLC was founded in 2006 at a point in time when Vaillant had an appropriate business size. As a first step, the affiliated company (AC) was responsible for the business development in Russia and support of external service partners. Since 2010, the AC is also fully responsible for all sales and distribution activities in Russia. In recent years, the Russian market has developed more and more sophisticated demand and also offers market opportunities for water heat pumps.

Russia: Opportunities for Growth

The attractive growth perspectives of the Russian market are based on the sheer size of the local market, the heat requirements, and the long-term development of the new construction and upgrading business, as well as a changing power system replacing long-distance heating by gasification.

The increase in new construction projects in Russia demonstrates the backlog demand in the housing market. The average living space per inhabitant is at 23 m^2 in Russia, which shows a significant underdevelopment vis-á-vis the European average of 33 m^2, or the German average of 45m^2. The trend towards higher standards of living comfort is in line with the increasing GDP per capita, and materializes in large construction projects and agglomerations offering higher standards of living in terms of heating, electrification and insulation.

Replacements and upgrades of existing or old heating units trigger further growth, as the modernization of old buildings has quadrupled since 2000. Most often a full replacement is required; more and more often, gas-fired and electric boilers - the core business of Vaillant Group - are installed in such projects.

Gasification means a fundamental system change in the heat supply. The comprehensive modernization of heat equipment progressively replaces the inefficient and outdated long-distance heating and triggers significant investments in new heating equipment, especially in the Eastern Russian provinces and regions such as the Urals, Siberia and the Russian Far East. More and more frequently, tailored heating solutions are also preferred in these regions, as they offer higher efficiency due to the consideration of the specificities of the buildings and usage. The share of households supplied with gas in Russia increased from 48 % to 60 % in 2011, whereas the share of households served by long-distance heating reduced at the same time. A very similar development was observed in the Eastern European markets of Poland, Slovakia and the Czech Republic a decade ago, which provided the grounds for a long-term market success. The heating supply of households over long distances in those countries is today at a penetration level of 40 % (previously 65 %) versus an EU average of 12 %. Thus, gasification provides a long-term opportunity for the core business of the Vaillant group.

Business performance in Russia. The Vaillant Group benefited from these long-term growth drivers and outperformed the relevant market with sales revenue growth of more than +20 % CAGR p.a., significantly above the market average at around +4 % p.a.

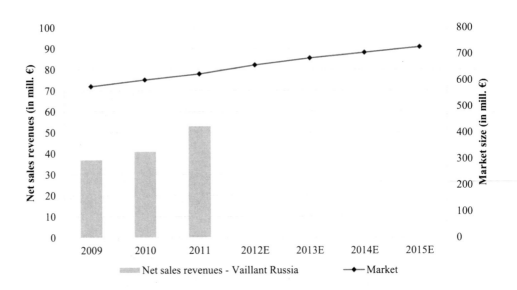

Figure 9.4: Sales revenues of Vaillant Group in Russia

The business plan for the following years assumes a market growth year-on-year in a corridor of +3 % to +5 %, as denoted by the red line in **Figure 9.4**. In this context, the management board of Vaillant Group drafted clear expectations for a continuation of the top-line development in Russia, in order to gain critical business size and deliver a positive operating result before taxes (EBIT) on this basis.

In 2011, the Russian AC realized once again a negative EBIT due to increased selling expenses versus the previous year and cost of sales at high levels, driven by the significant costs for transportation of the finished products from the factories in Central and Eastern Europe - most notably Slovakia - to the Russian distributors. The increase in selling expenses reflects investments in the build-up of a more regional distribution network with new sales representatives, sales offices and training centres in order to realize better market coverage.

The schematic profit and loss statement (P&L) of the affiliated company Vaillant Group RUS LLC is illustrated in **Table 9.1** and indexed on net sales revenues (=100). In addition to the higher selling expenses, the AC recorded an increase in sales deductions in 2011.

P&L Russia (in mill. €)	2010	2011
Gross sales revenues	102	104
Sales deductions	2	4
Net sales revenues	100	100
Cost of sales	88	83
General/Special warranty	1	1
Gross Profit	11	16
Marketing expenses	1	1
Selling expenses	19	21
OOI/OOC	1	0
EBIT (AC)	**-10**	**-6**

Table 9.1: P&L statement (schematic) of Vaillant Group in Russia

Brand portfolio in Russia. Vaillant Group is present with two differentiated brands in the Russian market, as illustrated in **Figure 9.5**. The premium brand Vaillant is positioned in the upper bound of the price range and targets one-off business, i.e., individual customers such as installers or even end-users. The brand offers the most efficient heating technology and optimal ease of use. This positioning fits the global brand strategy of the Vaillant Group.

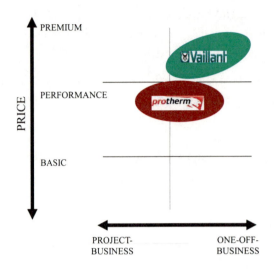

Figure 9.5: Brand positioning of Vaillant Group in Russia

The brand Protherm offers high-quality products at reasonable price levels, thus being perceived as a clever alternative to the Vaillant brand. The brand is positioned in the performance segment and targeted at project business, i.e., construction or modernization projects operated by institutional or private investors. Therefore, the Protherm branded product and service offers are targeted at planners, architects, trusts and investors.

Vaillant Group does not own any brands in the basic market segment. This segment offers very basic technologies at entry level prices, and is dominated by local Russian competitors.

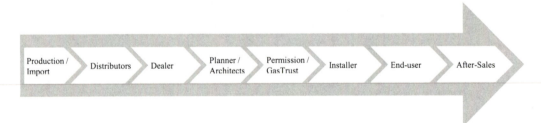

Figure 9.6: Distribution chain in Russia

Distribution in Russia. The sales and distribution of both brands is realized via an indirect multistage distribution chain, as illustrated in **Figure 9.6**. The Vaillant Group sells predominantly to distributors and to a lesser extent to dealers. Federal distributors with national market coverage represent the biggest customer group in terms of sales volumes, followed by regional distributors with limited distribution coverage within regions or provinces. All distributors sell the products of both brands to dealers and partly to installers. Federal distributors have a higher bargaining power vis-á-vis Vaillant Group in comparison to regional distributors, resulting in higher sales deductions. However, federal distributors provide nationwide distribution coverage and help to accelerate market development, especially in such provinces as the Far East as illustrated in **Figure 9.7**.

Architects and planners are often decision makers for heating solutions in the project business for construction or modernization programmes. They obtain their information from dealers or distributors, and integrate a specific heating system and brand in their projects.

Generally, installers purchase the heating and ventilation technology at their local dealer, and, depending on their business size, eventually at a regional distributor. In the case of larger building projects, installers are required to build in the brands and products as recommended by planners and architects. In the case of one-off business, i.e., tailored solutions for individual (mostly private) customers, installers usually consult their customers and recommend their preferred brand. Installers receive regular training provided by the manufacturers of heating systems or their service partners.

– Population: 147,5 Mio.
– Population density: 8 Pers. /km²; (Germany: 226 Pers./km²)
– Surface: 17,1 Mio km²
– Capital: Moscow (12 Mio. inhabitants)
– GDP p. capita: 15 k$; (Poland: 13k$; Turkey: 11k$)

Figure 9.7: Sales regions and macroeconomic data

MEETING THE BOARD OF DIRECTORS IN RUSSIA

The following week, Oliver Nehring arrived in Moscow to meet the directors of the Russian AC in order to discuss the strategic options for generating profitable growth. The directors presented different proposals and entered into a vivid discussion about how to make the business profitable.

The managing director of Vaillant Group RUS LLC emphasized in his introduction that Russia was a sustainable investment case in one of the most attractive emerging markets with a prosperous future, and that more time would be required in order to scale-up the business and become profitable. "We realize a long-term strategy in the largest market in the world and in one of the fastest growing markets, too. Our sales revenues grew by more than +20 % p. a. during the last few years, and we established leading market positions. However, we have an issue with our cost of sales due to production in Europe and extremely long distances for shipping our products to our distributors and dealers. This situation puts us at a disadvantage in comparison to other subsidiaries of Vaillant Group. That is why we need more time," he stated with emphasis. Oliver Nehring asked for the planned measures to improve the cost of sales. The supply chain director took over. "We need to build a production plant in Russia," he insisted to Oliver Nehring. "You know, the sheer market size and distances to the existing plants in Europe put us at a cost disadvantage in comparison to our competitors, too," he explained. Oliver Nehring remembered several discussions on this issue with the local management team and felt that the discussion was moving in the wrong direction, as he could not justify further investments in the local infrastructure. Thus, he suggested that it was not the right time to set up the group's own production plant in Russia.

"What is the current project status of our inventory optimization?" he asked, trying to steer the discussion back onto a positive course. "All relevant operative key performance indicators have been improved. Our forecast accuracy is above our targets and a comprehensive inventory management has been implemented. We just lack a realistic planning basis for optimizing our warehouse and distribution structure, which depends without any doubt on the location of a future factory", the supply chain manager noted. Oliver Nehring felt that they would not advance with this issue.

He turned towards the sales director. "How do you evaluate the options for reducing selling expenses?" he asked him. The sales director had been appointed to this position just a couple of months ago with responsibility for both brands at the same time. "We are currently installing the planned sales teams for both brands and are fully on plan. We concentrate on central regions, including the Volga district, and focus more and more on the eastern provinces with very strong growth potential and a backlog of demand in our core product ranges. If you ask me, do not cut a single euro, as our planned offices in Volgograd and Novosibirsk will scale-up our business soon," he replied. Oliver Nehring appreciated the enthusiasm of his sales director, but he knew very well the expectations of the management board at the headquarters. "Isn't there any chance to recalibrate our sales regions and optimize the sales budget allocation?" he asked. While listening to himself, he already knew the answer and accepted it. "The changes in the sales teams and structures need to become effective first. We cannot increase the speed of change any further without losing business," the sales director stated.

Oliver Nehring turned to the marketing director. "The marketing budget is marginal anyway; however, I do not see any opportunity for an increase if we do not find other means for cost optimization," he reasoned, and noticed that the marketing director was flustered. "We thought that we might differentiate our two brands, Vaillant and Protherm, even further in order to reach different customer segments more efficiently. We would require a moderate marketing budget for this repositioning. If we approach potential customers in a more differentiated way, we might move into a better bargaining position and influence the sales negotiations and deductions in our interest," he explained, in an attempt to save the marketing budget.

"That is a definite option," the sales director agreed. "We might optimize the sales negotiations as well, if we change our business model and implement a direct sales strategy step-by-step," he continued. Oliver Nehring knew that this was another long-term option, due to significant investments in building up an even larger sales force, and the fact that the existing relationships with distributors were put at substantial risk at a very early point in time. At this point, the managing director summed up the discussion. "We grow five times faster than our market and build a sustainable market position for the future of our business. We also need five times as much time and resources," he concluded.

Although Oliver Nehring did not fully agree with this conclusion, he reconsidered the different proposals on his flight back to the headquarters the following day. Most of the proposals made perfect sense in principle; however, they required significant investments in sales, marketing or production, with an immediate negative impact on the operative result. Was top management asking for too much, or did it need Russia to be made profitable first? Oliver Nehring decided to balance all available data and all the arguments raised, before preparing a recommendation to the management board of Vaillant Group. Back in his office, he gathered more detailed country information on Russia provided by BERI, Datamonitor, Euromonitor and the Economist Intelligence Unit, as well as the chamber of foreign trade. He did not have much time to develop his plans for making Russia profitable, and he kept asking himself: which strategic options should be prioritized? Which of these options should be bundled because they will reinforce themselves? Did he think of all options or had he missed out some? How could he orchestrate all the strategic options for good growth?

•••

Setting of the case: 2012; last revision: 2014.

10

A Brazilian Love Affair – Did ThyssenKrupp's Internationalization Strategy Fail?

Carsten Deckert, Alessandro Monti and Markus Raueiser

A PRESS RELEASE THAT SHOCKED THE WORLD

The announcement came unexpectedly and was antedated by four days. No-one seems to have seen it coming. Employees, industry experts and the financial press alike were all taken by surprise; some even claimed that there must have been a mistake. But the shocking information was true and it was front-page news: the leading German business newspaper *Handelsblatt* ran with the headline "Mismanagement"[1] and wrote of a "Grave of Billions" ("Milliardengrab")[2]. *Spiegel-online* referred to a "Heavy Blow"[3]; *Süddeutsche.de* called it a "Miserable Year"[4] for the company; *Manager Magazin* later diagnosed the company's illness as "Morbus Krupp"[5].

On Friday, December 2, 2011, four days before the expected presentation of the company's annual financial statement, ThyssenKrupp announced a huge net loss of EUR 1.783 billion for the fiscal year 2010/2011. Although order intake and group sales both increased (by 22% and 15% respectively), and the adjusted EBIT rose by 42%, the company had to make an adjustment to its book values which caused the reported EBIT to fall to EUR -988 million, compared to EUR 1.346 billion in 2009/2010.

This drop in margin was mainly caused by impairments on the asset value of the company's steel plant newly built in Brazil by the company's Steel Americas division. Of the total depreciation of EUR 2.9 billion, Steel Americas alone was responsible for 2.1 billion. The main reasons for this impairment, according to ThyssenKrupp, were cost overruns at the Brazilian steel plant, the relative strength of the Brazilian currency, and the weakness of steel markets, especially in the USA.[6]

The Brazilian steel plant was part of ThyssenKrupp's internationalization strategy, by which it aimed to enter the American market. This strategy was supposed to secure the flow of resources and strengthen the company's competitive position in North America, while at the same time avoiding the industry's apparent craze for mergers and acquisitions.

The question many spectators were asking now was: How could a strategy which at first looked so promising have turned out so wrong?

THE WORLD STEEL INDUSTRY

Steel is a basic material for industrial countries, with a wide area of application. It is produced by melting, secondary metallurgy, primary forming (typically continuous casting), forming (e.g., hot-rolling and cold-rolling for flat steel products), and, if necessary, finishing processes. The main methods involved in the production of crude steel are melting in a blast furnace and conversion into crude steel in a basic oxygen furnace. In the blast furnace, iron ore is reduced (i.e., oxygen is taken out) with the help of coke and other reducing agents. For the production of coke from coal, a coking plant is needed. The main outputs of the steelmaking industry are semi-finished products such as coils, sheets, pipes, wire, steel shapes, forgings and castings.[7]

Figure 10.1 shows the production process for flat steel products (coils and sheets). The main production stages can be described as Melting Shop (including melting, secondary metallurgy and continuous casting), Hot-Rolling Mill, Cold-Rolling Mill, and Finishing Shop. The material flow in the Melting Shop brings together many different ingredients as they are melted and mixed to form crude steel, which is then cast into a slab – a steel block which is the preliminary material for rolling. In the Hot-Rolling Mill and the Cold-Rolling Mill the slab is rolled several times until it reaches its final thickness, using intermediate annealing and pickling processes which affect the material's structure and surface. The slab is turned into a hot-rolled coil and then into a cold-rolled coil. The material flow is continuous. In the Finishing Shop the coil gets its final treatment to ensure surface quality and further characteristics, and is cut into its final shape (e.g., cut to width into sheets). The material flow at this stage is divergent.[8]

The steel industry is very vulnerable to business fluctuations. As a feeder of key manufacturing industries such as the automotive industry, the construction industry and the machine-tool industry, it is hit especially hard in times of economic downturn. Due to the financial crisis the sales revenues of the steel industry in Germany fell by 33% from EUR 51.5 billion in 2008 to EUR 32.8 billion in 2009, and capacity utilization fell from 91% to 66% in the same period. While capacity utilization quickly recovered, sales revenues remained lower than the pre-crisis value.

Figure 10.2 shows the world production of crude steel. The biggest producer is China (779.0 million tons), followed by Japan (110.6 million tons), the USA (86.9 million tons), and India (81.2 million tons). Germany is ranked seventh in this list, with 42.6 million tons. Thirty-eight of the Top 50 steelmaking companies in the world are from Asia, and 28 from China alone (measured in tons of crude-steel production). The biggest steelmaking company by far, however, is ArcelorMittal, whose headquarters are in Luxembourg and which produces a total tonnage of 96.1 million. According to the list, ThyssenKrupp is ranked 21st, with a total tonnage of 15.9 million. Within Germany, however, ThyssenKrupp is the biggest steelmaker, producing 12.3 million tons of steel in 2013. Other big steelmakers in Germany are Salzgitter (7.4 million tons), ArcelorMittal (7.3 million tons, only Germany), HKM (5.2 million tons) and Saarstahl (2.5 million tons). [9, 10]

	Melting Shop	Hot-Rolling Mill	Cold-Rolling Mill	Finishing Shop
Material Flow	converging	continuous	continuous	diverging
Main Processes	• Melting • Secondary Metallurgy • Casting	• Hot-Rolling • Annealing and Pickling	• Cold-Rolling • Annealing and Pickling	• Skin pass • Tension-levelling • Cutting
Outputs	Slabs	Hot-Rolled Coils (Black or White Strip)	Cold-Rolled Coils	Coils, Rings, Sheets

Figure 10.1: Production Process for Flat Steel Products

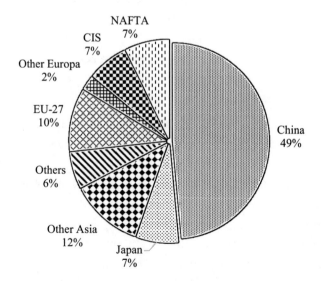

Figure 10.2: Crude Steel Production (2013)[11]

THYSSENKRUPP'S PATH TO BRAZIL

ThyssenKrupp emerged through several mergers and acquisitions carried out between the two main constituent companies of Thyssen and Krupp. The last of these were the acquisition of Rheinstahl AG by August Thyssen-Hütte AG in 1973, to form Thyssen AG, and the merger of Fried. Krupp AG with Hoesch AG in 1992, to form Krupp AG. Then, the two companies finally joined forces after years of cooperation and the combination of their flat steel production units to form Thyssen Krupp Stahl AG. The full merger, creating ThyssenKrupp AG, was realized in 1999.[12] One relict of the company's past is the Krupp Foundation, set up by Alfried Krupp von Bohlen and Halbach, the last of the Krupps to lead the company Fried. Krupp, and headed by Berthold Beitz, a close friend of Alfried Krupp, until Beitz's death in 2013. For decades the Krupp Foundation held at least a blocking minority of more than 25% of shares, which served as protection against hostile takeovers; the Foundation thus exercised effective control over the fate of the company.[13]

Today ThyssenKrupp is a diversified industrial corporation comprising the divisions Components Technology, Elevator Technology, Industrial Solutions, Materials Services, Steel Europe and Steel Americas. It employs more than 150,000 employees in 80 countries and generated sales of about EUR 41 billion in the fiscal year 2013/2014.[14] The steel plant in Brazil belonged to the Steel Americas division.

ThyssenKrupp planned to enter the American market by building a steel plant in Brazil to produce slabs, and by acquiring the Canadian steelmaker Dofasco to further process the Brazilian slabs into flat steel products for the North American market. However, a takeover battle ensued that pitched ThyssenKrupp against the Indian steel giant Mittal – and ThyssenKrupp eventually lost. After Mittal announced their merger with Arcelor at the beginning of 2006 to form ArcelorMittal – the largest global steelmaker by far – Mittal promised to sell Dofasco to ThyssenKrupp, only to claim later that year that this was legally impossible. At that point ThyssenKrupp decided to build a steel plant in Alabama, USA, to enable them to roll the Brazilian slabs on their own.[15][16]

So, for the first time since the Second World War ThyssenKrupp wanted to erect an entire steel plant, including blast furnace, coking plant, converter, power plant and deepwater port. The Brazilian plant was planned to produce five million tons of steel per year to be further processed by the old plants in Germany and the soon-to-be-built plant in Alabama. Low wage costs as well as access to raw materials from the iron-ore mines close by promised a good solution. A feasibility study by the consultancy firm McKinsey calculated an initial cost estimate of EUR 1.9 billion for the Brazilian steel plant. The forecasted cost of the Brazilian slabs was USD 55 per ton lower than for the slabs produced by the company in Duisburg, ThyssenKrupp's largest German manufacturing site. Furthermore, the North American market was in need of quality steel for automotive and machine-tool companies located in the South. The figures spoke for themselves: the risks seemed low. The decision seemed an easy one for the ThyssenKrupp management board.[17]

"I HAVE MADE MISTAKES"

The confession made the headlines. In an interview with *Handelsblatt* in January 2012 Ekkehard Schulz, former CEO of ThyssenKrupp AG, admitted personal mistakes concerning the project in Brazil. He claimed to have trusted the wrong people for too long, people who supposedly lulled him into a false sense of security until it was too late. But he called the allegations of deliberate deception by the supervisory board an "infamous insinuation". He also claimed that the construction costs for the Brazilian plant were calculated realistically and reported to the supervisory board on a continuous basis. The initial costs, which were quoted at EUR 3.5 billion according to Schulz, shot up to over ten billion.[18]

As a consequence of ThyssenKrupp's substantial losses Ekkehard Schulz had to resign both from the supervisory board and from the Krupp Foundation in December 2011. This was surely the lowest point in an otherwise bright career for Schulz – known as "Eisener Ekki" ("Iron Ekki") in the steel industry – who had led the group as CEO from 2001 to 2011. But the fiasco had further consequences.

Karl-Ulrich Köhler, former member of the management board and head of the steel division, had to leave ThyssenKrupp in 2008. As head of the steel unit he was largely responsible for the project in Brazil and had to face most of the blame and criticism. Köhler went on to become chairman of the board at Tata Steel Europe in 2010 and tried to turn Tata Steel from a producer of mass steel into a producer of quality steel for the automotive and machine-tool industries in Europe. This would lead him into direct competition with his former employer ThyssenKrupp.[19]

Gerhard Cromme, chairman of the supervisory board since 2001 and one of the 'fathers' of the merger between Thyssen and Krupp, announced his resignation from the supervisory board and the Krupp Foundation in March 2013 to make room for a "fresh start personnelwise". Cromme, who was the mentee of Beitz and had been expected to follow him as head of the Krupp Foundation, allegedly left the company due to the losses of the Brazilian plant and recent antitrust and corruption allegations against ThyssenKrupp. The disaster had thus touched even the man who was once called "the biggest Teflon pan of the Republic" by one speaker at a general meeting of shareholders.[20]

For the Krupp Foundation, ThyssenKrupp's huge losses meant financial trouble. Since the company could not pay dividends in 2013 the Foundation had to cut costs and had difficulty meeting its obligations. Seeing his life's work at ThyssenKrupp and the Krupp Foundation in danger, and having to let his close confidant Cromme go, must have been hard pills to swallow for Berthold Beitz, who would have turned 100 on September 26 that year.[21] But the next blow soon followed: ThyssenKrupp had to go for a capital increase in which the Foundation could not partake. This meant that the Foundation would hold less than 25% of shares and would lose its blocking minority. This step was realized in December 2013, after the death of Beitz in July of that year. The *Süddeutsche Zeitung* called it the "End of an Era".[22]

Meanwhile the situation in Brazil still did not look very promising. The plant was not operating at the planned capacity, and in 2012 the Brazilian slabs that should have been USD 55 cheaper than those from Duisburg were in fact USD 170 more expensive.[23] The market situation in North America also looked grim. ThyssenKrupp began to think about a sale or partial sale of the Brazilian plant.

INSURMOUNTABLE PROBLEMS
Macro-economic Problems

In 2013, the book value of ThyssenKrupp's operations in Brazil depreciated to a total of roughly EUR 3.3 billion.[24] An important variable in planning international investments and projects is the exchange rate between the local currency (in this case the Brazilian real) and the US dollar and the euro. ThyssenKrupp as an international company has to deal with many local currencies; but as a company reporting in euros, it has a vital interest in an optimal foreign-exchange currency strategy for its overseas investments. When ThyssenKrupp started its investment planning in early 2004, the Brazilian real was at the beginning of a consumption-driven boost, which attracted many foreign direct investments and thus flooded the country with money.[25] From January 2004 to early 2008, the real more than doubled in value compared to the US dollar, and significantly rose in value compared to the euro. At the time of the opening of the Brazilian plant in the summer of 2010, the real was at an all-time high compared to the euro. In other words, ThyssenKrupp had been caught off guard in its foreign-exchange currency strategy. Delivering steel to the United States was becoming more costly than ever – surely more costly than expected at the beginning of 2004. **Figure 10.3** shows the development of the Brazilian real compared to the US dollar and the euro, in a time-span ranging from 2004 up to late 2011.

Figure 10.3: Exchange rate of the Brazilian real in comparison to the euro and the US dollar, from 2004 to 2010.[26]

Another important macroeconomic factor to consider is the overall economic growth. In 2004, no-one at ThyssenKrupp could have predicted the financial crisis of the years 2008 and 2009. Those years contributed to negative economic growth in virtually all the major economies of the world, as **Figure 10.4** shows. The crisis of course did not stop at the steel industry, which is highly sensitive to economic cycles and vulnerable to fluctuations in the sector. When day-to-day operations are severely hit by economic downturns, there is obviously less room to plan for future operations. Assumptions about demand and supply, sales potential and price margins needed to be reconsidered at ThyssenKrupp.

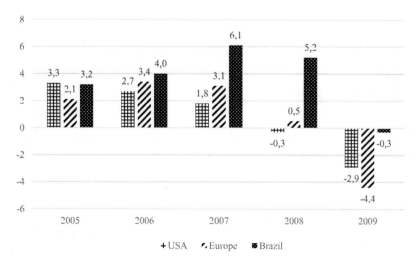

Figure 10.4: Annual percentage growth rate of GDP at market prices based on constant local currency.[27]

Labor costs in the respective countries have become increasingly important for investment decisions. As **Figure 10.5** shows, the hourly compensation in USD in Brazil in the manufacturing sector has increased significantly. When ThyssenKrupp took its investment decision in 2004, the hourly compensation was just slightly below USD /hour. When the plant opened in the summer of 2010, the average hourly compensation in Brazil had risen to more than USD 10/hour.

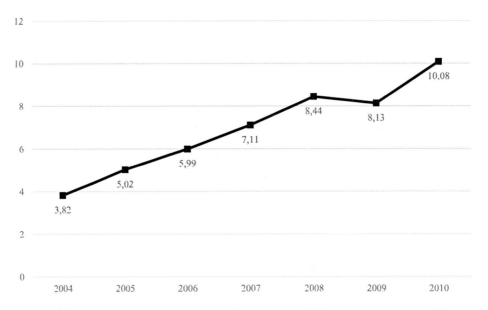

Figure 10.5: Hourly compensation in USD in the Brazilian manufacturing sector.[28]

It becomes more than evident that ThyssenKrupp made some rather optimistic macroeconomic assumptions based on all the relevant variables for an international investment decision: foreign currency development, economic growth, and labor costs. No cost-optimized and margin-oriented strategy to export high-quality steel from Brazil to the United States could be successful faced with these adverse macroeconomic conditions – transportation from Brazil to the USA was just as expensive as transporting material from Germany to North America.

Environmental Problems

The site of the steel plant in Brazil, near the village of Santa Cruz in Sepetiba Bay, is approximately 60 km from Rio de Janeiro. The advantages of this site include its direct vicinity to the Atlantic Ocean and a nearby railway line for carrying iron ore and coal for the furnaces from the Brazilian heartland.[29] Another important factor for ThyssenKrupp in choosing the Brazilian site were the apparently relaxed business environment and energy policies adopted by the Brazilian authorities. Environmental activists suspected that ThyssenKrupp were trying to exploit the chance to "avoid the regulations and policies regarding energy and environment that were distorting competition" in the company's home market in Germany.[30] It seemed that the Brazilians did not take environmental regulations on emissions and fine dust very seriously. The surroundings at the site, however, largely comprise mangrove forests, whose maintenance does require severe environmental regulation.

In order to counteract any environmental objections and pacify local opposition early on, ThyssenKrupp sought to highlight the advantages that such an investment would bring for the population and infrastructure. The company intended to create more than 3,500 jobs directly, with some additional 10,000 jobs being created indirectly around the production site.[31] The initial prospects seemed positive, as the company stressed the benefits of, e.g., new roads, schools, and kindergartens, and even proposed benefits for the environment (a disused zinc production site was continuing to pollute local waters, which would be taken care of when ThyssenKrupp began building landing stages for the steel mill).[32] A total of 129 stakeholder groups and their needs and wishes were considered in the course of preparations for the investment in the steel mill.[33]

Karl-Ulrich Köhler, head of the steel division at ThyssenKrupp, stated that the plant would satisfy "all international environmental standards".[34] But once the coking plant and its blast furnace were started up, a slimy ash began drizzling on the surrounding populated neighborhoods. The local people began calling the ash "silver rain"; they began experiencing breathing problems and skin rashes. The phenomenon of 'silver rain' stems from liquid steel being put aside in so-called 'emergency pits' in case the steel mill slows down or experiences an unexpected stall in its operations. The hot iron cools off while exposed to the air, and tiny particles peel away to be blown away by the wind.[35] Samples of emissions from the steel mill revealed above-average concentrations of calcium, silicon, aluminum, manganese, sulfur, titanium and zinc. All of these chemical substances are suspected of contributing to heart and lung diseases. Brazilian environmental authorities started to threaten severe sanctions, and ThyssenKrupp needed to comply with more than 130 new environmental obligations – guaranteeing, among other things, a new filtering system at a cost of EUR 20 million.[36] Many other individual lawsuits were filed against ThyssenKrupp, both by Brazilian prosecutors and local residents.

Operational Problems

The steel mill was the biggest private industrial investment in Brazil for 10 years at that time, and the first major steel mill to be built in the country since the mid-1980s.[37] The stakes for the investment were therefore very high, and ThyssenKrupp had not built a fully operated steel mill for decades. Nevertheless, ThyssenKrupp intended to build the production plant at reduced cost, aiming at an improved cost structure rather than shifting the focus towards reliable and sustainable quality performance. On this background, a Chinese subcontractor was engaged to build the heart of the steel mill – the coking plant. The subcontractor promised to deliver a turn-key solution to ThyssenKrupp at a fraction of the cost competitors would have charged. One of these companies was a subsidiary of ThyssenKrupp itself, ThyssenKrupp Uhde (now called ThyssenKrupp Industrial Solution), which did offer to build the coking plant for its parent corporation. Instead, the ThyssenKrupp management decided to rely on the external contractor, the Citic Group, which was appointed to manage the implementation of the core process for a total sum of approximately EUR 270 million.[38] The Chinese offer was EUR 60 million below the fee proposed by the German subsidiary.[39] For Citic, one of China's largest industrial conglomerates, the chance to play a role in such an important project was a huge opportunity, which raised hopes for future profitable business in the sector.

However, construction work did not proceed very smoothly. First of all, a major problem emerged when it was found that solid ground was a full 32 meters beneath the marshland on which the steel mill was supposed to be built.[40] Additional concrete poles of 50 meters length were therefore needed, which would each be rammed deeply into the ground in order to give the necessary stability to the foundation.

The factory plans envisaged the steel mill as an integrated production facility. Every single part of the plant and the construction process would be aligned and synchronized with the remaining phases of the process. If there were a flaw in one part of the process, all of the remaining processes would be affected. Meticulous planning and construction was therefore obligatory. The coking plant played a crucial role here: by producing the coke needed for the steel, it also served as a power generator for the whole plant via gas turbines generating up to 490 MW of energy.[41] ThyssenKrupp even stipulated contracts to feed energy generated out of the coking plant into the Brazilian network.[42]

However, as construction went on, technical problems continued to intensify. Materials, workmanship, processing – nothing seemed to be of satisfactory quality. Doors hanging off of their hinges, rust on critical equipment, welds poorly glued together with rubber, old instruments dating from the 1980s, and even fake Siemens logos were spotted throughout the construction site.[43] As a rule of thumb in the industry, production of one million tons of steel requires an investment of EUR 1 billion. ThyssenKrupp aimed to produce five million tons for an investment of less than EUR 2 billion – and now it paid the price.[44]

Due to the poor performance of the Chinese subcontractor, ThyssenKrupp was able to renegotiate the terms and conditions of the coking-plant construction with Citic, which led to an additional discount of EUR 100 million on the project price.[45] In December 2009, the problems and delays on the site were so evident that the ThyssenKrupp subsidiary Uhde took over responsibility for the remaining construction process.[46] But the errors and operational mismanagement were already so significant that, even after the efforts of the ThyssenKrupp Uhde experts, it proved to have become impossible for the coking plant to ever reach its intended capacity and utilization.

HIESINGER TO THE RESCUE – BUILDING THE NEXT SIEMENS?

In January 2011 Heinrich Hiesinger was elected the new CEO of ThyssenKrupp after a brief period as vice-chairman of the board alongside Ekkehard Schulz. Hiesinger, who had previously worked at Siemens, was tasked with leading the company out of the crisis and making it more resilient to business fluctuations. This probably meant that steel production, traditionally a core element of ThyssenKrupp, would lose its dominant position; the focus would shift to other sectors such as automotive components. Hiesinger was known for his lean, tight, and open approach to management.[47]

Hiesinger's strategy was to transform the steel corporation into a diversified and solid technology corporation, following the example set by Siemens. For this he sought to strengthen plant construction and automotive supply. His agenda included the centralization of decisions, the generation of clear responsibilities, tighter organization of foreign businesses, and a massive cost-saving program. Hiesinger was seeking to participate more substantially in the development of emerging countries, and to set the company back on a growth path.[48][49]

He was faced with serious financial problems. The equity ratio was low, and debts high. The sum of the value of the single business units was worth more than the value of the total group. The protection from mergers and acquisitions offered by the blocking minority of the Krupp Foundation was gone. Hiesinger sold ThyssenKrupp's stainless-steel division under the name Inoxum to Outukumpu in January 2012, but had to take back the Italian subsidiary Acciai Speciali Terni (AST) and VDM from Werdohl in 2014 because of antitrust regulations introduced by the European Union. The capital increase of 10% in 2013 and the accession of the Swedish private equity company Cevian as a main shareholder (11%) offered some relief.[50][51]

ThyssenKrupp also managed to sell the rolling plant in Alabama to a consortium of ArcelorMittal and Nippon Steel & Sumimoto Metal Corporation for USD 1.55 billion. A long-term supply contract with the consortium to purchase two million tons of slabs per year up to 2019 guaranteed a minimum capacity utilization of 40% at the Brazilian plant.[52]

But Hiesinger was still faced with the decision of what to do with the steel works in Brazil. He would have liked to sell it, but the plant, which cost more than EUR 10 billion, was in the books at over EUR 3 billion, and was not an attractive offer for potential

133

investors at that price. Another massive impairment of the value was potentially problematic. On the other hand, maybe it was better to keep the plant running, since the macroeconomic conditions were changing: business with North America was on the rise again, with increasing steel sales to the US automotive industry. The Brazilian currency had returned to the level of 2005 after a strong devaluation – the level it had been at when the supervisory board of ThyssenKrupp decided to build the plant. Taking into consideration the access to raw materials and the Brazilian wage costs, another option was to lead the plant to profitability – and then maybe sell it at a higher price. There remained the questions of plant performance and environmental cost. [53]

What might the company learn from its investment disaster? How could it ensure that a mismanagement of these proportions would never occur again?

•••

Setting of the case: 2015; last revision: October 2015.

NOTES

[1] Murphy, M. (2011). Missmanagement bei ThyssenKrupp [Mismanagement at ThyssenKrupp]. Handelsblatt 02./03.12.2011, p.1.

[2] Murphy, M. (2011). Brasilianisches Trauma [Brazilian Trauma]. Handelsblatt 02./03.12.2011, pp. 28-29.

[3] Spiegel-online (2011). Milliardenverlust: Stahlgigant ThyssenKrupp schreibt tiefrote Zahlen [Loss of Billions: Steel Giant ThyssenKrupp in the Red]. Spiegel. URL: http://www.spiegel.de/wirtschaft/unternehmen/milliardenverlust-stahlgigant-thyssenkrupp-schreibt-tiefrote-zahlen-a-801277.html

[4] Süddeutsche (2011). Miserables Jahr für ThyssenKrupp [Miserable Year for ThyssenKrupp]. Süddeutsche Zeitung. URL: http://www.sueddeutsche.de/wirtschaft/stahlkonzern-legt-zahlen-vor-miserables-jahr-fuer-thyssenkrupp-1.1224865

[5] Title page of Manager Magazin 5/12: 'Morbus Krupp – Der Ruhrkonzern kämpft ums Überleben' [Morbus Krupp – The Ruhr Corporation Fights for Survival]

[6] ThyssenKrupp (2011). ThyssenKrupp in fiscal year 2010/2011. Press Release 02.12.2011, URL: https://www.thyssenkrupp.com/en/presse/art_detail.html&eid=TKBase_1322818218006_1493599614

[7] Verein Deutscher Eisenhüttenleute (VDEh) (2002). Stahlfibel [Steel Handbook]. Düsseldorf: Verlag Stahleisen.

[8] Deuse, J., Deckert, C. (2006). Lean Steel Production – Schlanke Produktionsprozesse in der Stahlindustrie [Lean Steel Production – Lean Production Processes in the Steel Industry]. Stahl und Eisen 6/2006, pp. 84-86

[9] World Steel Association (2014). World Steel in Figures 2014. URL: http://www.worldsteel.org/statistics/top-producers.html

[10] Wirtschaftsvereinigung Stahl & Stahlinstitut VDEh (2014). Fakten zur Stahlindustrie in Deutschland [Facts of the Steel Industry in Germany]. URL: www.stahl-online.de/statistiken

[11] World Steel Association (2014). World Steel in Figures 2014. URL: http://www.worldsteel.org/statistics/top-producers.html

[12] ThyssenKrupp (2015).Thyssen and Krupp - companies going through change. URL: https://www.thyssenkrupp.com/en/konzern/geschichte_konzern.html

[13] Werres, T. (2012). Am Schmelzpunkt [At the Melting Point]. Manager Magazin 5/2006, pp. 28-35

[14] ThyssenKrupp (2015). Fact Sheet: ThyssenKrupp Group. URL: https://www.thyssenkrupp.com/documents/factsheets/ThyssenKrupp_Factsheet_Group.pdf

[15] Dohmen, F. (2006). Deutscher Sonderweg [German Sonderweg]. Spiegel 27/2006, p. 78

[16] Spiegel-Online (2006). ThyssenKrupp kommt bei Dofasco nicht zum Zug [ThyssenKrupp did not get a chance at Dofasco]. URL: http://www.spiegel.de/wirtschaft/stahlbranche-thyssenkrupp-kommt-bei-dofasco-nicht-zum-zug-a-429871.html

[17] Blasberg, M., Kotynek, M. (2012). Die versenkten Milliarden [The Sunk Billions]. Zeit-Online. URL: www.zeit.de/2012/28/DOS-ThyssenKrupp

[18] 'Ich habe Fehler gemacht' ['I have made mistakes']. Interview with ex-ThyssenKrupp boss Ekkehard Schulz. Handelsblatt 20./21.01.2012, pp. 1 and 8-9

[19] Murphy, M. (2011). Kampfansage an ThyssenKrupp [Declaration of War to ThyssenKrupp]. Handelsblatt 23.02.2011, p. 20

[20] Spiegel-Online (2013). Umstrittener Aufsichtsratschef: Cromme verlässt ThyssenKrupp [Controversial Chairman of the Supervisory Board: Cromme leaves ThyssenKrupp]. URL: http://www.spiegel.de/wirtschaft/unternehmen/thyssenkrupp-cromme-tritt-als-aufsichtsratschef-zurueck-a-887662.html

[21] Student, D., Werres, T. (2013). Die K-Frage [The K-Question]. Manager Magazin 04/2013, pp. 32-39

[22] Süddeutsche (2013). Ende einer Ära [End of an Era]. URL: http://www.sueddeutsche.de/wirtschaft/thyssen-krupp-stiftung-ende-einer-aera-1.1834821

[23] Blasberg, M., Kotynek, M. (2012). Die versenkten Milliarden [The Sunk Billions]. Zeit-Online. URL: www.zeit.de/2012/28/DOS-ThyssenKrupp

[24] Kaiser, A. (2013). Warum Brasilien plötzlich Standortvorteile hat [Why Brazil suddenly has Locational Advantages]. Manager Magazin. URL: http://www.manager-magazin.de/unternehmen/industrie/brasiliens-ploetzlicher-standortvorteil-fuer-thyssenkrupp-a-928130.html

[25] ibid.

[26] Retrieved on April 8, 2015. URL: http://www.oanda.com/lang/de/currency/historical-rates/

[27] Retrieved on April 8, 2015. URL: http://data.worldbank.org/indicator/NY.GDP.MKTP.KD.ZG/countries/EU?display=graph

[28] IBGE, Bureau of Labor Statistics (2011). Retrieved on April 8, 2015. URL: dx.doi.org/10.1787/888932924495

[29] Kaestner, U. (2008). 'Großbaustelle von ThyssenKrupp in Sepetiba', in: Topicos, Vol. 4/2008, p. 20

[30] Blasberg, M., Kotynek, M. (2012). Die versenkten Milliarden [The Sunk Billions]. Zeit-Online. URL: www.zeit.de/2012/28/DOS-ThyssenKrupp

[31] Schleidt, D. (2008): "Ein guter Fang", in: ThyssenKrupp Magazin, Vol. 1/2008, p. 42

[32] Schleidt, D. (2008): "Ein guter Fang", in: ThyssenKrupp Magazin, Vol. 1/2008, pp. 42-43

[33] ibid.

[34] Schleidt, D. (2008): "Ein guter Fang", in: ThyssenKrupp Magazin, Vol. 1/2008, p. 43

[35] Blasberg, M., Kotynek, M. (2012). Die versenkten Milliarden [The Sunk Billions]. Zeit-Online. URL: www.zeit.de/2012/28/DOS-ThyssenKrupp

[36] ibid.

[37] Bryant, C. (2011) 'Brazil plant tarnishes ThyssenKrupp's sheen', Financial Times, retrieved on April 8, 2015. URL: http://www.ft.com/cms/s/0/416c197e-20b7-11e1-816d-00144feabdc0.html#axzz3Wk4Vbrrq

[38] Murphy, M. (2011) 'Thyssen-Krupp zieht personelle Konsequenzen nach Amerika-Schock', Wirtschaftswoche Online, retrieved on April 8, 2015. URL: http://www.wiwo.de/unternehmen/industrie/hohe-verluste-thyssen-krupp-zieht-personelle-konsequenzen-nach-amerika-schock/5914110.html

[39] Blasberg, M., Kotynek, M. (2012). Die versenkten Milliarden [The Sunk Billions]. Zeit-Online. URL: www.zeit.de/2012/28/DOS-ThyssenKrupp

[40] Kaestner, U. (2008) „Großbaustelle von ThyssenKrupp in Sepetiba", in: Topicos, Vol. 4/2008, p. 21

[41] ibid.

[42] Blasberg, M., Kotynek, M. (2012). Die versenkten Milliarden [The Sunk Billions]. Zeit-Online. URL: www.zeit.de/2012/28/DOS-ThyssenKrupp

[43] ibid.

[44] ibid.

[45] Murphy, M. (2011) 'Thyssen-Krupp zieht personelle Konsequenzen nach Amerika-Schock', Wirtschaftswoche Online, retrieved April 8, 2015. URL: http://www.wiwo.de/unternehmen/industrie/hohe-verluste-thyssen-krupp-zieht-personelle-konsequenzen-nach-amerika-schock/5914110.html

[46] Bryant, C. (2011) 'Brazil plant tarnishes ThyssenKrupp's sheen", Financial Times, retrieved April 8, 2015. URL: http://www.ft.com/cms/s/0/416c197e-20b7-11e1-816d-00144feabdc0.html#axzz3Wk4Vbrrq

[47] Wildhagen, A. (2011). Unverblümte Mission [Blunt Mission]. Wirtschaftswoche 17.01.2011, pp. 54-55

[48] Murphy, M. (2012). Vorbild Siemens [Role Model Siemens]. Handelsblatt 01.03.2012, pp. 1 & 9

[49] Werres, T. (2014). Heinrich der Starke [Heinrich the Strong]. Manager Magazin 10/2014, pp. 42-47

[50] Werres, T. (2013). Schmelztiegel [Melting Pot]. Manager Magazin 07/2013, pp. 28-32

[51] Manager Magazin (2014). Der Fall Hiesinger [The Case of Hiesinger]. Manager Magazin 01/2014, pp. 10-11

[52] ThyssenKrupp (2014). Sale of ThyssenKrupp Steel USA completed. Press Release 26.02.2014. URL: https://www.thyssenkrupp.com/en/presse/art_detail.html&eid=TKBase_1393429094593_1585524485

[53] Kaiser, A. (2013). Warum Brasilien plötzlich Standortvorteile hat [Why Brazil suddenly has Locational Advantages]. Manager Magazin. URL: http://www.manager-magazin.de/unternehmen/industrie/brasiliens-ploetzlicher-standortvorteil-fuer-thyssenkrupp-a-928130.html

11

Searching for new Business Opportunities – The Strategy Process at Egrima Holding

Lukas Held, Bastian Schweiger and Sascha Albers

DKV Mobility Services' director of corporate development, Michael Stocker, is proudly looking back on the establishment of his newest business, Novofleet. Established in 2012 as a new division within EGRIMA Holding (renamed DKV Mobility Services in 2014), Novofleet has developed dynamically within EGRIMA's and DMS's portfolio. However, he was also reminded of the difficult situation he and his team faced at the time.

It was Friday, 5th October, 2012, when Stocker received the latest quarterly statements of all the company parts of EGRIMA Holding. As in the past, more than 90 % of the overall turnover was generated by EGRIMA's flagship business, DKV Euro Service (DKV) - the division that offers fuel cards for commercial truck fleets.

DKV, EGRIMA's root business for over 75 years, is the European market leader in its segment. However, it is currently under pressure due to rising gas prices, new competitors (gas companies offering their own fuel card systems) and an overall slowing economy. Once again, it became painfully obvious to EGRIMA's top management how much the EGRIMA group depends on DKV's performance. In light of an increasingly turbulent environment, Mr Stocker, was reassured in his belief that EGRIMA could no longer afford to rely solely on DKV for future success. A second high-impact business was sorely needed. But how could new business opportunities be identified and developed? Should EGRIMA expand into related businesses, or into completely unrelated terrain instead? If it should go for related markets, how could its existing knowledge and capabilities be effectively used to succeed there?

With the extent of the challenge beginning to dawn on him, Stocker was left wondering how to organize EGRIMA's strategy process going forward.

FUEL CARD SOLUTIONS IN GERMANY

The Product

Fuel cards work in a comparable way to credit cards, but are limited to the purchase of fuel and related services. The typical customer is a company that operates at least one vehicle that is used by its employees. In order to allow the drivers of their vehicles to easily access the necessary products and services to operate them, fuel cards are used. Since fuel cards eliminate the use of cash, they enable the fleet owner to keep track of every driver's expenses, hence reducing the danger of fraudulent transactions and the costs traditionally connected with administering a large number of bills. Instead of an unsorted pile of bills, users of fuel cards receive one invoice at the end of each month listing all fuel expenses of the previous weeks, broken down per issued card and/or driver. Overall, delaying payment until the end of each month and an according increase of liquidity is a major advantage of fuel cards for fleet operators. In addition, most fuel cards allow online, real-time tracking of fuel expenses, hence further increasing the level of transparency. While some cards charge monthly fees, others also grant discounts on fuel (either on a cent/litre basis or percentage), helping fleet managers to immediately lower their fuel expenses. Hence, the provision of fuel cards is a classical B2B business that can be split into two segments: passenger and pick-up truck fleets, on the one hand, and truck fleets on the other. Both segments haven traditionally been served by different service providers, and EGRIMA currently only offers a product for the truck segment via its DKV division.

The German Market Environment

In 2013 the German market for commercially used vehicles consisted of 7,063,792 registered vehicles, which are spread over the aforementioned segments as follows: passenger cars (62.4 %), pick-up trucks (< 3.5 t) (29 %), and buses and larger trucks (8.6 %). While the number of passenger cars and pick-up trucks grew by 2.4 % and 2.8%, respectively, over 2012, the segment of larger trucks shrank by 1 % (see **Figures 11.1a** and **11.1b**).

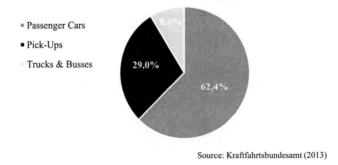

Source: Kraftfahrtsbundesamt (2013)

Figure 11.1a: Commercially used vehicles in Germany (2013)

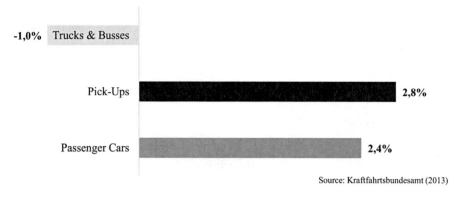

Figure 11.1b: Growth year-over-year by segment in % (2012/13)

These vehicles are owned by companies ranging from the local carpenter relying on a handful of trucks to logistics providers and rental services with fleets of hundreds or thousands of vehicles. In an environment characterized by increasing cost pressure and raised standards for transparency and governance, many of these fleet owners turn to external companies to help maintain and operate their fleet.

Not surprisingly, fuel cards are becoming increasingly popular, a trend especially pronounced for larger fleets. In order to manage the inherent complexity of larger fleets (> 50 vehicles), more than 90 % of fleet managers in this segment rely on a fuel card system to cut down administration costs. However, managers of smaller fleets (5-19 vehicles) too have discovered the advantages of fuel cards, and use them regularly (67.3 %). Simplifying the purchase of fuel is the prevailing motive among fleet managers for using fuel cards, since only half of them make use of the system to pay for additional services like car washes, toll payments or the purchase of oil.

The most obvious providers of fuel cards are gas companies using the payment method as a way to tie an attractive customer group to their network of gas stations. The network of gas stations in Germany saw a consolidation over the last decade in two ways (**Figure 11.2**): overall, the number of gas station was reduced from 16,324 to 14,373 (-12 %); on the other hand, in 2003, Shell merged its network with DEA (then no. 2 and no. 3), and in the same year BP's (then no. 6) stations were rebranded and joined the largest player: Aral. As a result, the three largest players (Aral, Shell and Esso) enlarged their combined market share from 34.3 % to 38.7 %.

However, nearly all closures were a result of the consolidation among the big players, while small- and medium-sized networks actually expanded in the meantime. Even though these small networks are considered independent, most still procure their gas from the international giants of the gas industry who in turn operate the three largest gas station networks under their respective premium brand (so called A-brands): Shell (Shell), Aral

(BP) and Esso (ExxonMobil). Smaller networks (or B-brands) are often positioned in less attractive locations and try to attract customers by offering lower prices, e.g., diesel prices are on average 3.1 % lower than at A-brand gas stations (**Figure 11.3**).

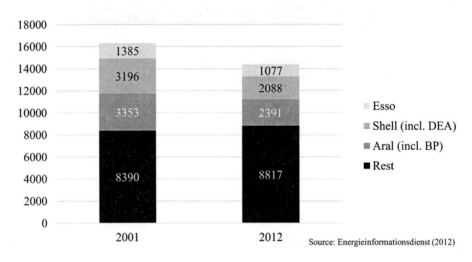

Figure 11.2: Number of gas station by operator in Germany

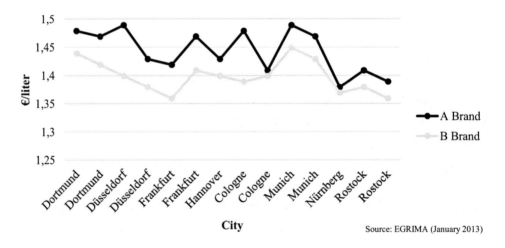

Figure 11.3: Gas prices A brand vs. B brand (2013)

The aforementioned prominence of gas companies is mirrored in the market for fuel cards in Germany (**Figures 11.4a** and **11.4b**). Aral is the market leader with a share of 24 %. Additionally, its fuel cards are accepted throughout the Routex network, in Germany mainly consisting of Eni (formerly Agip) and OMV. Shell is a close second with a market share of 23 %. Its cards (and vice versa) are accepted at Esso (8.5 %) and Total (4.9 %) stations, effectively making this cooperation the most widespread fuel card solution. The corresponding role of the independent gas stations is played by DKV, UNION TANK

Eckstein GmbH & Co. KG (UTA), and a large group of regional service providers in the fuel card sector. Where the small regional players have a cumulated market share of 9.5 %, DKV (12.2 %) and UTA (9.1 %) are the only meaningful independent providers of fuel cards.

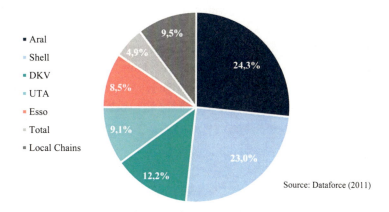

Figure 11.4a: Market shares for fuelcards by provider (2011)

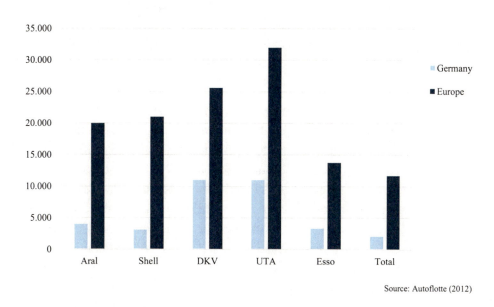

Figure 11.4b: Number of partner gas stations by fuelcard provider (2012)

Again, they are independent only in so far as they still rely on the gas companies to accept their fuel cards. Today, the fuel cards of DKV and UTA are accepted throughout all major networks and a large number of independent gas stations. In contrast to the fuel card solutions of the major gas companies, both DKV and UTA have specialized in providing an extensive service package for operators of truck and bus fleets. Fuel cards are only a part of this package and are supplemented by handling of toll charges, VAT1 refunds as well as a network of truck breakdown services. Like the fuel cards of the well-known oil companies, DKV and UTA fuel cards are accepted throughout Europe. Compared to these leading payment solutions, fuel cards introduced by mid-sized gas station networks (e.g., OIL!, Jet and Tamoil) are restricted to their own respective national network. Carriers of local gas stations struggle to keep up with the big networks.

THE COMPANY

DKV Euro Service as Part of EGRIMA Holding

Even though EGRIMA Holding was formed rather recently, on 1st January, 2011, its origins can be traced back to 1934, when its current flagship business DKV was incorporated in Düsseldorf, Germany. With the formation of EGRIMA Holding, named after DKV founder Ernst Grimmke, DKV recently moved to Ratingen, a northern Düsseldorf suburb. In the new and modern headquarters, all of EGRIMA Holding's divisions are united under one roof. The holding itself provides guidance on corporate development, HR and communications to its subsidiaries, as well as overarching financial solutions inaccessible to each subsidiary itself. Furthermore, it functions as a dedicated corporate strategy department (**Figure 11.5**).

In addition to DKV, three other subsidiaries and the EGRIMA Business Center are assembled under the EGRIMA umbrella. Mr Stocker was the driving force behind this move towards a holding structure intended to accelerate EGRIMA's diversification and the definition of each subsidiary's unique business area in the mobility sector. Whereas the Business Center seeks to create scale effects for all subsidiaries through consolidated back-office functions like IT and procurement, the other subsidiaries are strategically positioned around EGRIMA's capstone: DKV. MOS (mobility outsourcing service) optimizes accounting processes for fuel procurement and toll payments, both for domestic and pan-European operations. Remobis organizes the VAT and fuel tax refund for its customers. Remobis uses the DKV platform as its premium reseller. The acquisition of rights to handle invoices of different European toll systems is bundled in Tollstar, an exclusive supplier to DKV and MOS. The establishment of these subsidiaries and their individual business models is supposed to help identify specific target groups for each service. After creating separate businesses, a major concern was to guarantee the confidentiality of each customer's data. Since the customers targeted by the new businesses were operators of other fuel card solutions, and thus direct competitors of DKV, so called "Chinese Walls" were erected to prohibit the exchange of data between the subsidiaries. This absolutely waterproof data management was needed to guaranteetrust in the new subsidiaries.

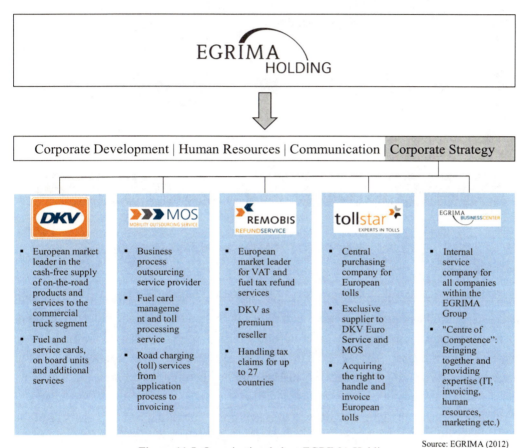

Figure 11.5: Organizational chart EGRIMA Holding

Source: EGRIMA (2012)

DKV's role as past and present centrepiece of EGRIMA is reflected in the current top management. Two out of three members of EGRIMA's management board also share the responsibility for managing DKV, and Mr Stocker, director of corporate development for EGRIMA, previously worked in the top management of DKV for five years.

Strategy Process - The EGRIMA Approach

The overarching strategy is developed by the corporate development department and is binding for all subsidiaries of the holding. The department follows a strict, predefined process to determine the strategy going forward (**Figure 11.6**).

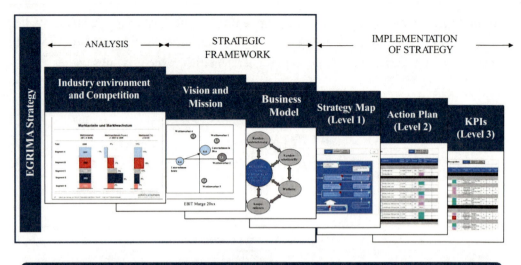

Figure 11.6: EGRIMA strategy process

The basis for the first phase analysis consists of the collection and analysis of current data sets, as well as future projections and trends within and outside the industry. In order to map its market environment, internal and external sources are used to analyse the relevant determinants. Part of EGRIMA's strategy process is to break the relevant environment down into three sectors: market and competitors, customers and suppliers, and technological evolution. The trends identified in these sectors are then consolidated to formulate the basic challenges EGRIMA will face going forward. From this analysis of the environment's future, a target positioning for the EGRIMA holding is deduced in accordance with the corporate vision: "Leadership in Mobility". The phase of strategic framework not only defines a firm target positioning, but also asks EGRIMA's corporate development team to design strategic options for how to achieve it. The major element of each strategic option is to define every subsidiary's contribution to the overall strategic positioning of EGRIMA, and hence its business model. Each respective business model lays out products, market and customer segments, and core competencies of each subsidiary, as well as the value chain. In the following implementation phase, a three-level approach helps to draw up a road map for how and when goals are to be reached. Each level employs a different performance management tool to ensure strategic goals are broken down in a consistent way. The first level is a strategy map providing operational translations of the strategic goals (e.g., increasing market share in Germany). The subsequent levels then consist of concrete action plans (e.g., recruiting gas stations in rural areas) and KPIs (e.g., visits by sales representatives per rural gas station) to allow constant monitoring of the progress for each project's contribution to the sub-goals.

GROWING IN A CHANGING INDUSTRY

For EGRIMA, this was the usual approach to assembling a project team to assess a strategic problem according to the company's predefined strategy process. The next day, Mr Stocker assembled this task force, consisting not only of his corporate strategy team, but also of trusted colleagues from different departments in EGRIMA. Mr Stocker and his team members Heiko Peters and Michael Morter were joined by Nick Nitpicker (Purchase), Jason Lemon (Sales and Marketing) and Pablo Alto (R&D). He asked each of them to gather all the information on EGRIMA's environment they could find during the next two weeks.

The First Strategy Meeting

In the task force's next meeting, Mr Stocker was eager to put together the pieces provided by each member in order to draw up the future of EGRIMA's environment. Heiko Peters opened the meeting by giving a detailed description of the current market. He was painting a picture of a fuel card market which was nearing saturation, which would lead to further increases in pricing pressure in the fight for market shares. In this immediate environment, the existing competitors, especially the major gas companies, were identified and profiled in detail. Morter added that through his network of informal industry contacts he was made aware of international competitors, especially from the US, who were offering fuel card payment systems and were preparing for expansion into Germany. While this was news to him, Mr Stocker was not surprised by it: he had long expected the entry of other players into the German market.

In order to get a complete view of the mobility market, its players and possible growth options, he asked Pablo Alto to present his findings. Alto, a technology enthusiast, warned against underestimating non-traditional competitors. He had spotted another development potentially creating competitors: converging markets were turning credit card companies, data driven companies like Google and other carriers, as well as online payment systems like PayPal into players worth keeping an eye on. Additionally, other companies operating in the transport or mobility sector, like OEMs3, were looking at new or changing business models. Heiko Peters agreed, pointing towards the fuel cards issued by Mercedes Benz (in cooperation with UTA) for its commercial customers, giving them better access to Mercedes' workshop network. Furthermore, Mr Stocker presented the results of his talks with EGRIMA's legal department on the future impact of regulatory changes.

Apart from this competition on the horizontal level, Mr Stocker also noticed trends changing the vertical value chain that EGRIMA was traditionally part of. He asked his sales specialist, Lemon, for the reasons for this shift. Jason Lemon reported in full about customers (fleet owners) who were increasingly demanding individualized services, and about an average payment amount clearly trending towards smaller payments, so-called micropayments. Nick Nitpicker realized that his findings perfectly mirrored these developments on the supply side. Here, new suppliers, such as energy providers, were about to emerge as electric vehicles became more popular. Nitpicker claimed that such a development would create more choices among suppliers, in turn strengthening EGRIMA's bargaining power. On the other hand, he reported, existing suppliers were taking an increasingly hard stance on card acceptance and granting discounts, as they were establishing their own cards. Just when Mr Stocker had summed up all these trends, Pablo Alto pointed out that underlying and influencing (at times even enabling) all these developments was a rapid technological evolution in terms of mobile payment (virtual wallet), contactless transmission (NFC) and connected vehicles. Mr Stocker thanked all participants for their valuable contributions and asked his team members Morter and Peters to prepare a presentation of today's findings for their next meeting.

Follow-up Procedure

After Peters and Morter had given their presentation (for an overview see **Figure 11.7**), which recapitulated the findings of the last session and underpinned them with solid data, a lively discussion ensued among the members of the task force. Quickly, two lines of argumentation emerged. Alto, Nitpicker and Morter all favoured, sooner rather than later, addressing the radical changes the industry presumably would face, and seeking out opportunities outside the current value chains. In contrast, Peters and Lemon pointed to EGRIMA's immediate surroundings as the area with the most potential for additional profits. After weighing up all the arguments, Mr Stocker used EGRIMA's mission ("assure success as the leading service provider for transport companies") as guidance, and ultimately decided that current customers, suppliers and immediate competitors have to be the focus of the new strategy. As a result, the five most basic challenges were broken down into: increasing customer individualization; supplier and pricing pressure; the saturated state of the market; and direct national and international fuel card competitors (**Figure 11.8**).

Based on these broken-down findings, Morter and Peters designed two solutions to reduce the dependence on DKV. Morter described the concepts as diversification and widening customer base. With diversification already addressed through the incorporation and strengthening of MOS and Remobis, the main focus shifted to broadening the company's customer base. Mr Stocker explained: "The rationale behind this proposition is that most of the identified basic challenges could be answered with a subsidiary targeting a new customer segment. With a differently positioned service, customer needs can potentially be catered to more precisely (that is, more individualized). Furthermore, a larger customer base helps increase the bargaining power vis-à-vis the suppliers, and thus lower procurement costs, allowing for more attractive gas rates for all fuel card customers of the EGRIMA group and/or the stabilization of EGRIMA's margins. The sub-problem of new entrants would also be mitigated to a certain degree by an increased market presence functioning as an entry barrier".

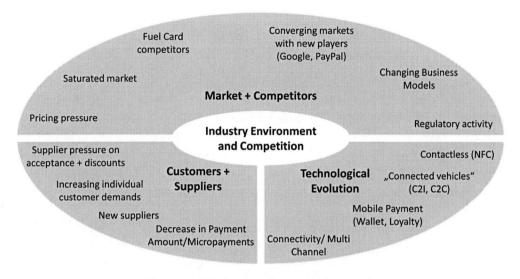

Figure 11.7: Industry environment – key trends

Encouraged that his idea was appreciated, Morter intensified his efforts: "Mr Stocker: Considering EGRIMA's (via DKV) current customer base is limited to fleets of larger trucks and buses, or 8.6 % of the overall market for commercial vehicles it becomes pretty obvious which customer segment represents vast potential for your growth initiative: the growing number of commercial passenger car fleets." Morter's conclusion convinced the task force, including Mr Stocker, and provided a clear target position for the new business. However, when the corporate development team moved to the next part of the strategic framework for the new business and laid out its business model, Peters informed his superior of a major obstacle: "A central part of any business offering fuel cards to owners of passenger vehicle fleets would be a close cooperation with various gas station networks. From the information I was able to gather from my industry contacts, the major gas companies would react extremely unfavourably to such a new business; some sources even hinted at a potential backslash against DKV." Mr Stocker realized how real this danger was, and postponed further steps. Back in his office, Mr Stocker asked himself: "Should we revisit the diversification concept? Or is there a way to move on with the current idea?"

In the team's next meeting, Stocker announced: "The major gas companies are obviously protecting their own payment systems at all costs, and any potential backlash against DKV would by far outweigh the new business's contribution. Still, I believe, the new business would offer the optimal combination of decreasing the dependence on DKV, while creating synergies by relying on the existing core processes and competencies of the EGRIMA group. In other words: we need to find solution to this problem."

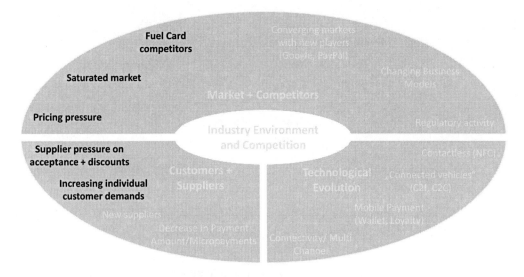

Figure 11.8: Industry environment – basic challenges

The Birth of Novofleet

After discussing and dismissing several workarounds, two measures were found to solve the issue while providing the new venture with a unique selling proposition. Lemon argued: "Isn't the most basic measure we can take incorporating the new service in a new subsidiary and under a new brand, in an effort to reduce the affiliation with DKV?" Mr Stocker and the rest completely agreed with Lemon's line of reasoning. Although Mr Stocker was happy with the progress, he reminded his team of the more fundamental challenge: finding willing and capable partners for the proposed business.

Finally, Mr Stocker himself came up with an idea: "If we have to avoid the larger gas companies, doesn't that leave the mid-sized and smaller operators as obvious targets?" Now things started to click. Nitpicker added: "I believe they would even be eager to join an overarching payment solution, since they have failed multiple times in recent years to launch a competitive system on their own." When Lemon reminded everyone that.

"Equally important, these players can also provide our system with a price advantage", it was clear they had found not only a way to avoid the larger players, but also a major selling point for the new system, even in an environment of rising gas prices and increasing price sensitivity among fleet owners.

The next and final step for Mr Stocker and his team was to present the new concept to the board. Following up on the idea of utilizing a new brand for the concept, Heiko Peters proposed: "Given its innovative nature in the vehicle fleet industry, why don't we call it Novofleet?" Mr Stocker and Heiko Peters start to design the final presentation for the Novo fleet concept. Stocker suggested starting the presentation with the description of the concept itself: "We need to show what the challenges are, and how Novofleet answers them. Of course, this includes the advantages, but also a list of risks as well as possible alternatives. I know our chairman always likes to compare a solution with its next best alternatives."

From his experience, he knew that they had to be prepared to answer questions regarding the process that led to their proposal: the board always wanted to make sure that sufficient data were gathered, that all possibilities were analysed and no options were discarded too easily. Of course, if the proposal was immediately clear, that would be obsolete. However, Stocker knew the intricacies of group dynamics in top management teams, so he liked to be better prepared. He told Peters: "We shouldn't forget to have a backup slide on how we went through the process, which analyses we made, and how we made sure we eliminated blind spots in our analyses."

Given how rapidly the environment in the industry was changing, specifically in terms of technology, competitors and regulation, Mr Stocker also wanted to use the meeting to start a discussion with the board on whether EGRIMA's current strategy process was still adequate: "Considering the dynamic market environment we are faced with, I think it is the right moment to discuss if we need to adjust our strategy process in order to increase flexibility and adaptability."

•••

Setting of the case: 2013; last revision: 2014.

12

Managing without Management – How Companies Succeed Without Hierarchy

Thilo Heyer, Lukas Seeger and Simon von Danwitz

On her way home, Mrs. Schmidt, the CEO of a medium-sized insurance company, cannot stop thinking about the workforce survey she received recently. Employees of her company were complaining about a lack of appreciation and innovation in their teams, while middle managers were having problems introducing new methods and finding people to work on seemingly exciting projects. From her perspective, the workforce across all levels seemed to agree that change was necessary, but was held back by a strong force of inertia.

Of course, this problem is not new to her. In the last two years, her management team has formulated and implemented many elaborate plans of action to foster innovation throughout the company. They have implemented new IT systems to encourage collaboration, created monthly cross-departmental meetings to enhance joint discussions, and conducted training to motivate employees to think 'out-of-the-box'. However, none of these measures seem to have borne fruit.

Mrs. Schmidt has started to question her own abilities to carry out the inevitable strategic realignment in due time. Will her company still exist in five years if it cannot drastically adjust its product portfolio, which is "inherited from the 90s", as one analyst put it?

The main issue Mrs. Schmidt currently encounters is a lack of innovation. Partly because insurance is a very conservative industry with little innovation, the company has lost the skills of looking forward and creating new products; it is unable to improve current processes or explore new business opportunities, instead being fixated on selling existing products through established processes to already-known customer groups. Thus, there is reluctance among the employees to embrace new ideas. In the few cases where the company tried to innovate or implement new ideas, these efforts failed due to a lack of support from employees.

When discussing these issues with a friend, Mrs. Schmidt is intrigued by the stories of two companies that seem to have no problems with innovation and change. Both claim to be 'hierarchy-free', places where 'everyone is a strategist' and where new ideas, products and services just seem to materialize on a daily basis. To her surprise, these companies are not tech start-ups or hip design agencies, but established companies operating in several markets and diverse industries. She wonders how these organizations get any work done without a conventional chain-of-command – would such an organizational set-up also work for her company? To help her answer this question, she tells one of her employees to write a report on the two companies.

KESSELS & SMIT – 'THE LEARNING COMPANY'

Kessels & Smit (K&S) is a consulting firm based in the Netherlands, Belgium, Germany, South Africa and India, with a special approach to organizing work and learning. It offers consulting services on learning, innovation and change processes to both public and private organizations of all sizes. Today, K&S employs around 50 consultants operating in five countries. The firm is set up as a heterarchical community of independent consultants operating under the common brand of Kessels & Smit. The company views itself as a laboratory where employees *"experiment and find own answers for learning and development issues that knowledge-based companies face"*[1]. Since K&S is convinced that continuous learning is the key driver for innovation, improvement and growth, their vision states that learning should be at the heart of the company.

Company foundation and ownership

The idea to create the company came to Joseph Kessels and Cora Smit, its founders, suddenly and to some extent unexpectedly. In 1977, when the two were working together on a joint project, they stumbled upon the fact that the monthly car leases of their directors were higher than their monthly paychecks. Neither appreciated working as an employee under these circumstances, so they decided to quit. Since some of their customers at their old employer asked about continuing to use their services as freelancers, the two founded Kessels & Smit. At that time, founding a company was seen as a necessity in order to bill their hours. The fact that neither of them had any aspiration to become a manager or owner might have been one of the reasons why they set up their company very differently to others. These differences are apparent in the company's principles, its organizing mechanisms, its approach to creating value and strategies, and its ownership structure.

When K&S was established both founders had equivalent shares. Over the years, especially from 1996 onwards when K&S and another consulting company, Profound, teamed up to form *Kessels & Smit, The Learning Company,* the team jointly created different ways to allow consultants to participate in the ownership of the company. In a two-way process, consultants are now invited to become a co-owner after some time with the company.[2]

The Kessels & Smit principles

The company is built on several principles, which serve as guidelines for collaboration at K&S. These principles are key to the company, as it operates with a hierarchy-free structure. The key principles are as follows:

- *Mutual attractiveness* – People work together because they like each other and because they are interested in the task in question, not because someone in the hierarchy tells them to do so.
- *Self-organization* – K&S has no formal hierarchies and no formal positions. As independent consultants, individuals are mostly only responsible to themselves, their projects, their working schedule and their paychecks.
- *Constant eagerness to learn* – K&S has a deep belief that learning is the key driver for innovation and growth. Through experimenting in daily practice, the company is constantly reinventing itself and its consulting services. As Joseph Kessels states: "Learning is at the heart of what we do".

The principles were established through continuous discussion, collaboration and refinement between the early members of the newly merged company in 1996. Taken together, they allow work to be organized to enhance collaboration and knowledge-sharing efforts, without the necessity for institutionalized hierarchies; however, the principles always remain open for discussion.[3]

Mechanisms to organize work at Kessels & Smit

In a heterarchical environment as promoted by K&S, the question arises as to how the firm organizes and distributes work, since there are no supervisors or strict rules about allocation. As it turns out, there are several mechanisms which K&S has put into practice over the years to sustain the hierarchy-free environment and keep formal positions out of the company.

The 'apple tree'. The 'apple tree' is an important instrument to enhance personal development and integrate new consultants into the company. K&S differentiates between two different kinds of apples trees: developmental and financial.

Both kinds of apple tree are set up as small networks of three to four consultants. The goal of the developmental apple tree is to offer support and advice about personal development. Normally each consultant is the central participant in his/her own apple tree, as well as belonging to some others.

The financial apple tree is basically identical to the developmental; the only differences are that the consultants entering the apple tree take personal financial responsibility for the central participant, who is typically a consultant new to the company. This means that they are personally responsible for the salary of the central participant in the financial apple tree. Furthermore, the financial apple tree is often slightly smaller than the purely developmental apple tree. Interestingly, all apple trees only exist as long as they are cultivated by their participants. There are no rules (e.g., telling the participants to meet so many times per year) to artificially keep the apple tree alive. Yet normally they are well kept, as the consultants are keen on personal development. Once a financial apple tree is set up between its mutually agreed participants, it also serves as a place for thought exchange and personal development in the short as well as in the long term.[4]

K&S's internal project market. At K&S, each consultant is in charge of the acquisition of new projects and their staffing. Once a consultant has acquired a new project, the search for suitable collaborators on the project begins. Due to the participation in apple trees and high interpersonal relationships, consultants use their networks within the company to ask other consultants to join their project. This way projects are always staffed with people excited about working together. If not enough colleagues are interested in a project, it will not be taken on, or other ways to work around the problem will be found. This creates a strong drive to create interesting projects that go beyond the routine and the obvious in collaboration with the clients.

The rule of thirds. Learning is at the heart of the organization. As mentioned, Josef Kessels and Cora Smit perceive the creation of knowledge as one of the core competencies of K&S. Therefore, each consultant may choose to adhere to the 'rule of thirds', which means that he/she is allowed to divide his/her working time into different thirds:

⅓ is routinized work, e.g., time spent on projects that do not take much effort and mostly generate a relatively predictable outcome.

⅓ is more complicated work, e.g., time spent on projects requiring innovative solutions and the development of new and advanced tools.

⅓ is devoted to the consultant's own development. This time is mostly spent on unpaid individual projects (e.g., pursuing a PhD or voluntary work).

Even though the rule is no longer strictly followed by every consultant, it illustrates the freedom and independence with which the consultants of K&S are supposed to operate.[5]

The strategy process at Kessels & Smit

In a hierarchy-free structure, formulating and deciding on strategies can be difficult, and a company can easily lose track of the direction in which it is heading. At K&S, the strategy process does not follow a pre-defined path. Instead, the strategy of the company evolves through multiple conversations within the organization and occasionally through two developed instruments: the 'K&S day' and 'round tables'. Nevertheless, K&S is not limited to these forms of exchange, and constantly seeks other opportunities and forms to improve and discuss different topics.

K&S days. The firm created K&S days to gather all consultants together on a regular basis and enhance knowledge and information sharing within the organization. The meetings are typically organized by a small group of eager consultants. Typically, such a group comes together randomly a few months prior to a predefined date to start planning the meeting.

K&S days are held in three different formats throughout the year. Once a year, every consultant is invited to participate in 'international' K&S days. At the end of August all the company's employees and consultants meet for three days to talk about projects, discuss new industry trends, and to get to know new colleagues. Additionally, the event also gives room to discuss the further development of Kessels & Smit. The format of the K&S day is defined in advance in order to give the consultants the possibility to take part in as many of the different discussions as possible. Nevertheless, there is always room to spontaneously start a discussion or openly debate a certain topic. Occasionally, external referents or discussants are also invited to gain an external view on certain topics.

Besides the international K&S days, there is also a 'continental' K&S day once a year, for consultants from across Europe, and several 'national' K&S days, which typically take place every six to eight weeks. The 'national' K&S days are, in contrast to the two bigger events, organized more flexibly as to the dates, but the topics discussed during the meeting are still pre-defined and decided in advance.

Round tables. One instrument that has worked well in the past is the so-called 'round table'. The consultants at K&S have the opportunity to individually set these up with the aim of discussing a certain topic with a larger number of participants. The round tables can be set up whenever an employee feels like it, and anyone can join the conversation. The round tables are either announced prior to a K&S day or spontaneously during the meeting, but they are not bound to the convention. Topics can be chosen freely and individually. Even the format of a round table is completely open to be changed by the consultant who initiated it. The only round table that has a fixed consultant in charge is the financial round table. Nevertheless, this does not mean that the set-up is fixed. As one consultant describes it: "Once in a while we come together when we notice a change in the approach of our financial process is necessary."[6]

New business units at K&S. As it turns out, several K&S days and many undertaken round tables as well as a simple trial-and-error approach based on randomly exerted discussions within the organization have led the company to establish several spin-offs operating outside the core consulting practice of K&S.

On the one hand there is a small property company, founded by a couple of K&S entrepreneurs who got together to jointly develop the underlying concept. The company is part of the K&S network and owns the K&S headquarters building in Utrecht. The core of the concept is to give K&S and other small companies and freelancers the opportunity to freely book and cancel individual office spaces, as well as rooms, at the building. This way the company tries to foster cooperation and knowledge sharing on an inter-organizational level.

On the other hand, three consultants with a special interest in learning through games and play established a firm called 'K&S Something'. The firm offers innovative ways of transferring knowledge on leadership, learning and development through design principles and playfulness.

Furthermore, the foundation of an Indian K&S subsidiary is also worth noticing. A client in India got to know Kessels & Smit via reading a Master's thesis written on behalf of the company. After initiating and successfully finishing a project in India, which had been planned to last a couple of months only, K&S established a branch in India. The branch was set up together with the client.[7]

After skimming through the information which her employee gathered on Kessels & Smit, Mrs. Schmidt was torn. Several mechanisms and instruments used by K&S sounded interesting to her, but could these approaches also work for her insurance company? For one thing, her company was considerably bigger than K&S. Luckily; she had also had her employee prepare information on the second company her friend told her about, Valve. This was a large, international company, and so she was curious to find out about their approach.

VALVE – 'WE'RE ALWAYS CREATING'

Valve is a video-game company that started its operations with the science-fiction shooter Half-Life in 1996.[8] Valve employs more than 300 people and its offices are located in Bellevue, Washington (USA). Until 2012 these were Valve's only offices, but since then the company also operates a subsidiary in Luxembourg. Besides creating video games, the firm also runs Steam, a digital game distribution platform that controls more than 50% of the market for downloaded PC games.[9] As a private firm, Valve's exact revenue is not public, as the founder Gabe Newell owns more than half of the company[10] and thus does not need to publish financial data. However, analysts estimate that Valve's total value is "*significantly higher than $5 billion*".[11]

Foundation and History

Before founding Valve, Gabe Newell dropped out of Harvard to take a position at Microsoft. He was Microsoft's 271st employee and spent 13 years with the company. Newell became a 'Microsoft Millionaire', and in 1996 he and his co-worker Mike Harrington left the company with the ambitious goal of developing new and innovative games.[12]

Thus, Newell and Harrington founded the Valve Corporation, and started working on Half-Life in 1996. In 1997 they started over, as they considered it to be "*not good enough for shipment*". To increase employee motivation, Newell promised to take every employee on vacation if the release of Half-Life was a success. After Half-Life was released in 1998, it won more than 50 Game of the Year awards. Valve went on its first company vacation with all employees, fully paid for by the company. In 2000, Harrington left Valve amicably and Counter-Strike was released, which became the world's number-one online action game in the following years.[8] After the turn of the millennium Valve started to diversify and explored options for the creation of online distribution platforms for video games. They released Steam in 2002 and have since gained more than 125 million active users.[13] In 2011, the multiplayer game Dota 2 premiered at Gamescom, the world's largest gaming trade fair, in Cologne (Germany). Keeping traditions alive, the whole company went on its 10th company vacation to Hawaii in 2012, including all employees' families.[8] In 2015 Valve was voted one of the Top Ten Most Innovative Gaming Companies.[14]

Nowadays, Newell's role could perhaps be described as that of a managing director of game development with a focus on technology. He was involved in the creation of Steam, but he also works as a talent scout and is in touch with independent game communities in order to discover new games. He also actively checks the message boards of Steam and other games in order to gain ideas and feedback from Valve's customers, and sometimes even to ask for assistance.[12]

Culture

Remarkably, Valve does not have any kind of formal hierarchy. The Valve 'Handbook for new employees', which is freely available on their website, describes the basic idea of the company and how employees should interact inside Valve. The firm considers hierarchy as a great tool for "*maintaining predictability and repeatability*" and controlling large groups from the top down, which makes it ideal for military organizations. But Valve aims to hire only the most innovative and talented people. Telling these people what to do demolishes most of their value. Thus, Valve wants to maintain an environment that facilitates creativity and innovation. As a consequence, Valve does not have any management or reporting lines. Newell is formally the president and CEO, but not the manager of any of the employees.[8]

In line with this idea, Valve does not designate any kind of formal job titles or descriptions. Some of Valve's employees actually have job titles on their business cards, but only to satisfy external stakeholders who are not used to the idea of people not having a job title.[15] It is common for software companies that employees are allowed to allocate a certain amount of time, typically between 10-20%, on projects they choose themselves; at Valve, employees allocate 100% of their time to projects they want to work on.[16] This idea is illustrated to the fullest by the fact that there are some projects Gabe Newell wants to realize, but since no-one has signed up for them they are so far not being pursued.[17]

Mechanisms to organize work at Valve

As a consequence of the heterarchical set-up of the organization the company's mechanisms and processes are built to support flexibility and responsiveness between employees. Three important mechanisms are the constantly changing roles of Valve employees, the concept of 'rolling desks' and the process of hiring new employees.

Roles within Valve

Inside the company everyone takes the role that suits their current task best. Thus every employee can be a designer, ask questions about others' tasks, or recruit others for their current project, from inside or outside the company. No-one gets told which project to work on or which task to perform, as every employee can decide on his or her own.[8]

Team leaders are chosen by informal consensus, but only act as an external point-of-contact without any directive authority. Furthermore, a leadership role is only temporary – a team leader of one project can be a contributor in another project. This way employees keep changing roles and perspectives.[17]

Rolling desks. All desks at Valve have wheels. These facilitate quick movement to colleagues and different project teams. But the concept of rolling desks is not only implemented for a quick alignment of new project groups; it also serves a symbolic function, constantly reminding employees to consider moving as an opportunity to create greater value for the company.[8] **Figure 12.1** shows an illustration of the desk movement for new employees.

However, constant movement makes it harder to find people within the offices. After identifying this problem Valve created a software that tracks positions as soon as employees plug in their work machines. This way colleagues can always see via the software where a potential collaborator is working at any given time.[8]

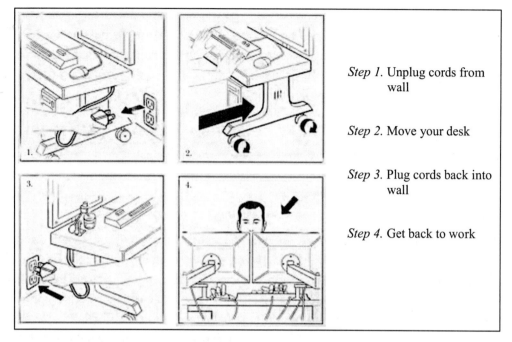

Figure 12.1: Method to move your desk[8]

Hiring new employees. Due to the lack of management control and supervision, "*hiring well is the most important thing in the universe,*" as it has a high impact on Valve's long-term value.[8] Therefore, Valve's '*Handbook for new employees*' explicitly states that someone who is working on hiring should ignore all of his or her other tasks and only focus on that. According to Gabe Newell, Valve does not look for the cheapest, but for the most expensive workers to do a certain job.[18] They look for collaborative people who have a broad general knowledge and are at the same time a specialist in one certain field. Valve employees are also required to hire people who are in some way more capable than themselves.[8]

During the hiring process, individuals are equipped with a very high degree of autonomy, and every employee is encouraged to participate in the process since there is no formal HR department. Normally, potential new entrees undergo an interview loop, having several interviews with different employees. The topics of these interviews are often highly context-driven. Yet, as a guideline, interviewees are told they should be able to answer the following questions afterwards:
1. Would I want this person to be my boss?
2. Would I learn a significant amount from him or her?
3. What if this person went to work for our competition? [8]

Interestingly, Valve has done a lot of remarkable hiring over the years. One example is Leslie Redd, a former school administrator who was hired to promote the use of Portal, one of Valve's games, to teach physics in schools. Another is Yanis Varoufakis, the former Greek finance minister who gained a lot of attention during the Greek financial crisis in 2015. He worked for Valve on game economics, applying game-theoretical approaches.[16]

The strategy process

At Valve, no manager tells his employees what to do or evaluates them, for the simple reason that there are no managers. Furthermore, the company does not give out promotions, job titles or assigned roles – but how does Valve manage to steer in the right direction regarding long-term strategies?[17] The answer to this lies with its employees.

Maximizing own value contribution. One fundamental approach at Valve is that employees decide what to work on by evaluating how they can maximize their own value contribution. Employees are not hired with a concrete job description, but have to find their most valuable work contribution themselves. There are lists of current projects employees can staff to, but usually the best way to get to know current projects is by talking to other colleagues.[8] When a team forms, everyone is an individual contributor taking different roles at the same time, leading the company in a potentially new direction because of the new content discussed in the project. To exemplify what 'maximization of own value contribution' really means to Valve, the example of Michael Abrash's approach serves very well. One day Abrash started working on wearable computing. Wearables are electronic devices that can be worn by users (e.g., Google Glass or smartwatches). After a lot of research on his own, he proposed his idea to a number of Valve's employees. After intense discussions some employees came to the conclusion that wearable computing was worth a try. As a consequence of these efforts, Valve, together with HTC, a large hardware company, announced their launch of a head-mounted virtual-reality display called 'Vive' in 2015. The headset can be used to play games, but will also enable users to interact with movies or TV shows.[19] For this approach, no formal approvals were necessary and no-one told Abrash what to do; he simply started his own project and gave it a shot. For him, it was probably only possible because at Valve failure is fine as long as the reasons for it are quickly identified, the lessons are learned and all involved people move on quickly.[17]

Exchanging information. As mentioned above, the best way to find out what is happening at Valve is to talk to other employees as often as possible. Many projects are staffed through employee conversations in the hallway, at the coffee bar or in a chill-out area. Therefore it is critical to the company's success that people are engaging in conversations almost anywhere at any time. **Figure 12.2** shows a cartoon from Valve's employee handbook which nicely illustrates how employees are encouraged to communicate in every situation possible, even in the bathroom.

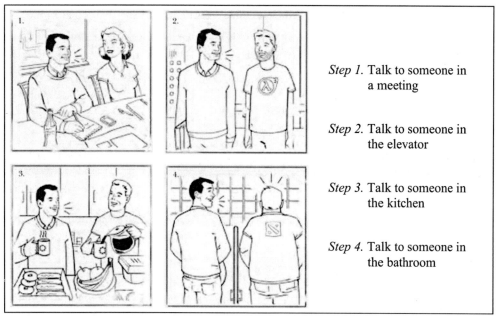

Figure 12.2: Methods to find out what's going on[8]

"Everyone is a strategist"

According to Valve, people tend to prioritize their work to favor projects that have a high and measurable return in the short term. The downside is that people lose track of long-term projects and goals when they are just switching between short-term opportunities and threats, where they react rather than act. Thus, it is the target of all employees to *"spend effort focusing on what we think the long-term goals of the company should be"*.[8]

Valve's approach of having every employee search for their own tasks and actively communicate with many colleagues finally boils down to one expression: *"Everyone is a strategist"*. This means that everyone is not only responsible for finding out what is best for themselves, but also what is best for the customers, the gamers, and respectively the company. With their own choices, employees implicitly steer the company in future directions.[8]

After studying Kessels & Smit and Valve, Mrs. Schmidt felt enthusiastic about the potential new approaches. Could they help her company overcome its inertia and seize new ideas and opportunities to create innovation? Which of the approaches could be transferred to her company and which requirements would have to be fulfilled in order to successfully implement these ideas? What would be a useful process of implementation? Should the management try to change the workforce from the top down or should there be workshops to encourage employees to develop ideas on their own?

Several different questions circled in Mrs. Schmidt's mind. When she arrived at home, she sat down at her desk and began to answer them step-by-step.

•••

Setting of the case: 2015; last revision: October 2015.

The authors thank Frauke Schmid-Peter and Arne Gillert of *Kessels & Smit, The Learning Company* for their valuable insights and support during the creation of this case study.

NOTES

[1] Quote from Joseph Kessels in: Laudenbach, P. (2008). *Die lernende Firma.* BrandEins, issue 5.

[2] Kessels & Smit, The Learning Company (2015). www.kessels-smit.de (accessed September 24, 2015)

[3] Hermann Gasse (2008). *Kessels & Smit – Wissensarbeiter werden immer frei sein* http://hermanngasse.com/2008/10/portrait-kessels-smit-wissensarbeiter-werden-immer-frei-sein/ (accessed September 23, 2015)

[4] Leutelt, J. (2010). *Hierarchiefreiheit in Organisation Und Kommunikation: Eine Untersuchung Am Beispiel Der Holländischen Unternehmensberatung Kessels & Smit.* Diplomica Verlag

[5] Roberts, A. (2011). *Being a true learning company and being free of management: living the dream* http://www.managementexchange.com/story/being-true-learning-company-living-dream (accessed September 24, 2015)

[6] ibid.

[7] Something, At Kessels & Smit Company. http://www.fueledbysomething.com/ (accessed September 24, 2015)

[8] Valve Press (2012). *Handbook for new employees. A fearless adventure in knowing what to do when no one's there telling you what to do.* http://www.valvesoftware.com/company/Valve_Handbook_LowRes.pdf (accessed September 23, 2015).

[9] Forbes (2011). *The Master of Online Mayhem.* http://www.forbes.com/forbes/2011/0228/technology-gabe-newell-videogames-valve-online-mayhem.html (accessed September 23, 2015).

[10] Forbes (2012). *Valve's Gabe Newell Is The Newest Video Game Billionaire.* http://www.forbes.com/sites/davidewalt/2012/03/07/valve-gabe-newell-billionaire/ (accessed September 23, 2015).

[11] Fortune (2014). *Valve Software shoots for the living room with Steam Machines.* http://fortune.com/2014/02/12/valve-software-shoots-for-the-living-room-with-steam-machines/ (accessed September 23, 2015).

[12] Giantbomb (2015) *Gabe Newell.* http://www.giantbomb.com/gabe-newell/3040-4498/ (accessed September 23, 2015).

[13] VG24/7 (2015). *Steam has over 125 million active users, 8.9M concurrent peak.* http://www.vg247.com/2015/02/24/steam-has-over-125-million-active-users-8-9m-concurrent-peak/ (accessed September 23, 2015).

14 Fastcompany (2015). *The World's Top 10 Most Innovative Companies Of 2015 In Gaming.* http://www.fastcompany.com/3041648/most-innovative-companies-2015/the-worlds-top-10-most-innovative-companies-of-2015-in-gaming (accessed September 24, 2015).

[15] The New York Times (2012). *Game Maker Without a Rule Book.* http://www.nytimes.com/2012/09/09/technology/valve-a-video-game-maker-with-few-rules.html?_r=3 (accessed September 23, 2015).

[16] Varoufakis, Y. (2012). *Why Valve? Or, what do we need corporations for and how does Valve's management structure fit into today's corporate world?* http://blogs.valvesoftware.com/economics/why-valve-or-what-do-we-need-corporations-for-and-how-does-valves-management-structure-fit-into-todays-corporate-world/#more-252 (accessed September 23, 2015).

[17] Abrash, M. (2012). *Valve: How I Got Here, What It's Like, and What I'm Doing.* http://blogs.valvesoftware.com/abrash/valve-how-i-got-here-what-its-like-and-what-im-doing-2/ (accessed September 24, 2015).

[18] Bloomberg Business (2012). *Why There Are No Bosses at Valve.* http://www.bloomberg.com/bw/articles/2012-04-27/why-there-are-no-bosses-at-valve (accessed September 24, 2015).

[19] Variety (2015). *HTC, Valve to Launch Virtual Reality Headset Vive in 2015.* http://variety.com/2015/digital/news/htc-valve-to-launch-virtual-reality-headset-vive-in-2015-1201444020/ (accessed September 24, 2015).

13

Strategic Planning at a University Department – A Meaningless Endeavor or Just Done in the Wrong Way?

Ingo Winkler

This is a story about Frank. He works as a senior lecturer in Management Studies at a university in the UK. The university has four faculties, each composed of five departments. I had the chance to interview Frank, talking about the strategy development process that his department has been through during the last year. Listening to his story, I learned how Frank and the other members of the department struggled to understand the management's decision to develop a new strategy for the department. I could sense that many of the staff members were rather critical of the very idea of using a management tool from the corporate world in the university, i.e., a public organization. Furthermore, I could see that the relationship between the professional academics and the department management was something worth looking into, since it strongly influenced the outcome of the story. I noted Frank's discomfort at his involvement in the strategy group, at his and the other academics' role, and at the role of the head of department and the consultants. Here is his story.

BEGINNING AND BACKGROUND

It all began in June at the annual one-day staff retreat. During the afternoon session the head of department (HOD) disclosed that the department was being asked to develop a new strategy outlining the direction that would be taken over the next five years. Having a new strategy in place, the HOD emphasized, is not only important because the university management requires it from each department. Like the department's strategy for the past five years, it would provide the staff with a sense of direction, indicating where to place the emphasis during the coming years. Furthermore, the strategy would enable the department to distinguish itself better from the other departments in the faculty of social sciences, thus strengthening its uniqueness and relevance. Listening to this kind of management talk always made Frank feel uncomfortable. It reminded him of the ongoing changes at the university. Over recent years he had observed that the university (like other universities in the country) was being run more and more like a private business. There is an economic logic creeping in to influence universities' structure, operations and performance. Frank was learning that the university, traditionally a professional and rather democratic institution, was turning into a managerial one defined by marketization, hierarchizing, and managerial measurement and control. As Frank had observed, students are increasingly treated as customers, courses are defined, advertised and sold as 'products' of university education, and the university and its departments have to participate in internal as well as external competition. This implies for instance that academic staff are urged to develop unique selling arguments for study programs and to profile and position their departments competitively, which includes developing business-like strategies at university, faculty and department level. Frank feared university managers, including his HOD, had already bought into this logic entirely. According to Frank, they tend to believe that proper strategic positioning will enable the university to achieve some sort of competitive advantage on the higher-education 'market', completely neglecting to observe that a university operates in the public sphere, not the corporate world. Furthermore, the university management seems to forget that the actual service of universities is to provide education, not simply courses and degrees. Within the faculty of social sciences, the management had implemented an internal competition for scarce resources, explained Frank. Departments were urged to develop strategic goals, including stressing unique value for the faculty and potential to contribute to the faculty's future development.

Back at the staff retreat, the HOD did not elaborate on the need for having a strategy, but went on by asking for ideas about what aspects should be included in such a strategy. Frank's colleagues promptly came up with various aspects covering all kinds of issues, such as redesigning some of the study programs, improving the collaboration between the three research groups, keeping the staff kitchen clean, fixing the problems within some of the offices, and implementing an alumni program. However, as it turned out this collection of ideas and problems was just the starting point. The HOD made it clear that he had no intention of developing the strategy alone. Instead he planned to implement a task force. This group would conduct a strategic analysis and afterwards formulate a strategy (deadline December). When he asked for volunteers the room was suddenly filled with silence. Apparently, none of the staff wanted to become included in the group. This lack of enthusiasm, Frank believed, was partly because everyone knew it would mean spending a lot of time on another administrative task. Although academic staff inevitably have to spend some of their working hours on administrative duties, neither Frank nor his colleagues are particularly keen on such duties. Frank explained that many of his colleagues think tasks like developing a strategy for the department are not part of their job. They argue that they, as academics, should do what they are best at, namely research and teaching. Moreover, Frank could also sense that his colleagues did not appreciate the management's imposition of the very idea of developing a strategy.

ESTABLISHING THE TASK FORCE

Since none of the department staff volunteered, the HOD announced that he would ask particular staff members to join the task force. Hearing this, Frank hoped he would get away with it. He did not, however. A couple of days later the HOD invited Frank to become a member of the group. Knowing that an invitation from the HOD usually equated to an order, Frank accepted, though hesitantly. So did five of Frank's colleagues. Soon afterwards the members of the so-called strategy group learned that they would receive help from the university's HR department in the shape of two internal consultants. The consultants had already developed a proposal about how to structure the process, which was distributed to the group. Frank thought that the contribution of these professionals could be extremely helpful. Having people on board who were apparently familiar with developing strategies in university departments, Frank hoped, would give the process both shape and drive.

The HOD recommended having a first meeting of the strategy group before the summer vacation, even if the strategy development process itself was not supposed to start before fall. During this constitutive meeting, which took place at the beginning of July, the HOD provided background information about the two internal consultants' role. It became clear that, although they were supposed to be responsible for the process, the HOD would remain as a member of the strategy group. After that, the subject of the meeting turned towards the consultants' proposal of how to structure the strategy development process. This led to a discussion of numerous workshops, both of the strategy group and the whole department, that were scheduled for the autumn. Some of the group members expressed their concern that there would be too many meetings; others, however, thought that this would provide the opportunity for extensive discussion. During this first meeting, it turned out that hardly anyone in the strategy group had any idea what the term 'strategy' actually meant, let alone what it meant to 'develop' one. The group members held rather vague conceptions of the term; even the HOD was unable to provide a clear explanation of strategic planning. Frank proposed that a short text explaining the concept would be helpful to achieve a common understanding among the group. The group perceived his suggestion as a promise to produce such a text. Although this was not Frank's intention, he agreed to do so. He e-mailed a brief and, as he believed, easy-to-understand text from Wikipedia to the group members later in the afternoon. The constitutive meeting ended with everyone agreeing that no further action was necessary before the kick-off meeting in September. Great, thought Frank, because this would allow him to use the summer to focus on his research, i.e., the 'real' work.

THE STAFF'S SENTIMENTS

During the summer, Frank also took the opportunity to speak to his colleagues to learn what they thought about the strategy development process. The HOD had announced to all department members that during the autumn they would all be given various activities related to the development of the department's new strategy. While talking to his colleagues, Frank became confronted with their concerns regarding both the very idea of having a strategy and the suggested process for developing one. He found that the notion of having a strategy did not make much sense to them. A strategy, they argued, belongs to the corporate world, i.e., the world of private companies, and maybe it provides a good management tool in that sphere. But they stressed that a university is not a business but a public organization; the purpose of a university was not to sell products and make profit but to educate young people. How on earth did it make sense to apply methods from the business world in a public institution of higher education? Other colleagues referred back to the department's last strategy – this had effectively been just a piece of paper that perhaps served mainly to satisfy the management. Its usefulness for the department was questionable; hardly one of Frank's colleagues could see how their activities in the past five years had been informed by the strategy. Regarding the development process, many saw it as a waste of time. Frank's colleagues challenged the idea of becoming involved in the development of the new strategy. They argued that if the management wanted a strategy for the department, it should be the HOD's job to develop one. Surely this was true? Were not university managers such as the HOD responsible for things like developing strategy? Was it not better for them to leave the academic staff alone to do what they are best at, namely research and teaching? Some of Frank's colleagues particularly emphasized that they were professional academics. They were aware of the challenges of their work and how they should address them. They did not need someone who calls himself a manager telling them what to do and thereby limiting their autonomy. In any event, to try and 'herd' academics and manage the organized anarchies of universities was a mission impossible, some of Frank's colleagues said. In short, during the summer Frank learned that his colleagues thought that it did not make much sense for them to invest their time and resources into the development of the department's new strategy. Perhaps some of them already had thought about ways to circumvent the requirements expressed by the HOD of active participation in the process. Frank was looking forward to fall in order to see how the strategy development process would unfold.

DOING STRATEGIC ANALYSIS

What happened first was another meeting of the strategy group at the beginning of September, this time led by the two consultants. They outlined that the first step should be to analyze the department and its environment; secondly, priority areas should be identified, followed by the definition of strategic initiatives in order to address these areas. The consultants also presented an updated schedule for the process, which was projected to last until the beginning of December. The process would include a set of joint meetings (among others, one one-day and one two-day workshop for all department staff). The consultants wanted to learn from the strategy group what the department actually wanted, what the strategy should accomplish, what it should be good for, and finally what their role should be. The HOD, who was the first to respond to their questions, stated that the strategy should promote the department's development, and, in doing so, serve the staff members. From what the other members of the strategy group said, however, it became apparent that they expected the strategy to solve all sorts of problems. One group member argued that the three research groups needed to be better integrated. Another raised the problem of declining student numbers in the department's study programs. A third group member was concerned that the department had become too big after the recent employment of six new academics. Finally, one of the group members pointed to the need to discuss the contents of the study programs.

While listening to these numerous and diverse issues, Frank had the impression that it dawned on the consultants what a difficult task they had actually agreed to. Furthermore, the group members were still unfamiliar with the idea of a 'strategy' and what it should be good for. It seemed to Frank that most of the group members thought it could be a means to solve both the small and the large problems in the department. One of the consultants reminded the group that a strategy could not solve all of these challenges, but rather had a long-term orientation.

At the end of the kick-off meeting, the consultants asked the group members to develop a SWOT (Strengths-Weaknesses-Opportunities-Threats) analysis. They argued that one should firstly analyze the department's present situation before thinking about future directions. The members of the group agreed to carry out such an analysis individually by the next meeting, since they were unable to agree on a procedure to do so collectively. One of the group members was quick to deliver her thoughts. Others soon followed, including Frank, since he did not want to be the last one to hand in his analysis. Looking at the different papers Frank observed that, apart from him, only one other group member had described any issues with the way the department was currently managed. In hindsight this was perhaps a question of politeness, since all group members (and therefore also the HOD, who did not provide his own analysis) had access to the individual analyses. Frank explained that it was the vice-chancellor, the deans of the faculties and the heads of the university departments who constituted the authoritative body. These managers had the prerogative to steer the university, to take decisions about hiring and firing, and to decide how to distribute resources. Although the staff were continuously encouraged to provide their opinion, and even their criticisms, the management was not always willing to listen to critical voices.

The individual SWOT analyses constituted the input for the strategy group's next meetings. The consultants compiled a list of all the strengths, weaknesses, opportunities and threats that had been mentioned. During the session, the group was firstly asked to discuss them. Frank was not able to fully participate in this discussion because he had to leave for an hour to teach a class. When he returned to the meeting, the others were just about to prioritize aspects, meaning that each group member had to mark the three most important items. After they had done this, Frank noticed once again that hardly anyone had mentioned management problems as being among the most important issues. This was a bit puzzling for him, as each time he chatted with his colleagues in the corridor or in the coffee room, many of them criticized the department management.

The result of the prioritizing exercise was that the group members determined the challenges deemed to be the most important ones that should be further addressed during the strategy development. These problems included how to attract more international scholars, how to improve the quality of the study programs, how to strengthen collaboration with other universities, and how to organize more interdisciplinary seminars. As a consequence, all the apparently 'non-important' items were removed from the agenda. Although Frank felt rather frustrated about this outcome, particularly the circumstance that management-related problems were taken off the agenda as well, there was not much he could do about it. Organized as a participative exercise, everyone had her/his chance to point out the most important items. The aspects that were named most often were taken to be the joint outcome of this activity, and were therefore accepted as the legitimate result. This might perhaps be one reason why Frank did not directly object but simply accepted the result, albeit with disappointment. However, he hoped that during later meetings, in which all department members would become involved, some of them would address the more serious problems again.

With regard to these meetings, the consultants considered it important that a strategy development process should be done in a participative manner, because this ensured acceptance and successful implementation. They were therefore appreciative that the HOD had invited all department staff to the workshops. What they did not realize, and what was not revealed to them, was that the department members had understood the HOD's invitation to mean the workshops were mandatory.

INVOLVING DEPARTMENT STAFF

About one month later (in October), the one-day workshop took place, a meeting in which most of the department's staff participated. During this meeting the staff did the same exercise the strategy group had done at the previous meeting: they conducted a SWOT analysis and used the results for defining strategic actions. Over the day, the department members worked in smaller groups, which, after discussing issues, briefly presented their results and answered questions. The amount of time that they had for discussion, presentation and responding to questions was fairly restricted. As a member of one of the groups, Frank found himself actively contributing to the discussion, both defending what had previously been done in the strategy group and adding new aspects. The discussions and the presentations led to a fairly heavily revised SWOT analysis together with a list of possible strategic initiatives, which looked rather different from the initiatives that the strategy group had suggested.

Towards the end of the workshop, the participants had the opportunity to evaluate the day. Despite the fact that almost all had been engaged in the exercise, some of Frank's colleagues made the criticism that there had been no attempt to establish common ground. The consultants had not sought agreement but only collected the various topics and aspects that had been raised during the meeting. Furthermore, it was mentioned that there was too little time for discussion. Several staff members argued that there had been a lot of disagreement and that this had led to an outcome that might not mean much. Others suggested that both the discussion and the results were colored by the interests of the participants, and therefore not representative of the whole department. From listening to the feedback, Frank could sense that the most of the staff members were not satisfied with the outcome of the meeting. The HOD did not respond to these criticisms. The consultants made notes of the aspects raised, but also ignored them. After the meeting they merely summarized the various contributions made during the day, identified what they thought were the most important strategic aspects and challenges, and presented these as the collective result of the day, which should subsequently form the input for the further steps in the process. The staff's critical comments had been omitted.

A couple of weeks after the one-day workshop, the department members travelled to a location outside the university in order to take part in a two-day retreat to further develop the strategy. Almost all of the 30 staff members participated. Only a few had been able to come up with excuses, such as teaching, fieldwork, or illness. After summarizing the results of the first workshop the consultants attempted to move forward. They asked the staff members to further develop what the consultants called strategic intentions and initiatives, as well as an action plan. It appeared, however, that despite the consultants' best attempts to explain the purpose and the content of the workshop, the academics had enormous difficulties understanding what they were expected to do. Most of them did not know what the consultants meant by such terms as 'strategic intention' or 'strategic initiative'. Frank and his colleagues sensed, however, that they were supposed to engage in some kind of forward thinking, thus developing something that could contribute to the future of the department. Hence, they started to think about how they wanted the department to be, some focusing on the near future and others on the remote future. Some developed ideas about improvements to the study programs, while others considered the ideal conditions for conducting their own research. Due to the lack of understanding, probably not all of these thoughts deserved the label 'strategic'. In fact, most of the participants were thinking about existing problems and how short-term solutions could be developed. These problems, as well as the proposed solutions, reflected the great diversity among the department members, particularly in their disciplinary backgrounds, which included sociology, history, geography, economics, business administration and anthropology. The discussions during this two-day workshop also brought to the surface many of the underlying conflicts that the HOD usually tried to suppress. Some of the staff began fiercely arguing with each other, some even shouting, thereby ignoring the otherwise respected social norm that working at a university department implies politeness and engagement in scientific argument rather than open disputes over practical matters or personal animosities. Some staff members stormed out cursing. As a consequence, the consultants found there was not much material to work with in order to develop a first draft of the strategy. Most of the discussion was not helpful for generating any integrated long-term orientation that could provide a direction for the department. However, they had to come up with something, because they had been appointed to do so. Furthermore, the HOD was encouraging them to move on, since there were deadlines to meet. So, they did their best to put the various bits and pieces together to produce a strategy draft.

DISCUSSING THE STRATEGY DRAFT

The final workshop took place in December. During this half-day meeting of the department staff, the HOD and the consultants presented what they called a 'first draft' of the strategy paper. Discussing the content of the draft, it soon became apparent that hardly anyone could identify with its content. Both the strategy and the steps proposed to implement it were heavily criticized. Frank's colleagues argued that the paper addressed the wrong aspects, neglecting more important ones, and provided unrealistic suggestions for implementation. Having been through such a laborious process, Frank could understand why the outcome of the strategy development process was disappointing for the department members. The members of the strategy group did not appear to be overly satisfied with the draft, either. Frank sensed that many of his colleagues saw their expectations fulfilled, in that developing the strategy had turned out to be just another meaningless exercise imposed upon them by the management, which had not resulted in any useful outcome. Personally, Frank thought that the strategy draft meant something to the staff, but only to the extent that it was regarded as irrelevant, failing to address the real issues, essentially as something that definitely did not have any legitimacy to affect their daily work.

THE FINAL STRATEGY

Unfortunately, Frank was unable to provide any information as to whether the criticisms expressed by his colleagues during this final workshop found their way into the final version of the strategy paper. Although the HOD promised to finalize the document during the Christmas holidays, the staff have still not seen the finished paper.

•••

Setting of the case: 2014; last revision: October 2015.

14

Online Food Retailing in Germany – Sleeping Giant or a Niche Market?

Simon von Danwitz and Bastian Schweiger

For a long time, food shopping in Germany was almost exclusively done in shops. While few people still visit street markets to buy fresh groceries, the majority of customers favour supermarkets for their daily shopping. In fact, a recent survey among German shoppers shows, that more than 90 % stated that they are highly satisfied with their usual grocery shopping[1]. Given the relatively high store density and intense rivalry in Germany, grocery shopping is very convenient; however, any dysfunction may also quickly change a customer's preference for a certain grocery chain. Consequently, food retailers go to great lengths to optimize virtually every aspect involving their store, from logistics and facility design through to in-store marketing campaigns. Almost every German retailer sees bricks-and-mortar stores as the heart and soul of their business.

However, the ongoing digitalization of retailing, as seen in other markets such as fashion, electronics, books or even tires, allowing companies to supplement existing sales channels and create novel, more immersive forms of customer interaction, has the potential to disrupt long-standing conventions and market typologies in the German food retail market[2]. On the one hand, online food sales in other European countries, pioneered and led by the United Kingdom with shares of a considerable 4.5 % (2010) of the total UK food market, clearly indicate the attractiveness of this segment. On the other hand, new market entrants ranging from small, agile food retail start-ups to ongoing rumours about entries of big pure online retailers such as Amazon are able to shake up established market structures in the food sector. Both developments are posing significant threats to the traditional retailers, which are constantly struggling to grow in this highly competitive market.

THE GERMAN GROCERY MARKET

The total German food market generated roughly €164 billion in sales in 2013 (see **Figure 14.1**), making it the second biggest market in Europe behind France. All major players have nationwide stores and distribution networks, covering both metropolitan and rural areas. In the last 30 years, food retailing has been a business strongly focused on bricks-

and-mortar stores, where all customer-facing activities (e.g., store design, stacking, selling, customer service and returns) are carried out. Consequently, today, more than 99 % of sales are generated within stores. The most common store format is the *discount store* of less than 1000 m², solely offering self-service and with a focus on goods with quick turnover, followed by *supermarkets* of between 400 and 2500 m², featuring full-line grocery and varying non-food assortments. Furthermore, *hypermarkets* also account for a major share of food sales, rendering *drugstores* the least important format. Many suppliers of the retailers are regional medium-sized companies, such as butchers, bakeries and dairies, but an increasing share of products is procured from multinational food and drink companies, like Nestlé, Unilever and Coca-Cola. To counter this trend, most retailers are engaging in upstream integration, operating their own food processing operations and managing a base of suppliers.

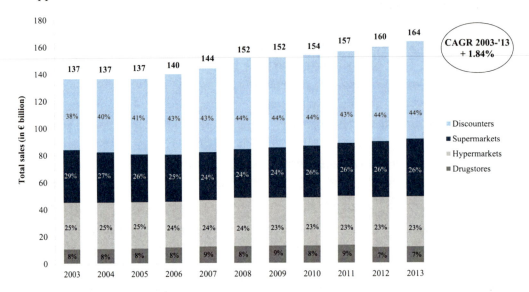

Figure 14.1: Grocery sales by retail format from 2003 to 2013 (€ billion)

The current market structure of the German food market is highly concentrated on five large players. The EDEKA Group (36 %) holds the brands EDEKA and Netto, while the REWE Group (21 %) operates its prime REWE chain, but is also the mother company of Penny. Originating from the discount sector, the Schwarz Group (19 %) owns both Lidl and Kaufland, while ALDI (17 %) is pursuing a pure discount, single-brand strategy. Finally, Real and Metro C+C are led by the Metro Group (10 %). Together, these nine big brands (representing the top five companies) hold 77 % of the total market, which illustrates a market saturation comparable to other European food retailing markets.[3]

Despite these clear-cut ownership structures of key food retailing chains, the business strategies employed by their respective sub-brands are in most cases quite different. On the one hand, nearly half of the market (44 %) is dominated by four discount brands (ALDI, Lidl, Penny and Netto), which are all following an uncompromising cost-based strategy with limited product assortments, high standardization of operations and store designs geared towards efficiency. On the other hand, a variety of full-line retailers (with REWE, EDEKA, Real and Kaufland as the largest) are competing in terms of differentiation, using strategies such as more extensive product offerings, diverse store formats (variety of supermarket and hypermarket formats), and regional or organic products. These companies control about 49 % of the market. The remaining 7 % of food sales is covered by drugstore chains, but their market share diminished in recent years (see **Figure 14.1** for an overview of annual sales by retail formats).[4] In this saturated market environment, there seems to be little room for other companies to position themselves between the two main groups of discounters and full-line retailers.

Limited Growth Opportunities after Years of Price Competition

Food retailing in Germany has a long tradition of intense price competition, especially driven by strong discount brands. The famous "ALDI-principle", focusing on narrow, cost-efficient product assortments, bulk procurement and lean distribution, has clearly shaped the industry for a long time. In recent years, many initiatives by key players were directed towards cost savings, neglecting moves to extend the differentiation of existing retail chains. Most food retailers concentrated on optimizing their operational efficiency and reliability of in-store processes and logistics systems. All full-line retailers reacted to the strong price competition from discounters by introducing their own, low-price private label product lines as a supplement to the extensive selections of premium brands. As a result of such cost savings, customers are highly price-sensitive, expecting both low prices and uncompromising quality, especially for day-to-day commodities such as dairy products, bread and meat. However, full-line retailers are continually struggling to justify premium prices, as indicated by a recent shift of market share towards discount chains.

To that end, many experts perceive the German food retailing market as saturated. Due to the aggressive expansions of established retail chains in the last two decades, today Germany holds one of the densest networks of grocery stores worldwide, in which even most rural customers can reach a nearby supermarket in less than 10 minutes[5]. Further, the overall market is slightly growing (CAGR 2003-2013: 1.84 %), highlighting the amplifying need for food retailers to explore new possibilities to grow.

In response to these developments, full-line retailers go to great lengths to evolve their supermarkets to become "real marketplaces", featuring a wide assortment of regional products, tasting promotions and entertainment events, supplemented by extensive opening hours. In a recent interview with the *Handelsblatt*, REWE CEO Alain Caparros stated that his company needs "to offer a shopping experience in as many stores as possible - a bistro, a café or a sushi bar."[6] Customers need to be convinced by a fascinating and diverse in-store atmosphere, combined with an omnipresent product assortment plus convenient, reliable services, expanding into fields that established discounters cannot or are unwilling to offer. Yet, the value-added of such differentiating services is subject to ongoing discussions among industry experts and store managers, and clear answers are still lacking. But Alain Caparros is sure that a new course is inevitable: "If we do not pay attention, the supermarket will become obsolete. Finally, we are simultaneously attacked from two sides: by online retailers and discounters."[6]

Online Food Retailing (OFR) in Germany

Put simply, OFR can be defined as the electronic ordering and physical distribution of goods that customers can buy in a traditional supermarket. More specifically, it describes retailing of predominantly grocery product portfolios through online interaction channels, in which a customer places an order online, and a retailer subsequently packs together the desired goods and prepares them to be picked up by a customer, or delivers them to his or her home (see **Figure 14.2**). Such products commonly include six product categories: non-fresh, fresh, ultra-fresh, frozen, beverages and near-food products. "Ready-to-eat" food services such as pizza delivery are excluded, due to the distinct market of such products (see **Figure 14.3** for OFR product groups).

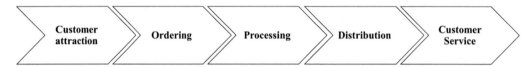

Figure 14.2: OFR value chain

Despite the remarkable success stories of online retailers in virtually every other retail category such as fashion, electronics, books and furniture, the German OFR sector has remained almost unexploited by Internet-based sales formats up to now. In a 2013 study, the consulting firm A.T. Kearney estimated that only 0.5 % (equalling €1.2 billion) of total food sales in Germany are accounted for by the OFR market. This is a slight increase in market share compared to 0.2 % in 2011[7], showing that OFR in Germany is still performing as a niche market.

However, this share is unanimously expected to grow over the coming years, largely driven by potential new market entries and innovations in ordering and logistics activities. Based on an extensive survey featuring more than 1,200 respondents from the German market, a study by the University of Cologne, in cooperation with A.T. Kearney, recently forecasted that the market share of online food will rise to approximately 3.3 % (€7.2 billion) by 2020, which represents a CAGR of +30 % (2013-2020).

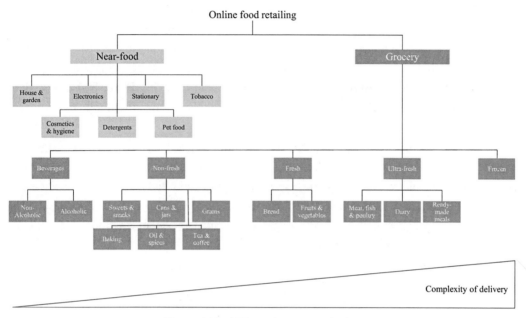

Figure 14.3: OFR product categorization

In its best-case scenario, comprising more extensive service roll-outs and bolder market entries, the study even estimates a share of 4.6 % of the overall food market. If these predictions come true, OFR will soon gain importance for the overall German food sector comparable to today's market realities in the United Kingdom, where online food retailing is widely accepted and offered by effectively every major food retailer.

While the importance of OFR is expected to increase, today's offerings can be described as flagship projects or pilots. A variety of established German food retailers began to experiment with the concept of OFR, mainly full-line retailers. Although established players generally hold a nationwide presence of retail stores, their online food services are mainly limited to certain regions or cities. Besides the traditional players, a second group of agile food start-ups, often focusing on clearly defined niches, such as specialized product portfolios limited to organic food, wine, frozen food or delicacies claim, now their stake in the OFR market.

Both groups try out novel ways of ordering and delivering food by constantly changing and optimizing their operational processes to serve customer expectations. For example, the shopping websites of REWE or food.de recently received major overhauls, adopting more convenient and straightforward online ordering services. Other companies are cooperating with local couriers to deliver baskets quickly, while at the same time managing their own fleets of trucks to deliver less urgent orders in a consolidated way.

Nevertheless, until today, German online food retailers still mostly struggle to set up distribution chains able to attract customers from the grocery mass market. One key problem in that regard is the storage and transportation of fresh goods. Based on the broad product assortments of German food retail stores, shoppers are very accustomed to buying fresh, non-fresh and non-food products jointly, all of which are commonly available in today's grocery stores. Customers take it for granted that they can do all their day-to-day shopping in a supermarket, and equally also demand this one-stop shopping convenience for online food shopping. While e-retailers have gained extensive experience in distributing non-food and non-fresh goods, this clearly does not apply to fresh products. Logistics service providers also struggle with this task. They are, on a large scale, unable to offer delivery services in a way that guarantees the flexibility and reliability customers are used to from shopping in a store, where they can touch, feel and inspect their desired goods. Therefore, many retailers and industry experts perceive the logistics component to be at the core of a compelling online food service.

EXISTING BUSINESS MODELS IN THE OFR MARKET

The distribution solution employed by OFR companies is seen as of crucial importance to the nature of their business model and its long-term success. Consequently, retailers are approaching the developing online food channel with a variety of different concepts, leaving several options for the customer to receive their desired shopping baskets by online ordering. The main distinction from a customer's point of view is the choice of fulfilment: does the retailer deliver goods to the customer's home, or is he/she expected to collect the packed baskets at a pick-up location, such as a store or warehouse? Both concepts are currently being tested in the German market. However, they involve substantial advantages and disadvantages for the retailer as well as for the customer which need to be considered.

Companies need to decide on two basic operational configurations when designing their business model. First, a retailer needs to identify the right location of picking and packing of the ordered goods, which can be done at a warehouse or inside an existing retailer's store. Second, a company needs to determine what kind of distribution fulfilment options it wants to offer: either a home delivery service, a pick-up of the pre-packed goods by a customer, or both. As a result, the current OFR business models in the German market can be distinguished into four different operational approaches, each addressing different customer needs and retailer logistics structures (see **Figure 14.4**).

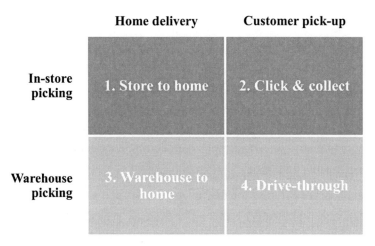

Figure 14.4: Existing OFR business models[8]

The most common approach for existing food retailers is *store-to-home*. In this case, the goods are picked in a store close to the individual customers, and sent to their home address. This model allows retailers to utilize existing inventory and personnel in a store to serve local customers with a more convenient way of receiving their goods. However, the operating companies need to either hold and manage their own delivery fleet, or outsource the delivery to a third party, such as DHL.

The second business model can be described as a *click-and-collect* solution, in which an established retailer uses its existing store network to fulfil online food orders. In this approach, the goods are picked inside a local store and prepared for subsequent pick-up by the respective customers. In the German market, this model is only applied by the REWE chain.

As a third option, retailers can offer home delivery, but prepare the shipment of ordered goods in one or several central warehouses. This *warehouse-to-home* approach is commonly taken by food retailing start-ups due to its relatively low investments, maintenance costs and complexity compared to a nationwide network of stores. Nevertheless, this model generally entails long delivery distances (and therefore long delivery windows), and may be less suitable for perishable goods.

Consequently, the remaining fourth business model is represented by a *drive-through* solution. Here, a customer orders goods online, and the picking is done in a central warehouse; then, customers drive to a specific warehouse to collect their basket, often without leaving the car. This concept, clearly inspired by common "drive-in" solutions, has the lowest operational complexity of all solutions, but also implies limited interaction with and convenience for the customer. In Germany, this model is utilized by the two retailers Real and Globus, both full-line retailers with very large store formats.

THE COMPANY PLAYERS

In mid-2014, more than 25 companies were doing business in the German OFR market. However, many of these retailers only offer a narrow product assortment, mostly limited to non-fresh, beverage and near-food products (e.g., LIDL, Kaufland, Tchibo, Netto and Plus). In addition, some are focused on a distinct product category (Bofrost and Eismann for frozen food), while others only supply certain types of products (e.g., mymuesli, Gemüse-Tüte, bringmirbio and basic).

Today, 10 retailers are offering a wide range of fresh and non-fresh products in their online food stores, able to (mostly) replace the need to visit a physical store for daily grocery shopping. These companies can be differentiated into two main groups, namely the online food branches of established supermarket chains and start-ups trying to establish themselves as viable alternatives to the traditional incumbents in the German grocery market. Overall, only three of these pure online retailers (Allyouneed, eCola and myTime) are serving the entire German market with their products, whereas the remaining companies are limited to one or a few regional areas.

Established Supermarket Chains

Almost all incumbents in the grocery sector, operating an existing store-based distribution infrastructure, have tried OFR. However, most of them were reluctant to offer their entire product portfolio in their online shops, instead concentrating on durable and long-lasting products, simple to store and ship. The companies providing supermarket-like product assortments are EDEKA (EDEKA24), Globus (Globus Drive), Kaiser's Tengelmann (bringmeister), real (real Drive) and REWE (REWE online).

REWE is one of the most active players in OFR services. Its CEO, Alain Caparros, recently claimed that REWE, as a premium supermarket chain, needs to and will be the "pioneer" of OFR, helping it to become the market leader in the overall food market. To be the number one online food retailer is of high importance, as Caparros explains: "If you type in a search term on Google, you click on one of the first hits. You do not scroll to the second page". The Cologne-based retailer just recently bundled its online business units in a new, hip office, many kilometres away from corporate headquarters. So far, REWE offers services in 16 regions in Germany, expanding gradually. The company aims to "make history" with its e-commerce services, becoming the go-to place for online food shopping. REWE is experimenting with many different forms of ordering (website, apps and phone) and distribution, testing what is most attractive for customers. As of yet, all of REWE's infrastructure revolves around existing stores, where the picking of goods is carried out by distinct personnel. For the distribution of orders, the company is experimenting with both pick-up at stores, and a home delivery service with trucks operated by a logistics service provider.

EDEKA, the largest full-line retailer in the food market, on the other hand, is following another OFR strategy. It is gradually rolling out its online services, called EDEKA24, with a limited assortment of only non-fresh products. While the company has offered nationwide home delivery services in cooperation with DHL for a long time, its pick-up services are fairly limited, serving only individual regions or cities. Autonomous retailers of the EDEKA chain are each developing their own order applications and websites, allowing customer interaction processes to be tailored to specific demands. For pick-up services, the picking is done in store, while home delivery orders are picked in and dispatched from a small, dedicated warehouse.

Driven by the cooperative structures of the two big German full-line retailers REWE and EDEKA, offering high autonomy for individual stores in terms of product assortments, pricing and operational processes, many initiatives in the direction of OFR are championed by individual store managers, rendering their implementation and success dependent on individual commitment and resources. Whereas such independent efforts allow for flexible and innovative approaches to OFR, these retail chains often lack cohesiveness and a joint vision in their ambitions for offering food online. Although OFR operations of both chains can be regarded as functional and working, the companies are hesitant to broadly promote such services, let alone run large-scale marketing campaigns.

The third big retailer, Kaiser's Tengelmann, has long-standing experience with the delivery of food. While being initially only focused on phone orders, its first non-store services were launched in 1997. Even back then, it chose a different way to enter the OFR market. Instead of transferring its brand image to online food operations, it chose to build a dedicated brand and infrastructure solely focused on the home delivery of food, called bringmeister. Through its elaborated online services, customers can order the full range of products available at the big Kaiser's Tengelmann supermarkets, and have them delivered to their homes during a desired time slot. However, today such services are only available in Berlin and Munich, two of the most populated metropolises in Germany.

The remaining two major food retailers, Globus (Globus Drive) and real (real Drive), are offering store-based click-and-collect services. Both concepts are only available in cooperation with individual stores of the chains, each accepting online food orders in just two, smaller German cities. Customers can order their food to be prepared for a pick-up area, where it can be collected as early as two hours after the order is completed. If products are of bad quality, or customers change their mind, these products can conveniently be excluded from the order basket.

Until the middle of 2014, no German discounter is currently operating or has announced plans to roll out a large-scale OFR service. LIDL is the only exception in this regard, since it is operating a nationwide online shop, but its services are limited to non-fresh products, focused on established online retail categories such as fashion, machinery and electronics. Despite the major presence of discounters in the overall German food market, in the short to medium term, none of the companies is expected to expand into OFR of fresh, day-to-day products due to a mismatch with their overall cost-focused strategy.

Online Food Retailing Start-ups

The early stage of the OFR market development provides a breeding ground for innovative business ideas. Several start-ups try to set their footprint in the market by occupying specific food segments, where they can attract customers for a concentrated or full-line product assortment. Interestingly, almost all start-ups focus their service on the home delivery of goods, clearly aiming to attract customers with the convenience of ordering and receiving desired food products without leaving their homes. Furthermore, there is a trend among start-ups towards offering organic food, which usually also entails higher product margins. By taking a closer look at the start-up companies in the market, it is possible to segment them into three groups of OFR retailers, differing in their range of product assortment and the area of delivery.

The first group (Allyouneed, bringmirbio, eCola, myTime) is characterized by a large product variety and a nationwide delivery services. These companies offer the full range of products one can buy in a supermarket (including fresh and ultra-fresh food, and in the case of myTime even many non-foods products), and often present themselves as truly supplementary alternatives to traditional store shopping experiences. All four companies are cooperating with one or many different specialized logistics service providers to carry out the distribution of their goods, and provide incentives such as free shipping to customers to encourage the use of their services. Interestingly, the most mature player in this group, eCola, operates two web platforms (gourmondo and lebensmittel.de), both offering similar products but under different brands, to increase its chances of finding the right service to attract customers. The company is collaborating with more than six different logistics companies for distribution, sending all orders from one central distribution centre in Hanover, Germany.

A second group of the OFR start-ups (e.g., Die grüne Bohne, Emma's Enkel and food.de) also offer a supermarket-like product assortment, but are purposely limiting their delivery services to certain regional areas. In that regard, some companies focus on only one urban area (Emma's Enkel and Die grüne Böhne), delivering from an existing retail store, while others are even able to serve multiple large areas across Germany (food.de), preparing customer orders from the pooled inventories of cooperating retail outlets in the respective cities. Commonly, these companies employ their own drivers and trucks for the distribution, which gives them better control over the delivery process. By concentrating on key regions, they may also be able to specifically design their services for the needs of local customers, offer highly regional food, and provide more reliable time periods of delivery to their clients.

Finally, the third group of start-ups in the online food retailing sector are made up of companies with a highly specialized selection of products, clearly targeting niches, which can often already be recognized from their brand names. Gemüsetüte, for example, is offering a pre-packed selection of vegetables and fruits for a fixed price to be sent to an urban pick-up location, to be collected by customers on a weekly basis. Other start-ups from this group are online alcohol shops (e.g., Belvini, Weinversand) and shops with international products from certain regions, which are usually limited to non-fresh products, and make use of conventional ways of delivery typically also employed by other online retail categories. Overall, there is no single origin from which the products in this group come, ranging in means of distribution from manufacturer- to store- to warehouse-based solutions.

Figure 14.5 gives an overview of selected online food retailers and the business models they are operating at the moment. It also shows a selected group of food retailers who do not yet offer grocery categories online.

Figure 14.5: Selected German OFR players and their business models

CUSTOMER NEEDS AND OPERATIONAL CHALLENGES

Most existing OFR propositions try to highlight the superior convenience of ordering food online compared to buying in store. Customers are not required to spend the time and energy going to a store, selecting and picking their desired products, and carrying the potentially heavy goods home, but instead can perform this process independent of opening hours and physical presence via their computer, smartphone or tablet. By ordering food online, customers can save time, avoid stressful situations in a supermarket (congestion, long waiting times) and can choose products in a relaxed atmosphere. Although this promising outlook may appeal to many potential customers, the expansion of OFR appears to be hindered by a wide range of challenges in marketing and operations for retailers, along all phases of the customer purchasing process.

Today, most German online food shoppers are in their middle years, technology-literate and receiving a medium to high income. The majority live in urban areas and have already had extensive experience of and made frequent use of other opportunities for online shopping. Regular customers primarily decide to shop for food online because of the perceived time-saving and the option for delivery without the need to leave their homes. The home delivery option particularly attracts German customers. In an A.T. Kearney survey, 38 % of participants named the home delivery option as the main reason for purchasing food online. For nearly half of the shoppers, lower prices than in store are also a major factor. About 55 % of the buyers have already used a mobile device (either smartphone or tablet) to order groceries online.[9]

The Need for a Sophisticated OFR Infrastructure

To serve the expectations of the German customers, OFR companies are required to build up specialized distribution structures and often partner with logistics service providers, an endeavour traditional food retailers usually have little or no experience in. In general, companies need to make sure that the products are delivered at the right temperature, in a promised time frame and in a healthy and pleasant condition. While they may be able to sufficiently control such factors when the customer picks up the goods at a store or a warehouse, the retailers' service level and quality is highly dependent on the respective logistics service provider if the goods are to be delivered. Therefore, a few retailers went on to establish and maintain their own transportation fleets and personnel, made up of drivers of cars or trucks.

At present, the market players are far from settled on a standardized or similar procedure for how the shopping experience looks, how the packaging is done or what payment options are offered to the customer. The websites and mobile apps of the retailers appear to have different structures and functionality, provide diverse order fulfilment options, and their services are often restricted to certain regions or even individual stores.

Of course, the product assortment also differs significantly, ranging from portfolios consisting exclusively of non-fresh products, to a focus on premium products, to product offerings comparable to store assortments. The payment is often done electronically during the order process, but is also occasionally possible when picking up the goods at a store or warehouse.

Furthermore, several home automation technologies, allowing household devices to be connected with Internet-based services, are providing great opportunities for an even more convenient and automated order process, but at the moment these are only found in high-end products and, more importantly, are completely missing technical interfaces to interact with the scattered options for IT ordering solutions for online food.

Hurdles for the Established Grocery Chains

From a managerial perspective, traditional food retailers need to adapt structures and processes capable of adequately aligning with the characteristics of this developing market, which is especially challenging for established retailers. To begin with, the fast-changing service processes require autonomous and quick decision-making to adapt, untypical for many large business organizations. Further, the build-up of new distribution channels (for online retailing) demands huge investments in both infrastructure and marketing, while the risk of low profitability, or even persistent losses, might remain acute for a long time. If executives are interested in taking a stake in the OFR market, they will definitely need to find ways to convince their store managers, their personnel and, of course, their customers to show an interest and commit to the online food trade on a large scale, while the future outlook still seems arguably uncertain.

Finally, the companies need to attract personnel with leading expertise in food retailing, electronic commerce and logistics to create appropriate services aligned with customer needs. Often, these individuals are highly skilled and demand an engaging work environment, and, of course, an attractive salary. Retailers need to provide the right incentives and create inspiring tasks to win the right people.

HOW TO REACT TO THE GATHERING STORM?

Despite the wide range of choices, uncertainties and challenges the current market players face, some market experts expect one key event to turn the market and its dynamics literally upside down. A single international player, equipped with exceptional logistics and distribution capabilities, extensive market experience and high brand loyalty, may be able to not only disrupt existing market structures, but may also claim large shares of the potential profits current incumbents have dreamed of. The described player is, of course, Amazon, the vastly dominant e-retailer in virtually all online sales categories in most international, developed markets. Amazon has already gained major practical experience in the online food retailing sector through Amazon Fresh. Its OFR service started in 2007, but is currently limited to selected US cities only. However, according to recent rumours, the e-retailing giant might expand such services into the German market as early as 2015.

But how might the current players react to such a market entrance? Amazon is known to go "all in" on its target markets, cross-subsidizing new markets with deep pockets, large enough that even multinational retailers need to obey. Should the German players now focus on niches of the market, establishing a strong but narrow market positioning? Many observers question whether they can win a battle against Amazon; only a few dare to fight. Are the current offerings and the brand loyalty of German shoppers even strong enough to compete with the services of an e-retailer known for simplicity, convenience and low prices?

With such worrying issues in mind, many executives of traditional retail chains are even rethinking their entire online food services, questioning if it is really worth it. Until now, the OFR services only asked for large investments and management attention, but scarcely reached any profits. Customers also seem to be happy with store-based shopping, and unlike in other retail categories, sales do not really seem to have taken off. Should they perhaps just refocus on what they are best at, a strategy many of their store managers have endorsed for a long time?

Of course, similar thoughts also arose among start-up founders. If home deliveries are at the core of their business models, how might they be able to outperform Amazon's leverages from their existing customer base, and their enormous product assortment? Many small firms are afraid that the bold moves that may be induced by Amazon's market entrance will render their limited services unnecessary, causing them to sink into oblivion. Can they keep their purely online role in the marketplace, trapped between the established retail chains and the overly powerful e-retail giant, Amazon? And how should they argue against such risks to their future investors, who are asked to provide the capital that is so essential for the investment-heavy OFR market?

•••

Setting of the case: 2014; last revision: 2014.

NOTES

[1] A.T. Kearney, & Department of Business Policy and Logistics, (2014): *How big will the cake be?*, University of Cologne, Germany.

[2] DVZ, (2014): *Abkehr vom klassischen Handelsgeschäft*, URL: http://www.dvz.de/themen/e-commerce/single-view/ nachricht/abkehr-vom-klassischen-handelsgeschaeft.html, (accessed May 15, 2014).

[3] TradeDimensions, (2013): *BVE Jahresbericht 2013/2014,* Berlin, Germany.

[4] GfK, (2014): *Consumer Index Total Grocery 04/2014*, Nuremberg, Germany.

[5] Flinzner, K., (2014): *Lebensmittel online. Ein deutsch-französischer Vergleich*, URL: http://www.mehrsprachig-handeln.de/blog/2014/01/20/lebensmittel-online-ein-deutsch-franzoesischer-vergleich, (accessed June 16, 2014).

[6] Ludowig, K., & Kapalschinski, C., (2014, Januar 27): *Kampfzone Supermarkt*, Handelsblatt, pp. 1, 4-7.

[7] A.T. Kearney, & Department of Business Policy and Logistics, (2013): *Online Food Retailing: Challenges and Solutions for the German Market*, University of Cologne, Germany.

[8] Warschun, M., Delfmann W., Albers, S., & Müßig R., (2012): *A Fresh Look at Online Grocery*, A.T. Kearney.

[9] Warschun, M., Krüger, L., & Vogelphol, N., (2013): *Online-Food-Retailing: Ein Markt im Aufschwung*, A.T. Kearney.

15

Kölner Stadt-Anzeiger and the Digital News Revolution

Sascha Albers, Stefanie Dorn and Felix Limbert

The German newspaper industry is facing a crisis. The renowned press agency dapd has declared bankruptcy and two further pieces of news shocked the industry in the autumn of 2012 when the Frankfurter Rundschau (FR) declared insolvency and Gruner + Jahr decided to close down the daily Financial Times Deutschland. However, the Federation of German Newspaper Publishers (BDVZ) and the German Federation of Journalists (DJV) have strongly objected to statements such as "death of newspapers," as most German newspapers have survived the introduction of the internet, despite bleak predictions. Nonetheless, some industry experts have predicted the end of the era of printed newspapers.

For the Kölner Stadt-Anzeiger (KStA), a family-run daily regional newspaper with a rich tradition of reporting on contemporary topics in and around Cologne, it is becoming more and more difficult to maintain a strong position within the news market. In bargaining meetings with their advertising clients, sales managers at KStA are repeatedly confronted with questions about the future of the printed newspaper. The internet has been established as the daily medium for communicating and gathering information, offering consumers a variety of new possibilities. For instance, the internet allows consumers to search for specific content and facilitates interaction with other readers. After initial hesitation, advertising clients are spending much more on online ads and benefiting from the manifold opportunities to place their products and messages, along with a reduction in spending on traditional advertising channels. This dynamic new environment presents challenges for the traditional newspapers, whose reach is steadily decreasing (see **Figure 15.1**). Hence, advertising clients are tending to place fewer ads in traditional newspapers in an attempt to reach as many potential customers as possible (see **Figure 15.2**). Additionally, the online advertising business is dominated by such internet giants as Google and Facebook. Still, many newspapers have aimed to play out their journalistic and editorial expertise with online appearances or tablet editions and elaborated apps. However, investments for establishing and maintaining digital appearances are substantial and therefore involve risks. Moreover, newspapers are still struggling with the "for-free" mentality of their readers and advertising clients which has resulted from the introduction of the internet. Right from the beginning of private internet use, nearly all online content was free of charge. One reason for this was the relatively simple and cheap possibility of presenting online content, and consumers were not willing to pay for such simple content. A second reason for the "for-free" mentality was the absence of a micro payment system that would allow for the easy and secure settlement of small sums. As a result, traditional media underestimated the commercial potential inherent in the internet. So what does the future hold for newspapers that are confronted with a declining print section and an extremely competitive online market?

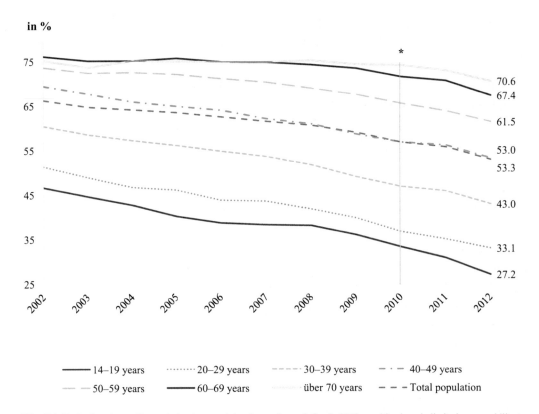

*The "Media-Analyse (ag.ma)" association increased the observed population in 2010, resulting in only limited comparability to the values of prior years

Source: ag.ma/BDZV/ZMG

Figure 15.1: Development of the reach of regional subscription newspapers in Germany in percent by age groups, 2000–2010

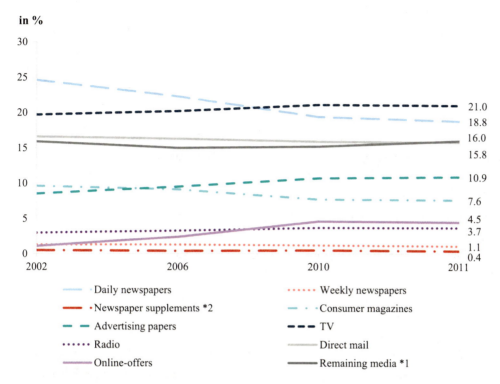

Figure 15.2: Spending on advertisement in Germany market share of different media types in percentage, 2000–2010

NEWSPAPER JOURNALISM IN CRISIS

Experts have claimed that within a few years, the European newspaper market might witness trends similar to those currently being experienced by the North American market. In particular, local daily papers are affected by the so called death of newspapers. In May 2012, the renowned Times Picayune from New Orleans had to be closed down, leaving that city without its own daily paper. Two further examples for victims of the digitalization and its inherent developments are presented by the Canadian Halifax Daily News and the American Kentucky Post. Altogether, a total of 14 local North American dailies have ceased publication since March 2007. However, nationwide media are equally affected as well. Only recently, the US American IAC Group announced the complete termination of the printed version of the traditional weekly Newsweek by the end of 2012. Due to a dramatic decline in readers and advertising clients, Newsweek reported losses of up to 40 million USD. In the future, the magazine will be operated as an online version under the label Newsweek Global. In Europe, similar developments are beginning to emerge. The French publication France Soir had been on the verge of bankruptcy when the paper was first kept alive by private investors, then changed to online in December 2011 before it completely vanished from the market eight months later. The Spanish media group Prisa, suffering from a high amount of accumulated debt, had to cut over one third of its staff at El País, one of the leading daily newspapers in Spain.

The German newspapers are observing the developments on the international markets with concern, because they are struggling for their own survival. Thus, regional competitors of KStA or papers with a similar local focus are increasingly opening up to online business. Although online business opens up diverse opportunities for the news industry, hardly any publishing company manages to earn money from their online appearances. Even if the situation in Germany is not as dramatic as on the North American market, more and more publishers are planning to reduce resources for their printed media. In autumn of 2012, however, two pieces of uncomfortable news emerged. Firstly, media group M. DuMont Schauberg announced the insolvency of the renowned Frankfurter Rundschau. Secondly, Gruner + Jahr announced the termination of its economy section: Financial Times Deutschland will be abandoned, whereas the economic magazines Impulse and Börse Online will be sold. According to media reports, Gruner + Jahr will also reduce up to 10 percent of its staff at the leading women's magazine Brigitte. Furthermore, Hamburger Jahreszeitenverlag announced it would cut down the printed version of its city magazine Prinz.

Like its competitors, KStA is struggling with these recent trends. The circulation of KStA has decreased by a constant rate of two to three percent per year over the last ten years. Even more problematic than the declining sales revenues is the resulting loss of important advertising clients. Regional newspapers are exposed to a self-reinforcing effect, since for the newspapers lucrative local advertising battles regularly ensue among local retail rivals (such as supermarkets) which now become less numerous and also involve less clients. The traditional rule that 40 percent of newspaper industry revenues are generated through distribution to customers (readers) and 60 percent through the advertising business no longer applies; in fact, the ratio has even been reversed (see **Figure 15.3**). A further problem can be identified in the fact that some formats, such as the free advertising paper Einkauf Aktuell, compiled by Deutsche Post, the German postal service provider, and distributed on Saturdays, become more and more attractive to advertising clients. These papers do not contain elaborate editorial content and offer advertising clients a guaranteed and constant reach, at least up to the customers' mailboxes.

As a result of these threats, nearly all traditional newspapers are trying to secure another revenue source via internet and mobile applications. For several years, the online media world has been an important pillar for KStA, in addition to its traditional printed edition. With the introduction of its iPad app, which is subscribed to by over 3000 readers, the KStA is one of the pioneers among local newspapers when it comes to tablet computers.

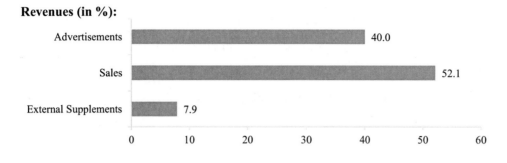

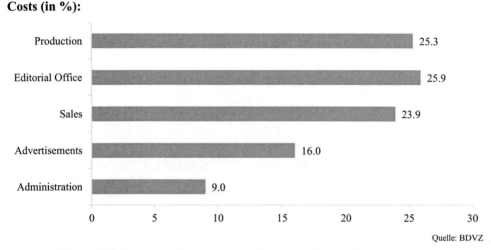

Figure 15.3: Revenue and cost structure: Average values of subscription newspapers in West Germany in percentage, 2010

REVOLUTION OF NEWS CONSUMPTION

Traditionally, Germany has been a newspaper bastion. As part of an everyday breakfast ritual, in the train, or in the office, more than 70 percent of Germans aged 14 and over kept up-to-date by regularly reading a weekly or daily newspaper. In 2011, approximately 23.8 million daily newspapers were sold in Germany per day of publication, most of which (approximately 80 percent) were daily newspapers. Around 70 percent of these are local subscription newspapers, with Sunday and weekly newspapers completing the offering. In 2011, the reach (one of the key performance indicators for the newspaper industry) amounted to 68 percent of Germans aged 14 and over. Put another way, more than two-thirds of all Germans read newspapers (see **Figure 15.4**).

By age (in %):

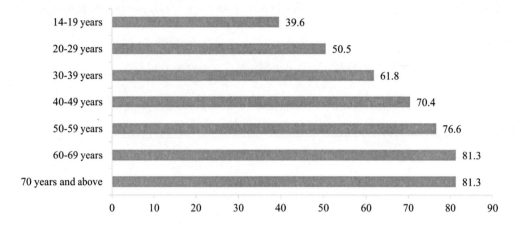

By sociodemographic target groups (in %):

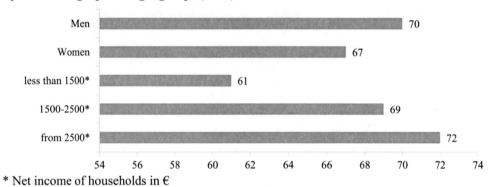

* Net income of households in €

By types of newspaper (in %):

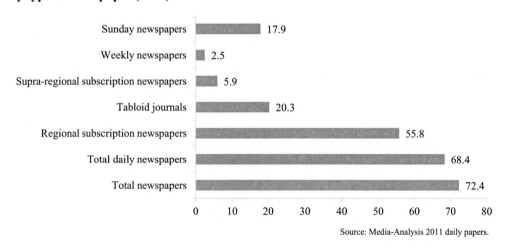

Source: Media-Analysis 2011 daily papers.

Figure 15.4: Reach of daily newspapers, 2011. Base: German-speaking population aged 14 and above

An important feature of the German newspaper market has always been the extremely diverse range of daily and weekly newspapers (see **Figure 15.5**). This diversity is reflected in the highly fragmented market structure. However, the industry is dominated by three big publishers: the Axel Springer Group, with its widely known newspapers like Bild and Welt is the clear market leader with 17.8 percent. It is followed by the WAZ Group, with 4 percent and the media group M. DuMont Schauberg with 3.5 percent. The remaining 74.7 percent are composed of numerous small publishing companies (see **Figure 15.6**).

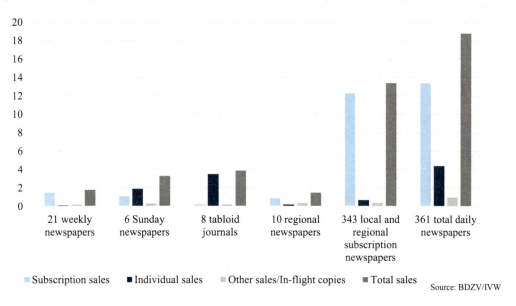

Figure 15.5: Newspaper sales in Germany in the 2nd quarter of 2011 (in millions of units)

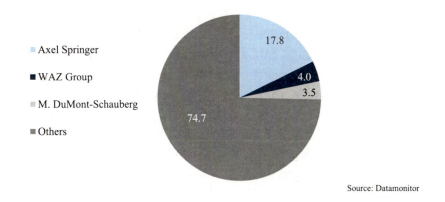

Figure 15.6: Market shares of the largest German publishing companies

All publishers are now obviously facing serious technological change, which is considerably affecting the usage patterns of the readers.

Changed social structures are the major reason for the decline in circulation. The typical newspaper reader tends to live in small or medium-sized cities and the typical household of newspaper readers is composed of at least two persons so that a joint newspaper subscription is economically viable. Nowadays, however, especially younger people live in big cities, which means that the number of single person households is steadily increasing. Furthermore, the increased tendency towards mobility has created a problem that the newspapers have to face. The German newspaper market is characterized by a strong reader newspaper bond, meaning that readers tend to stay loyal to their newspaper – literally from the birth announcements to the obituaries. In the German newspaper market, newspapers are more than just a medium for information; they reflect a certain ideology and are important instruments for the formation of opinions. Due to the increased mobility of potential readers, combined with frequent changes of their locations, the relevance of local newspapers in particular has declined (see **Figure 15.8**). Additionally, according to market analysts, readers either decide at a young age to stick to the newspaper medium, or they probably never will.

Analogous to the development and dispersion of broadcasting in the 1980s, publishing companies face the challenges of current technological innovations that demand an adaption of traditional value chains. The internet allows other players, such as radio and broadcasting companies, or companies that are traditionally from outside the media industry, such as Google and Facebook, to become direct and relevant competitors for traditional newspapers. In doing so, radio and other broadcasting companies enrich their journalistic content with additional text, and their web pages and streaming offerings represent attractive advertising platforms. However, the internet enterprises in particular have revolutionized traditional market structures and generated a new battle over advertising budgets (see **Figure 15.8**). These companies are clearly leading in the distribution of advertising sales in the digital market, as they can offer soliciting firms added value compared to standard print placements. By examining user profiles and patterns on their websites, the advertisements are placed in a way that precisely fits the consumer, leading to a more individual direction of the sales message. Recently, modern advertising has achieved a dynamic character, for which the companies are willing to pay premium prices. Google, for instance, generates 99 percent of its sales via the advertising business. From a publisher's point of view, this situation is somewhat delicate, since search engines such as Google or Bing show abstracts of online press contents to make the users curious and to motivate them to click on the search results. The money that is generated in this manner is not shared with the authors of the content, but instead directly flows to the search engine.

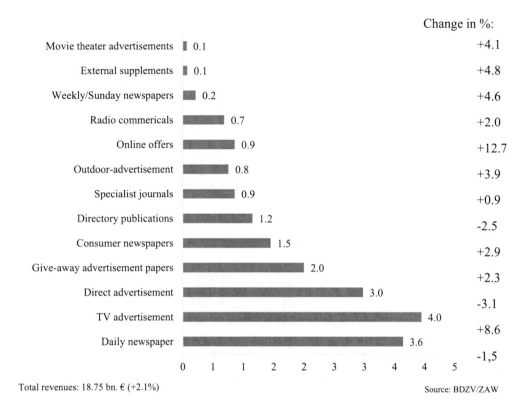

Total revenues: 18.75 bn. € (+2.1%) Source: BDZV/ZAW

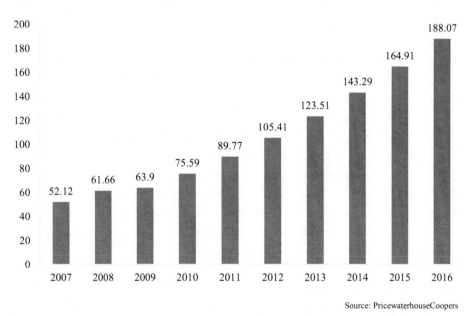

Source: PricewaterhouseCoopers

Figure 15.7: Online sales revenues worldwide until 2010 and forecast until 2016 (wired and mobile; in billions of US dollars)

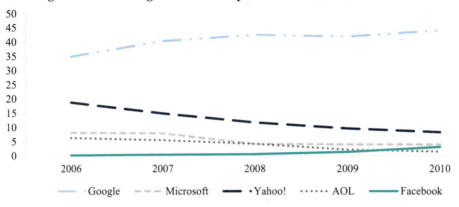

Figure 15.8: Net advertising sales of measurable advertising media 2010 in billions of Euros

The continued existence of the printed media has been challenged by the ongoing digitalization of information. Newspaper reach is shrinking dramatically and newspaper circulations have had to be sized down. Some experts have spoken of a publishing house crisis, while others have even predicted the "death of the newspaper". Despite these opinions, the digital world also holds great opportunities for newspaper publishers. The number of readers that consume information and news via the internet continues to grow and almost all newspapers maintain a website. Because they are competing with other sources of digital information availability, publishers must assert their own online offerings. Therefore, many newspapers, including the KStA, have decided to make selected contents of print issues available by putting them on their internet page with some time lag, without charging. Since almost all newspapers ran their online offerings this way for many years, it is now difficult to get readers used to paying for online contents. This is even more important as the substitution of print media by digital media becomes more prevalent. The same applies for advertising clients. Originally, when booking advertisements in print media, an advertisement in the respective online edition was included for free, as a large online reach also tends to foster the advertising business in print media. On the one hand, the success of other online newsportals left no opportunity for the newspapers; on the other hand, this led to the development of an exceedingly problematic "for-free" mentality of the advertising clients, since printruns have declined steadily.

In response, newspaper companies have applied various strategies to tackle the digital challenge. Nearly all newspapers run an online version that contains the essential contents of the print edition, albeit mostly in a shortened way. The texts, which are usually free, are supplemented by photos, short video clips, and functions to comment on the article. The diffusion of tablet computers has again differentiated the demands for digital offerings of the newspapers; due to their portability, online newspapers have become even more attractive. More and more newspapers have developed apps that adapt the offerings of the newspaper to the potential of mobile devices using upscale, multimedia contents. Also, the technical specifications of such apps, which have to be downloaded onto the device, simplify the charging of money. Due to this and the improved range of applicabilities and services, the newspapers hope to counteract the "cost-free" attitude of the users by raising readers' willingness to pay.

While traditional newspapers are coping with these challenges, completely new and online only newspapers have also been established. A business model that has been successful so far – at least from the founders' point of view – is The Huffington Post, which went online in May 2005 in the form of a political weblog. For a long time, the newspaper was accused of "cheesy journalism", not least due to the relatively poor renumeration of its journalists. However, with the awarding of the Pulitzer Prize in 2012, the Huffington Post proved that online reporting can be produced at a high quality. Some experts are certain that digital offers are the only way newspaper companies can survive within the market in the long run. Anyway, the implementation and the long-term maintenance of an online strategy for traditional publishing houses are easier said than done.

THE TRADITIONAL PRINT VALUE CREATION MODEL AT KStA

KStA is the leading daily newspaper in Cologne and proudly looks back onto a long tradition (see **Figure 15.9**). With a circulation of about 215,000 newspapers sold (100.000 of them in Cologne) it targets urban Cologne readers and realizes a reach of about one million readers on average (see **Table 15.1**). KStA is one of eight daily newspapers published by M. DuMont Schauberg (see **Figure 15.10**). The family-led media group yielded revenues of about €710 million in 2010 and has roots that can be traced back to the 17th century. Because of its diverse involvements, the publishing company covers a large array of media types.

The most important distribution form of the KStA is currently the classical print version – the daily newspaper. Revenues of the newspaper are created both by sales to readers (either through individual purchases or through a subscription) and by the sale of advertisements and commercial supplements inside the newspaper. Its regional quality reporting is KStA's core value proposition. The content is produced by an elaborate daily research of about 100 staff writers and about 60 independent writers. While the reporters conduct their research, photographers are out in the city to gather images to illustrate the stories. Police reporters, who are often contacted by the police itself, also work at night to collect important information about accidents, fires, or other instances on-site. In addition, investigative research regarding stories that are important to the Cologne region is carried out.

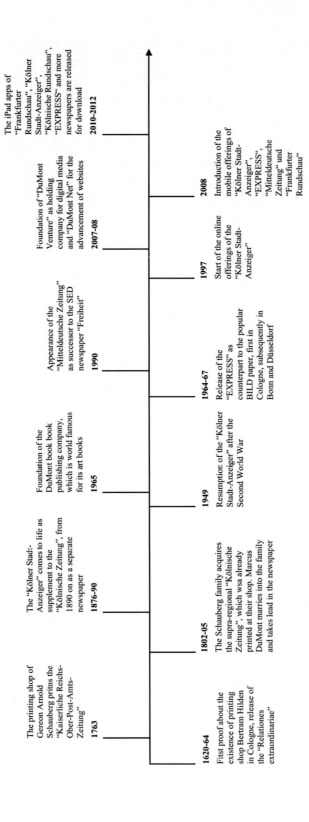

Figure 15.9: History of KStA as part of the MDS Group

The researched data and facts are processed in the editors' office. The employees are divided into an editorial office and five district offices (Euskirchen-Eifel, Leverkusen, Rhein-Berg/Oberberg, Rhein-Erft, and Rhein-Sieg/Bonn). Accordingly, the KStA is published in five different editions; apart from the Cologne edition, there are specially adapted versions of the paper for the five districts (for example, the Leverkusener Anzeiger as a regionally adapted version of the KStA). Each variant of the KStA consists of five so-called "books". Across all editions, four of these books are edited centrally by the "umbrella" editorial office (German: Mantelredaktion). Three of those compose the so-called "umbrella", one is the Cologne local section. Within the different districts, a fifth "book" with regional news of the respective districts completes the newspaper. Twice a week, the fifth part is exchanged through suburban news of the respective districts. Additionally, page one is designed individually according to the local news of the distinct districts.

	3/2012	of that: ePaper 3/2012	2/2012	of that: ePaper 2/2012	+/-
Distribution	307,808	893	329,779	734	-6.66%
Sales	301,592	893	322,885	734	-6.59%
Subscription	265,166	564	269,718	484	-1.69%
EV sales	19,738		21,355		-7.57%
EV delivery	43,502		45,693		-4.80%
Returns	23,764		24,338		-2.36%
In-flight copies	861		879		-2.05%
Other sales	15,827	329	30,933	250	-48.83%
Print run	346,365		368,549		-6.02%

EV: Pieces delivered to retail outlets, less unsold goods.

Source: IWV - Informationsgemeinschaft zur Feststellung der Verbreitung von Werbeträgern e.V.

Table 15.1: Sales development of KStA and Kölnische Rundschau, 2012

An important and economically necessary part of the newspaper is the advertising section. The advertising department acquires new advertisements and processes orders, which are usually placed by agencies hired by the corporation that runs the campaign. Private advertisements are usually received by phone at the service center.

Once the newspaper content is finally produced, laid out, and revised, the paper is handed over to the printing department. Offset printing is carried out in-house in a central and modern printing line with a capacity of about 80,000 newspapers per hour. The large print run of the KStA including its regionally adapted version allows for an efficient capacity utilization of the printing line, which enables profitable production. Before bundling the individual "books", advertising supplements are placed in the middle of the newspaper. Subsequently, the finalized newspapers are distributed overnight: subscribers can expect their copy of KStA to be in their mailbox by 6:30 a.m. at the latest. Moreover, the KStA is available at kiosks, stores and gas stations for €1.30 (weekdays) and €1.70 (weekend edition) from early morning.

Source: Mediengruppe M. DuMont Schauberg

Figure 15.10: Daily newspapers offered by Mediengruppe M. DuMont Schauberg, 2012

KStA´s ONLINE STRATEGY

Like most other newspapers, the KStA developed and implemented new strategies in order to survive in the long term in the new dynamic environment. For about the last 15 years, the KStA has offered an online version in addition to its traditional print format. Until 2011, excerpts of the print version of the day before were published on the paper's homepage, ksta.de. However, after recognizing the internet's future significance, KStA's executive team decided to improve its online appearance, to provide additional resources for the online offerings, and therefore to make it more attractive. Accordingly, in 2001, a dedicated online editorial team was created to develop content specifically tailored for the website. This content was not only shorter and more concise, but differed considerably from that in the print version. One of the directives from the main editorial office was to only adopt about 50 percent of the online articles from the print version.

The website's significance increased steadily and, since 2008, the internal principle has been: "online first". This is supposed to match the readers' changed reading habits. As it turned out, the readers still obtain their basic daily information from the printed version, but also expected to find the most current news on KStA's website. Today, the share of printed texts in the online version accounts for only 30 percent. In addition, the editors of the print version are encouraged to write comprehensively in order to ensure efficient utilization of information across several media channels. In the best case, KStA informs its readers online shortly after a relevant event has happened in Cologne or the surrounding area. The daily newspaper discusses topics in-depth and the print editors can enrich existing articles on the website.

A milestone of the online strategy's development is the introduction of the KStA app. The tablet version of KStA is the third pillar of the publishing company's hybrid strategy between print and digital distribution. At 8:00 p.m. each day, users with mobile devices can read the most important stories from the next day's newspaper, enriched with pictures and charts, as well as video and audio files. The iPad app, which was the first app of a German regional newspaper, was introduced in 2010. Since 2011, the app has also been available for Android tablets. The daily edition of the app costs €0.79 and subscriptions are available starting at €17.90 per month (see **Figure 15.11**). However, KStA's pioneering role did not come without some difficulties. The medial design, which includes many audio and video recordings, poses a great challenge for newspaper staff. Preparing and creating this content requires professional software systems that support the content and format of the tablets. Furthermore, newspapers must develop new distribution channels. Apps can be distributed via different channels, which differ substantially in their contribution margin. When sold via the Apple AppStore, 30 percent of the price is retained by Apple. These costs do not occur when the purchase is made on KStA's own website. Therefore, KStA offers its iPad version on its own website for download; as of 2012, approximately 3000 subscriptions have been sold. Roughly 50 percent of iPad subscribers have bought the subscription bundled with the tablet, sold directly through the newspaper company. A further 15–20 percent of iPad subscribers have switched from the print version to the iPad version. Very few users purchase the iPad version directly through the AppStore – this is beneficial to KStA, as not only does Apple retain 30 percent of the price if the purchase is done via the AppStore, but KStA also misses the direct customer interaction on this distribution channel. Apple does not pass on any customer data to the creators of the app. Also, due to the regional focus of the newspaper brands, the global visibility and availability via the App Store is not seen as a key sales facilitator.

With the increased importance of online reporting, an online editorial team was established. Ten employees are responsible for the contents of the website ksta.de and the production of the tablet app. This team starts working at 6:00 a.m. – long before their colleagues of the print version – because this is the time that the first readers want to be informed about the latest news via mobile devices. The online editorial team is involved in all of the important editorial conferences. For the app, three illustrators are part of the editorial team to cut the multimedia content for the iPad. Depending on the news, several additional freelancers from external agencies are used to support the core team under high loads. Each of the named editorial desks has one responsible editor, who leads the production of the certain unit.

	Print	App
Unit price per issue	€1.30	€0.79
Monthly subscription price (duration at least 1 month)	€28.40	€17.90
Subscription incl. tablet computer	---	€28.80

Figure 15.11: Pricing scheme of Kölner Stadt-Anzeiger, updated November 2012

ONLINE STRATEGIES AT MDS AND ITS RIVALS

The online activity of KStA is considered as an extremely successful strategy within the company portfolio of M. DuMont Schauberg. On the way to a multimedia press house, the websites of KStA are becoming more and more complex. Besides the online presence and apps of KStA, the online television service www.ksta.tv and the online community www.stadtmenschen.de, which is based on user-generated content, are also part of the online strategy. The company plans to generate at least a quarter of its revenues via online offerings by 2013. In 2008, digital media already held a 10 percent share. Thereby, the KStA management focuses on cooperation with other regional newspapers, such as the online platform Kalaydo, which is ranked among the top 10 German e-commerce offers, in which also other regional newspapers like the Westdeutsche Zeitung, the Solinger Tageblatt and many more are involved.

Moreover, within the group's structure, M. DuMont Schauberg focuses on multimedia share, amongst others in publishing as well as on radio or TV (see **Figure 15.12**). Even investments in the online segment play a significant role within the corporate involvements. Here, the subsidiary DuMont Neue Medien is responsible for offering services in the online sector. The enterprise DuMont Venture, on the other hand, deals with specific investments in start-ups. DuMont Net considers the continuous improvement of all corporate websites, such as ksta.de and express.de. In this manner, all of MDS's newspapers were extended by websites of different kinds. For instance, the online appearance and the app of DuMont's Kölnische Rundschau are completely designed as a simple e-paper, while the Express and the KStA are operated with multimedia tools that are integrated in the respective websites and apps. In addition, both papers attempt to directly contact their readers after current events through social networks such as Facebook and Twitter.

M. DuMont Schauberg Expedition der Kölnischen Zeitung GmbH & Co. KG, Köln

District Köln
- Düsseldorf-EXPRESS GmbH & Co. KG (50%)
- RZZ Logistik GmbH (100%)
- Rheinische Zeitungs-Zustellgesellschaft Köln mbH & Co. KG (100%)
- RZZ Köln/Leverkusen GmbH (100%)
- RZZ Köln linksrheinisch GmbH (100%)
- RZZ Rhein-Berg GmbH (100%)
- MDS Creativ GmbH (100%)
- DERTICKETSERVICE.KT GmbH (100%)
- Kreative Medieninnovation GmbH & Co. KG (100%)
- MAS, Medien Archive Service GmbH & Co. KG (100%)
- Disktret GmbH (100%)
- MVR Media Vermarktung Rheinland GmbH (100%)

District Halle — Mitteldeutsches Druck- und Verlagshaus GmbH & Co. KG, Halle
- MZZ-Mitteldeutsche Zeitungszustell-Gesellschaft mbH (100%)
- MZ Logistik GmbH (100%)
- MZ Dialog GmbH (100%)
- mz-web GmbH (100%)
- TIM Ticket GmbH (100%)
- MZ Druckerei GmbH (100%)
- AROPRINT Druck- und Verlagshaus GmbH (95%)
- TV Halle Fernsehgesellschaft mbH (74,8)

District Berlin/Hamburg — Druck- und Verlagshaus Frankfurt am Main GmbH, Frankfurt (50% Anteil der DuMont Beteiligungs GmbH, Köln)
- BVZ Berliner Medien GmbH (100%)
- BV Deutsche Zeitungsholding GmbH (100%)
- Berliner Verlag GmbH (100%, via BV Deutsche Zeitungsholding)
- Morgenpost Verlag GmbH (100%, via BV Deutsche Zeitungsholding)
- DZH Digital Media Holding GmbH (100%, via BV Deutsche Zeitungsholding)
- Berlin Online Stadtportal GmbH (100%, via BV Deutsche Zeitungsholding)

District Frankfurt — PMB Presse- und Medienhaus Berlin GmbH & Co. KG, Berlin
- MainSign Redaktions GmbH (100%)
- FR Publishing GmbH (100%)
- Verlag Frankfurter Stadtanzeiger GmbH (100%)
- FR-ComLog GmbH (100%)
- Mediendepot Frankfurt GmbH (100%)
- Janz und Fritzsche Medienvertriebsgesellschaft mbH (100%)
- Zeitungs-Vertriebs GmbH FR Ost (100%)
- 5 Zeitungsvertriebs GmbH (51%)
- Kalaydo Rhein Main GmbH (100%)

Section Beteiligungen

Verlags-Beteiligungen
- Rheinische Anzeigenblatt GmbH & Co. KG (50%)
- K.I.-Mediengesellschaft mbH (100%)
- Wochenspiegel Verlagsgesellschaft mbH & Co. KG (100%)
- MSG Media-Service GmbH & Co. KG (50,2%)
- DuMont Verlags-Beteiligungen GmbH & Co. KG (100%)

Sonder-Beteiligungen
- DuMont Kalenderverlag GmbH & Co. KG (100%)
- DuMont Venture Holding GmbH & Co. KG (100%)
- DuMont Net GmbH & Co. KG (100%)
- DuMont Shop GmbH & Co. KG (100%)
- DuMont Systems GmbH & Co. KG (100%)
- mypage GmbH & Co. KG (100%)
- DERTICKETSERVICE.DE GmbH (50%)
- Centerty Heimatfernsehen Köln GmbH & Co. KG (100%)
- DuMont Anzeigenverwaltung GmbH (100%)
- DuMont Auslandsbeteiligungs GmbH (100%)
- Bonner Zeitungsdruckerei und Verlagsanstalt H.
- DuMont Buchverlag GmbH & Co. KG (100%)

Beteiligungen Funk und Fernsehen: DuMont Funk und Fernsehen GmbH & Co. KG
- HSG Hörfunk Service GmbH (88%)
- RRB Rheinische Rundfunkbeteiligungs GmbH & Co. KG (100%)
- DuMont Digital GmbH & Co. KG (100%)
- DuMont Neue Medien GmbH & Co. KG (100%)

Figure 15.12: Structure of M. DuMont Schauberg media group

To enable efficient working at these different economic activities, information is exchanged between the publication units of MDS. The so-called editorial unit (German: Redaktionsgemeinschaft – ReGe) within the MDS ensures efficient reporting, particularly among the newspapers Berliner Zeitung, Mitteldeutsche Zeitung, and the KStA. The ReGe is concerned with nationwide investigations concerning politics and economy, and provides the aligned texts for the individual publication units of MDS. The publisher's different newspapers can adapt the information to their own requirements. Accordingly, Hamburger Morgenpost and Express cooperate closely and share information and texts.

A factor that has grown in importance recently is for newspapers to sustain efficient structures. The Axel Springer Group (a.o. Die Welt, BILD) has already earned one third of the digital market, with a turnover of nearly €3 billion (compared to €962 million in 2011)). Next to the development of their newspaper brands, such as the Welt Online HD app for tablets, the publisher relies on a diversified portfolio of online services. For example, the group operates as a service provider on the digital advertising market or at the online job board. The Rheinische Post, a local newspaper that also competes with the KStA outside the city of Cologne, relies on multimedia editing of news. The tablet app RP+ is published once a week and can be purchased as a single edition (€1.59 per issue) or as a subscription (30 days for €4.99, three months for €14.99, six months for €29.99 or 12 months for €49.99). The RP+ is currently only available via the Apple AppStore and exclusively for the iPad. The website rp-online.de is extremely successful and has one of the widest reaches of any regional German daily newspaper in terms of online services. Beyond that, the newspaper arranges its site as a regional portal, where users have the opportunity to add new contents. For tablets, the paper develops a digital magazine under the brand RP+. In a similar manner, most of KStA's competitors are exper-imenting with a wide variety of online strategies – from rather simple e-papers to complex multimedia apps. Whereas some strategies of the industry turn out to be successful, others fail. For example, the sales of e-papers as a simple online issue of the printed paper are quite low, so that it is not regarded as a promising strategy for future online appearances of newspapers.

To maintain a print- and online edition at the same time, the newspapers must implement efficiency raising methods. KStA had to adjust its strategy. First, it increased the price of the printed edition by €0.10. Second, the editing and layouting of the district editorial teams will be centralized in 2013 to simplify the concentration of editorial contents. The seriousness of the situation can be seen in the example of the sister-newspaper Frankfurter Rundschau, which had to announce insolvency in autumn 2012. The owners initially tried to ensure the continuation of the newspaper with the help of a €1 million investment and the staff relinquishing parts of their salaries. However, considering the massive losses in the advertising business, the FR had to file for insolvency proceedings.

THE WAY AHEAD

The future role of KStA's print edition is uncertain. Fundamental reading habits have changed due to young, technology-oriented consumers who do not want to devote themselves to the traditional print format. The publishing houses are evolving into media companies and are increasingly investing in the digital business to fulfill consumption habits in the long term. In the short run, however, the newspaper companies are looking for a suitable pricing model for their online contents in order to counteract consumers' expectations of cost-free content. The German public broadcasting corporations, on the other hand, are hampering the intended move by the publishers, given that they publish free electronic press offers with a high proportion of texts, multimedia support, and background information on the stories, which go far beyond the broadcasts and thereby put these companies in direct competition with the online-offering of the newspapers. According to the Interstate Broadcasting Treaty (German: Rundfunkstaatsvertrag) the dissemination of press-like information or such information that does not directly relate to the broadcast content is prohibited to the fees-funded broadcasters, thereby avoiding distortions in competition. However, the interpretation of the attributes "press-like" and "program-related" is currently still subject to a comprehensive dispute between publishers and broadcasters. Recently, the Cologne court decided in favor of the publishers assessing one issue of the Tagesschau news app by the German broadcaster ARD as "not sufficiently program-related". In October 2012, the ARD appealed against this judgment. In addition to these disputes, in the long run the publishers must enforce a payment model for their online content to compensate for declining revenues in the printed sector. One option that is already tracked by some newspapers is to offer archived content for a fee. If the apps and internet pages of the newspapers manage to assert themselves in the long run, more and more print editions might vanish from the newsstands.

Still, some experts disagree with these predictions. They believe strongly that the print editions of the newspapers will be accepted as an elitist premium product in the future, due to lower circulations and therefore higher prices. If this is true, the decision of some newspapers to stop their print editions might turn out to be a mistake. Unlike other formats, local newspapers in particular have the advantage that they are difficult for their readers to substitute, especially their local advertising customers. However, the dropping sales volume shows that the KStA cannot rely on this advantage. Furthermore, the effort of retaining the high standard of quality journalism exists, next to pursuing arrangements that increase efficiency, such as staff cost savings, to align the costs to the decreasing revenues. The situation in Germany is getting worse and questions remain, such as how the Kölner Stadt-Anzeiger can most suitably meet the new digital challenges, and the extent to which the current newspaper crisis can be viewed as a new opportunity.

•••

Setting of the case: 2012; last revision: October 2015.

16

Reissdorf Kölsch: Regaining Momentum

Sascha Albers and Bastian Schweiger

It was Friday afternoon when Michael von Rieff, managing partner of the Privat-Brauerei Heinrich Reissdorf GmbH & Co. KG, looked at his latest sales figures. Times were tough for his company. The beer market was a mature, even a shrinking, market, and customers simply declined to drink as much beer as in the good old days. From its peak in 1991, when Germans drank 114 million hectolitres, beer consumption had decreased by 20 % to 94.6 million hectolitres in 2013 (see **Figure 16.1**).

Reissdorf, a medium-sized company with strong regional roots and a long family tradition, had hitherto been in a rather comfortable position: even though the German beer industry had witnessed declining sales, the Cologne-based company had achieved a respectable sales growth of 28 % from 2000 to 2008. But now it seemed that Reissdorf could no longer escape the market trend, von Rieff thought. But Reissdorf had shown that it could outperform the market for quite a while. Had they lost track? And what should they do?

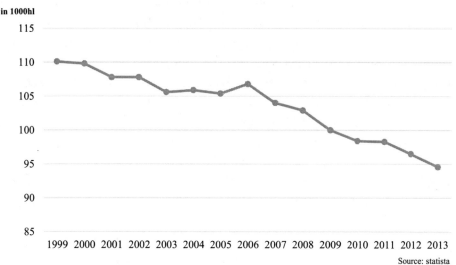

Source: statista

Figure 16.1: Quantities of beer sold in Germany (in mill. hl)

THE MARKET ENVIRONMENT

The National Beer Market in Germany

With one brewery for every 62,000 of its residents, Germany has one of the highest brewery densities per capita worldwide. The 10 largest German breweries account for 27 % of the national industry output, illustrating the rather fragmented market structure. In the past, German breweries focused their attention on sales volume growth rather than on profitability. The dramatic decline in beer consumption over the last few years has led to high overcapacities. Despite the highly competitive situation in the market, in 2007 80 % of the companies still claimed that their top priority was to increase their output. Additionally, with the 2001 acquisition of Beck's by Interbrew (now Anheuser Busch-InBev), international competitors have been able to enter the formerly rather closed German beer market. Moreover, Anheuser-Busch InBev, the Netherlands' Heineken and Denmark's Carlsberg have been continuously annexing German beer brands, thereby intensifying the competitive situation for German breweries.

The formerly rather closed nature of the German beer market stems from its historical heritage and the socio-cultural importance of the brewery craft. The first evidence for beer brewing on German soil dates to 800 B.C., but it was in the ninth century when Benedictine monks especially started to systematically and continuously enhance the brewing processes. Over the centuries, brewing families enjoyed high social standing, were wealthy people with their own land. They were socially well embedded, forging ties with the regional nobilities, clergy and monasteries, as well as with other brewers in their area. For a long time, the brewing trade stood for a closed elitist group of wealthy families and monks.

Today, the German market is more and more dominated by large brewery groups which manage a portfolio of both national and regional brands. Among them are national, privately owned brewery groups like Krombacher, Bitburger and Warsteiner, the Radeberger group, which is the beverage holding company within the German Oetker conglomerate, and global giants such as Anheuser-Busch Inbev, which holds two of Germany's top 10 premium brands: Beck's and Hasseröder. Heineken, another international brewery giant, indirectly holds 24.9 % of Bavaria's Paulaner brewery. The Germany top 10 premium lack of only mono-product breweries such as Erdinger Weißbräu. Erdinger, a family-owned Bavarian brewery. Erdinger produces about 1.6 million hectolitres of wheat beer annually, which is not only available all over Germany but is also exported to more than 70 countries around the world (see **Table 16.1 and 16.2** for the largest breweries in Germany and worldwide).

Rank	Company	Sales in GER in (in 1,000 hl)	Change in sales GER (in %)	Sales in other countries (in 1,000 hl)	Total
1	Radeberger Gruppe KG	11,230	-1.8	570	11,800
2	AB-InBev Deutschland	7,400	-6.3	3,000	10,400
3	Bitburger Braugruppe	6,900	-1.2	500	7,400
4	Oettinger Gruppe	6,800	-3.1	3,000	9,800
5	Krombacher Gruppe	5,565	+1.0	187	5,752
6	Brau Holding International	4,500	+2.3	1,000	5,500
7	Warsteiner Gruppe	3,945	-0.6	615	4,560
8	TCB/Frankfurter Brauhaus	2,900	+7.4	200	3,100
9	Carlsberg Deutschland	2,880	+8.2	140	3,020
10	C. & A. Veltins	2,529	-3.5	172	2,701
	Total	54,649		9,384	64,033

Table 16.1: The top-ten breweries in Germany in 2013[1]

Rank	Brewery	Country	Production volume in mill. hl	Percentage of world beer production
1	AB-InBev	Belgium	352.9	18.1%
2	SABMiller	United Kingdom	190.0	9.7%
3	Heineken	Netherlands	171.7	8.8%
4	Carlsberg	Denmark	120.4	6.2%
5	China Resource Brewery Ltd.	China	106.2	5.4%
6	Tsingtao Brewery Group	China	78.8	4.0%
7	Grupo Modelo	Mexico	55.8	2.9%
8	Molson-Coors	USA/Canada	55.1	2.8%
9	Yanjing	China	54.0	2.8%
10	Kirin	Japan	49.3	2.5%
...				
	Total		1,951.3	100%

Table 16.2: The largest brewing groups worldwide in 2012[2]

To reach their consumers, breweries use bottles as well as cans which are sold to customers via retail channels, bars, hotels, restaurants and clubs. Though typically serving both segments, every brewery, however, leans more towards either the bottled or the draught segment (see also **Figure 16.2**). Contribution margins for the draught segment are generally higher than those of the bottled segment, but since breweries own many of their restaurant and bar outlets, which they lease to their tenants, capital requirements are quite high, especially since the financial situation of their tenants is often unsatisfactory. Additionally, breweries bear a high failure risk in the very cyclical and dynamic restaurant scene. These advantages and disadvantages are mirrored by the bottled beer segment. Here, capital requirements are lower, but margins are, too.

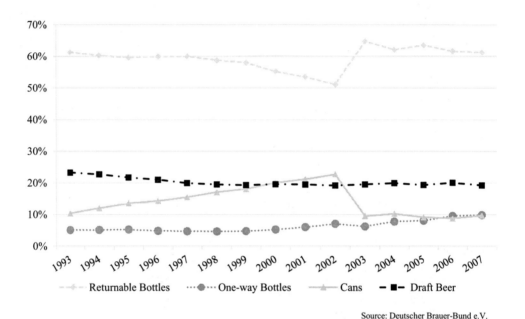

Source: Deutscher Brauer-Bund e.V.

Figure 16.2: Beer packaging in Germany (shares in %)

For both segments, breweries have various options in designing their distribution system. In addition to directly delivering their products to retailers and bars and restaurants, indirect distribution channels including national or regional wholesalers are used. The indirect channel accounts for 80 % of the total beer distribution in Germany. The wholesalers are usually specialized according to the segment they predominantly serve. Hence, bottled beer wholesalers serve all kinds of retailers, such as convenience stores, specialized beverage stores, discounters and food retailers. Draught beer wholesalers deliver beer to bars, hotels, and restaurants. Market analysts suggest that sales through the traditional, multi-tier distribution channels will continue to decline over the next years and that discounter retailers will represent the only (slightly) growing market segment due to their aggressive price policy. Discounters, however, represent an opportunity predominantly for large national and international brewery companies which are able to realize economies of scale in brewing, transportation and marketing, and which can counterbalance the retailers' bargaining power. Many regional breweries are struggling to resist the temptation to directly deliver to the retailers. Instead, they prefer indirect distribution channels that include regional wholesalers, as these can buffer the continuously increasing bargaining power and the increasingly unfavourable terms and conditions of the large German retail chains. Only companies with exceptionally strong brands have hitherto been successful in this regard. Brewpubs, small or financially weak regional breweries, and contract breweries, however, will have to quickly remodel their distribution networks and find new opportunities to stay competitive against the upcoming pressure in the market.

Yet there might be some promising strategies for breweries to keep their pot boiling. While the sales volumes of the traditional beer varieties like Pils, Kölsch, Alt and Export are declining, wheat beer and non-alcoholic beer, as well as beer-soft drink mixes have become popular among consumers. (In the early 1990s, light beers were popular, too, but have since disappeared from the market.) The Krombacher brewery, for example, extended its product line successfully: in addition to the traditional Krombacher Pils and its non-alcoholic version, a Radler (beer flavoured with citrus lemonade), a non-alcoholic Radler, a wheat beer and a non-alcoholic wheat beer are offered. To attract young consumers, Krombacher launched a new brand family called Cab, currently available in four flavours: cola and beer, lemon and beer, blood orange and beer, and banana and beer.

The Kölsch Market

In 2008, Kölsch breweries accounted for 1.6 % of the total German beer sales through retail and beverage store distribution. Different from most other types of beer like Alt, Pils or wheat beer, Kölsch has a legally defined certification of origin. The association of Kölsch breweries maintains that only breweries in Cologne or members of the association are permitted to label their beer as Kölsch. Kölsch is exclusively distributed in the area of Cologne, Germany's fourth largest city, situated close to the former West German capital city of Bonn in the Rhineland region. Beyond this core Kölsch region, this type of beer is only available at boutique-style retailers and selected bars and restaurants.

While this strong regional focus limits the geographical scope of the Kölsch market, the deep regional roots and rich tradition represent an advantage for Kölsch breweries. Traditionally, people around Cologne prefer to drink Kölsch instead of other kinds of beer. For many of them, Kölsch is more than a tradition. It is, instead, ingrained in their identity and this part of their regional culture. "Kölsch" is not only the name of the local beer, but also the word for the local German dialect, hence the saying that Kölsch is the only language that you can drink. Through the regionally limited sales area, its status as a cultural asset and its special brewage recipe, the Kölsch market has a unique position in Germany's beer landscape.

Remarkably, Kölsch beer started to become the beer of the Cologne area just 40 years ago. In the first half of the twentieth century, it was more a niche product than a top seller, because consumers preferred other beer varieties such as Export, Lager and especially Pils. Particularly, Bitburger, Weihenstephan and Löwenbräu were popular brands in the 1960s. But consumer preferences changed over time, and today formerly renowned beer varieties are exotic, while Kölsch beer is the first choice in Cologne restaurants, pubs and clubs.

Because of the concentration on the same market in a rather compact geographical area and the collective growth of the industry after the Second World War, a social network among the brewers arose of necessity. Over time, many friendships and personal connections among Kölsch brewers, distributors and suppliers have been established. The Kölsch convention in 1985 strengthened this network by a unanimous contract. Several industry-sector-specific institutions were created. For example, Cologne's brewery owners meet quarterly at conferences of the Kölner Brauerei Verband (founded in 1919), which is a local chapter of the German Brewers' Association in Cologne. The Cologne Brewers' Association is currently chaired by Heinrich Becker, co-owner and managing director of the Gaffel Kölsch brewery. The technicians, i.e., the brewery engineers of the Kölsch breweries, also meet regularly in order to discuss industry issues. But the ties among the breweries also extend beyond business: for example, the former managing director of Sünner Kölsch (at about 40,000 hectolitres, a middle-sized Kölsch brewery), Ingrid Sünner-Müller, is the wife of one of the former Früh Kölsch owners, Hermann Müller.

Over the last two decades, though, the general trends of the national beer market were reflected in the Kölsch beer segment as well. In this period, the market for Kölsch beer and the national beer sales shrank by 20 % from 1991 to 2008 (for detailed information, see **Figure 16.1**). The changing customer preferences were reinforced by retailers' purchasing strategies and consolidation. This evolving pressure was primarily caused by increasing market power on the discounter and retailer side. Discounters attracted customers by price or promotional campaigns, while retailers increasingly engaged in launching their own label brands. In addition to the loss of customer allegiance, it became very difficult for specialized beverage stores to survive (see **Figure 16.3**). Once attracted by the vast assortment and convenient service, consumers now seem to favour low prices, one-stop shopping, various forms of package designs, and the ability to purchase their beverages along with their fresh vegetables, cheese and milk at large retail outlets or discounters. This tendency affects regional beer brands negatively because they strongly depend on these specialized retailers as one of their primary outlets: specialized beverage stores alone account for one-third of the total beer sales in Germany. But it is not only beverage stores that struggle through the increasing market power of discounters; beverage wholesalers, too, are impaired by these new developments. However, some beverage wholesalers attempt to solidify their market position. Market observers assume that alliances (franchise, partnership agreements, licensing) among wholesalers and beverage stores will spread as a promising solution which offers the opportunity to gain higher profits, cut costs and enhance consumer service. For example, Appelmann (a beverage wholesaler located in Cologne) offers beverage stores partnership contracts, which include supporting services in marketing, promotion, accounting and IT. By this measure, Appelmann hopes to help its partner stores achieve efficiency gains in order to survive on the retail market, and thus also act as important intermediaries representing Appelman's connection to its customers. **Figure 16.4** gives an overview of the Kölsch distribution channels.

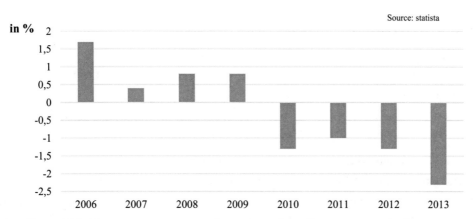

Figure 16.3: Year-on-year percentage change in number of beverage stores in Germany

The overall market conditions for Kölsch breweries can thus be described as increasingly unfavourable, and indeed many regional breweries like Germania, Schöffen and Gereons Kölsch have exited the market. Today, only nine out of 20 original independently-owned Kölsch breweries have survived this consolidation process.

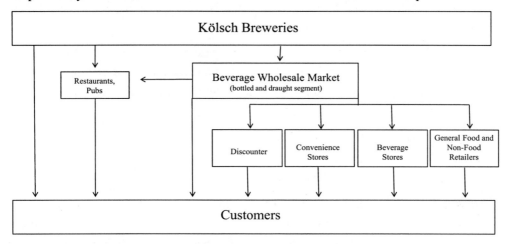

Figure 16.4: Kölsch distribution channels

THE COMPANY PLAYERS

Three actor types can be identified on the Kölsch market: first, there are the family-owned leading local breweries Reissdorf, Früh and Gaffel Kölsch, which together account for approximately 60 % of total Kölsch production. Second, there is the Kölner Verbund Brauereien GmbH & Co. KG with its Kölsch brand assortment, part of the large German Oetker Group, an (also family-owned) conglomerate that is active in such diverse fields as instant pudding, frozen pizza and shipping. These two groups account for about 80 % of the total Kölsch market. Third, there are the smaller, family-owned breweries like Malzmühle, Päffgen and Sünner Kölsch, with an annual sales volume of around 10,000 to 50,000 hectolitres.

Privat-Brauerei Heinrich Reissdorf GmbH & Co. KG

The Privat-Brauerei Heinrich Reissdorf GmbH & Co. KG was founded in 1894 by Heinrich Reissdorf. Originally located in Cologne's Serverinsviertel district, the Reissdorf tavern with its affiliated brewery became well established in Cologne and its environs. Since its foundation, Reissdorf beer has been sold around the area of Cologne; its reputation as a quality beer was well entrenched throughout the Rhineland.

Reissdorf's subsequent growth was characterized by common twists of fate, and especially by the Second World War in which most of its brewery premises were destroyed. After the War, it took Reissdorf until the 1960s to regain significant economic momentum. At that time, the demand for Kölsch was rapidly growing. In the late 1980s, the company site in the Severinsviertel was no longer capable of serving the increasing demand. The company relocated to less confined premises. Michael von Rieff explained the rationale behind the company's rather aggressive growth strategy in 1995:

> "I believe that the Kölsch market is in the early stage of a concentration process which will put many Kölsch breweries out of business. We want to stay autonomous by enlarging our business and attracting more customers for our beer. To strengthen our position in the market we need sustained growth. Therefore, it is necessary to find a new home for our production plant."

In 1996, Reissdorf decided to move its headquarters as well as its production site further south to Cologne-Rodenkirchen. The relocation was a major step in modernizing production technology and extending infrastructure which could serve the increasing customer base.

Between 1993 and 2007, Reissdorf was able to increase its annual output against the market trend, taking over market leadership in 2004 from Kölner Verbund with a market share of approximately 30 % of the overall (draught and bottled beer) Kölsch market.

Reissdorf was the first Kölsch brewery to offer Kölsch in bottles (1936), and still concentrates on the bottled beer segment, selling 80 % of its total production in bottles through retailers and only 20 % as draught beers. Although very capital intensive and risky for Reissdorf, the draught beer segment is seen as important for representing the brand in Cologne's restaurant sector.

Still located in Köln-Rodenkirchen, the company achieves an annual output of about 630,000 hectolitres and employs 90 staff today. The company is jointly owned by the Reissdorf and von Rieff families. Whereas the Reissdorf family is not actively involved in the company's management, Michael von Rieff is leading the enterprise as managing director and joint-owner, one of the fourth generation. He occupies the central role in Reissdorf's organizational structure (see **Figure 16.5**). Reissdorf is structured by function into the areas of sales and marketing, accounting and productions. Reissdorf's top management team has a solidly technical background - historically, the owner-managers are graduate brewing engineers (even though this situation is about to change with the fifth Reissdorf generation: Christian von Rieff, Michael von Rieff's son, graduated in management and brewing engineering).

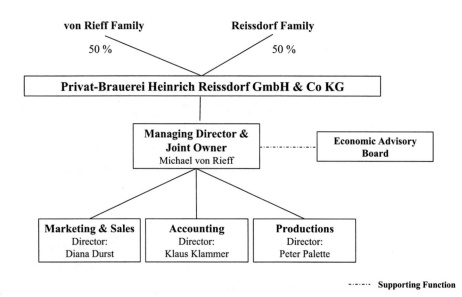

Figure 16.5: Organisational chart of Reissdorf

Reissdorf is well established as a premium Kölsch brand, and traditionally follows a mono-product strategy: Reissdorf Kölsch has been its sole product for the last 40 years [2]. Reissdorf Kölsch is positioned in the premium segment and emphasizes its quality and unique taste. Many customers purchasing Reissdorf state taste, quality, brand image, tradition and especially local authenticity as the main reasons for their choice. The company owners believe that the concentration on the core product (the Kölsch) is the basis for Reissdorf's success, and the most suitable strategy in a maturing market. A strong emphasis is put on maintaining modern, automated and technologically advanced production processes and facilities - for both quality and cost reasons. Despite the temptation to create trendy beer-mixed drinks or to combine beer taste with sports and fitness aspects during the last ten years, Reissdorf did not extend its product line until recently. In February 2010, Reissdorf launched its first non-alcoholic Kölsch, Reissdorf Alkoholfrei, positioned as an isotonic and low-calorie sports drink rather than a beer, with the aim of attracting new customer groups and simultaneously keeping the core customers attuned to the real and pure Reissdorf Kölsch.

Reissdorf considers the long-lasting, loyal partnerships with its beverage wholesalers and its suppliers a major reason for its success. This loyalty can be illustrated by Reissdorf's 1994 acquisition of Nollen Getränke. Reissdorf acquired Nollen as one of its long-time wholesalers when its owner and CEO retired. However, even though part of Reissdorf, Nollen is treated as an autonomous, self-contained business unit which delivers products of other breweries, too. Reissdorf benefits from Nollen's integration not only because of its competence in draught and bottled beer distribution, but also because it can serve as its extended point of contact with retailers and restaurants.

Competitors

Privatbrauerei Gaffel Becker & Co. OHG. Founded as a classical guild house by the Becker brothers, the history of Gaffel began in 1908. In 2004, all Gaffel products together accounted for an output of more than 500,000 hectolitres. In the draught beer sector, Gaffel is currently the market leader for Kölsch sales volume in Cologne. Like Reissdorf, Gaffel is a premium Kölsch brand. In addition to the traditional Kölsch, the product portfolio of Gaffel includes a light and a non-alcoholic beer, as well as a non-alcoholic sports drink. Gaffel is particularly committed to sports promotion and marketing around Cologne. Besides the sponsoring of the 1. FC Köln, the biggest local football club and member (usually) of Germany's premier football league, Gaffel is the official beer supplier of the Cologne Falcons (American football), ASV Köln (athletics) and Fortuna Köln (football), as well the local rival Bayer 04 Leverkusen (football).

Cölner Hofbräu P. Joseph Früh KG (Früh Kölsch). Similarly to Reissdorf, Früh was founded in 1904 by Peter Josef Früh. Today, the company operates the traditional brewery as well as a restaurant and a hotel next to Cologne's major tourist attraction, the cathedral. With a production of more than 390,000 hectolitres, Früh is among Reissdorf's biggest competitors. Früh Kölsch is a premium brand; the product portfolio comprises the traditional Kölsch and a non-alcoholic variant. Traditionally, Früh also relies more on the bottled market segment, but has recently redoubled its efforts to gain a stronghold in the draught beer segment. In contrast to Reissdorf, Früh puts more effort into advertising, merchandising and promotion.

Kölner Verbund Brauereien GmbH. Unlike the traditional, privately owned breweries, the Kölner Verbund Brauereien GmbH is an umbrella organization of a variety of Kölsch brands within the nationally active Radeberger beverage group, which is in turn part of the privately held German conglomerate Oetker Group. Radeberger's Kölsch portfolio encompasses five brands with a cumulated sales volume of 765,000 hectolitres annually: Sion (145,000 hectolitres) is its premium brand, and is sold predominantly (80 %) in the draught beer segment, whereas Küppers (260,000 hectolitres), positioned in the consumer segment, is mostly distributed through the retail channel. Gilden Kölsch (260,000 hectolitres) produces a lot of draught beer besides its bottled beer, and is positioned in the upper price segment. It is a partner of the local ice hockey club, Kölner Haie, supports one of Cologne's famous music groups, De Höhner, and is involved in many big and small folk festivals around Cologne. Sester Kölsch (45,000 hectolitres) is positioned in the low-price segment. To serve the customers around Bonn, Kurfürsten Kölsch (55,000 hectolitres) is also part of the group. With the strong financial background of Radeberger and Oetker Group, Kölner Verbund is in a convenient position to run sales promotions, special price offers and other sales campaigns for its different Kölsch brands. Unlike the other Cologne brewery companies, Kölner Verbund is led by employed and non-local managers.

RETHINKING REISSDORF'S STRATEGY

At nine o'clock on Monday morning, Michael von Rieff opened the strategy meeting with his top management team. After a short introduction and a comment on the last sales and revenue figures, the managing partner began to open the discussion. Von Rieff encourages open criticism and suggestions from each member. Diana Durst, Reissdorf's marketing director, started: "Perhaps we should evolve our brand identity into another direction. Fitness and sports! Gaffel and Gilden showed us how that works. Sponsoring sports events should be a good platform to begin acquiring a new public perception. Sports excite emotions in customers and influence their purchase decision." Peter Palette, Reissdorf's production director, replied: "The big sports events and clubs have contracts with other breweries. Moreover, we have no experience in sports. But you are right, Diana, the fitness trend is obvious."

"What's more, we could break new ground. Why shouldn't we expand our sales region? Our export initiative to the United States went very well, didn't it? We sell 1,500 hectolitres per year to the US! Admittedly, I'm talking about small volumes, but, hey, the margins are great. Kölsch itself is becoming a well-known brand, so let's use this evolution for our success," Diana said. Klaus Klammer, Reissdorf's accounting director, responded, "It's not that easy, Diana. We have to take into account what we are. We have a strongly rooted tradition. This tradition is strongly connected with Cologne. Kölsch is Cologne. That's the basis of our success. Bigger is not necessarily better! I would prefer to suggest expanding our presence in the draught beer segment. We have a great product, people like our beer; so let's give them more opportunities to drink it!"

Peter replies: "We had all this before - these are huge investments we need to make and you know that it's not easy to sort out the shaky tenants. Let's stick to our knitting, with regard to our distribution area, too. Within the brewery association, we all agree that it does not make sense to distribute Kölsch outside Cologne. Everybody who tried finally failed!"

Diana tried again with a new idea: "OK, OK. Perhaps this might be too big for us. But as Michael said, we need to do something which helps us sustainably." After a short break, Diana continued, "If we consider the situation of our distribution channels, we have to recognize that the loss of many beverage wholesalers and stores strikes us hard. Just a few wholesalers will survive and they will demonstrate their new bargaining power. They will squeeze our margin to a minimum. But we have the option to contract with a discounter. Discounters are particularly popular at the moment."

Klaus responded, sensitively, "I agree that we must consider the shifting in the beverage wholesalers sector, but I believe that discounters cannot be a solution. We would damage our reputation as a renowned premium Kölsch brand. Beyond that, discounters will smash our margin, too. And we have never done that before." Peter added: "You know that the discounters sell beer in those plastic PET bottles. Cologne's restaurants and pubs as well as our core consumers won't be pleased if everyone can buy our Kölsch in PET bottles. I'm sorry, Diana, but that can't be a solution." Diana looked frustrated. "Perhaps we are really not ready to detach ourselves from traditional enmeshments."

Michael observed the discussion thoughtfully. On the one hand, he admired Diana's willingness to think in new directions. On the other hand, it was exactly the feeling for tradition and no-nonsense strategy that had enabled him, his father and grandfather to lead the company to become the Kölsch market leader. But the environment was changing so dramatically. They had to act. What were they missing? What should they do?

•••

Setting of the case: 2010; last revision: 2013.

NOTES

[1] Lebensmittelzeitung, (2013): *Top 10 Brauereien Deutschland 2014*, URL: http://www.lebensmittelzeitung.net/business/daten-fakten/rankings/Top-10-Brauereien-Deutschland-2014_500.html, (accessed June 26, 2014)

[2] The Barth-Haas Group, & Hansmaennel, G., (2013): Beer Production - Market Leaders and their Challengers in the Top 40 Countries in 2012, URL: http://www.barthhaasgroup.com/images/pdfs/report2013/Barth_Beilage_2013.pdf, (accessed June 26, 2014)

17

Higher Education as Rocket Science: Private Business School Taking Off or Hitting the Ground?

Markus Raueiser and Volker Rundshagen

One Saturday night in late August, the annual graduation ceremony of Big City School of Business (BCSB) took place in town at the Grand Hotel. In the imposing ballroom, proud families and friends, as well as many faculty members, applauded as the deans handed over Bachelor and Master degree certificates to some 300 students. Just before midnight, all graduates, wearing their gowns and ready to throw their hats up into the air, gathered on the stage for a group photo; a documentation of this moment of successful completion of a precious episode of their life: their student era. Certainly, this was a moment of pride but, even more so, a moment of reflection for the president of BCSB, Ms Ribeauvillé.

The private institution has seen impressive growth over the last two decades, which she had pointed out in her opening speech, a few hours earlier in the ballroom. But in times of growth and success the need to see the bigger picture of the market shifts that will eventually threaten the very business model that has enabled the current success are often set aside too easily. Ms Ribeauvillé's eyes were still on the enthusiastic graduates on stage but her thoughts wandered to the school's future. The political environment has brought about significant changes, resulting in heightened pressure, caused by regulatory constraints and the dependence on public authorities or quasi-governmental bodies, as well as by increasing expectations about the role of private universities in society. In addition to that the latest projections indicate a slight decline in the enrolment figures in the years to come, a result of the demographic factors in Germany but also of the increasing competition from more domestic and foreign business schools opening up new campuses. Beyond these political and competitive challenges, professional traditions and academic habits limit the leeway for managerial decisions even further. The time might have come to rethink BCSB's strategy.

INSTITUTIONAL ENVIRONMENT OF HIGHER EDUCATION IN GERMANY

European higher education reforms

The German higher education landscape is in transition. One of the major reasons for this change is the profound transformation which has been initiated at a European level. Arguably, this development started in 1992, when a landmark, in terms of new business opportunities across Europe, was established through the signing of the Maastricht treaty by 12 states, including Germany. The Maastricht Treaty consolidated the three European Communities of Euratom, ECSC and EEC. It, furthermore, institutionalised cooperation in the areas of: foreign policy, defence, police and justice under one umbrella: the European Union. The main idea was the further economic integration among the member states of the European Union, based on the four freedoms: the free movement of capital, people, goods, and services; the latter formally comprises the area of higher education.

More thorough and direct changes to this area resulted from the, so-called, Bologna process. On June 19th, 1999, the Ministers of Education of 29 European countries, including all EU member states, convened and created a joint declaration.[1] The declaration states six objectives of primary relevance, in order to establish the European area of higher education and to promote it worldwide:
- Adoption of a system of easily readable and comparable degrees
- Adoption of a system essentially based on two main cycles, undergraduate and graduate
- Establishment of a system of credits: European Credit Transfer System (ECTS)
- Promotion of mobility
- Promotion of European co-operation in quality assurance
- Promotion of the necessary European dimensions in higher education

Furthermore, the EU has committed to create "the most competitive and dynamic knowledge-based economy in the world capable of sustainable growth with more and better jobs and greater social cohesion" (proclaimed at the European Council meeting at Lisbon in March 2000). Meanwhile, the project of increasing the competitiveness of higher education, in accordance with Bologna, is connected with the overall European economic project, according to Lisbon.[2] Thus, higher education has become a key area for strengthening the knowledge-based economy on the continent.

Especially the Bologna process-induced two-tiered path, with programmes leading to a Bachelor's level and a Master's level degree, respectively, has led to fundamental changes in university degree programme provision in Germany. It has resulted in tightly structured programmes, which has also enabled the model of the private business school in the first place, as the traditional German university degree system with its rather unstructured programmes delivered at huge institutions mainly pursuing basic research would overburden the financial and personal resources of privately funded organisations. With regard to the Bologna process implementation, higher education institutions are recommended to focus on employability (and, therefore, on skills directly associated with job market demands), modularisation and output orientation.

The legal basis of higher education in Germany

The nature of higher education in general, and of the institutions to which the right of conducting it is granted in particular, is elusive. However, there is a legal framework act for this sector, providing national legal guidelines: the *Hochschulrahmengesetz (HRG)*, introduced in 1976 and last updated in 2005. It establishes major tasks of higher education institutions, such as development of the arts and sciences through research, teaching, scholastics and further education. It, furthermore, distinguishes several types of academic institutions, composing of the higher education sector in Germany. There are *Universitäten* – universities, *Pädagogische Hochschulen* – teacher-training colleges, *Kunsthochschulen* – art colleges, and *Fachhochschulen* – polytechnics, more recently officially translated as universities of applied sciences.[3] Whereas the first three have been, more or less, traditional institution types, the latter were introduced in the early 1970s, primarily designed to serve the labour market by offering shorter, clearly structured programmes with an at least partly vocational orientation. Due to the latter, and also due to the absence of basic research, they were considered of lower academic status. However, they have greatly benefitted from the value the Bologna process placed on the vocational goals of higher education much more than the previous German system. In addition, this process has ignited a trend of convergence within the German institutional scenery: the government increasingly expects institutions of lower academic status to also conduct research, whereas traditional universities have to orientate more towards vocational aspects of academic education, which allegedly leads to the 'schoolification' of universities.

German federalism adds to the complexity of the sector. The 16 states (*Bundesländer*) are primarily responsible for education. Hence, they have the discretion to enact their own legislation governing higher education matters in more detail. HRG explicitly allows them to establish or approve higher education institutions with other legal forms than that of a public body. The states also decide on the tuition fees students enrolled at public universities have to pay. There have been fierce political debates concerning this quite recent issue. Much of the controversy is rooted in the tradition that university education in Germany had always been tuition-free. In the last decade several German states had implemented tuition fees of 500 Euros per semester on average.

However, partly as a result of strong controversies and public debates, and partly following changing state governments and electoral campaign promises, the states have, one by one, abolished these semester fees again. At least the studies towards a first degree (Bachelor programmes) and for students residing in the state where they enrol are now, once again, tuition-free in every state. There is only a small semester contribution fee to pay for students to support student unions and other social institutions related to universities, as well as to cover expenses for a semester ticket, granting the use of public transportation.

In recent years, the German *Bundesländer* have adopted Bologna and, in particular, Lisbon-related goals with an emphasis on the overarching paradigm of competition to which now also universities are subjected. There are explicit policy tools for resource allocation, in general, and for research funding, in particular, emphasising competition. It is also reflected in the admission of private institutions to the higher education sector. Furthermore, competition is now the principal criterion governing the accreditation system.

Accreditation

The concept of accreditation is complex and multi-layered within the German higher education landscape. On the one hand, it is part of the legal framework, on the other hand, it goes beyond that with its quality assurance and communication properties. Basically, there are the two levels of institutional and degree programme accreditation. The former is required only for private institutions to achieve or maintain state-recognition, whereby detailed rules differ again across the German states. The science council, or so-called *Wissenschaftsrat*, conducts institutional accreditation on behalf of the federal and the state governments. It is composed of top-level academics, hence it is not a government body, but assumes a quasi-governmental role. Failure to receive approval in the institutional accreditation process will result in removal of state recognition and, thereby, the loss of a viable operation, as recognised academic degrees can no longer be awarded. The obligatory science council accreditation process, which costs the school ca. 25,000 Euros, verifies the scientific performance potential of private providers, to ensure a level of quality that justifies participation in the higher education sector, still dominated by public universities that have proven their academic credibility over decades or even centuries. Particular focus lies on the capability of conducting and publishing research and on the organisational structure, which has to ensure that the management of the school and academia are separate, so that the academic freedom (teaching and research) granted by the constitution, the German *Grundgesetz*, is honoured.

The level of degree programme accreditation applies for public and private institutions alike. Formally, every Bachelor or Master degree programme has to be accredited, but so far this requirement has not been consequently enforced at public universities. There are six competing agencies awarding accreditation. This accreditation system sparks controversy, as the agencies face conflicts of interest. Their role is comparable to that of rating agencies in the finance sector: they charge the institutions (ca. 20,000 Euros per programme under review), and there are competitors, so that there is some pressure toward positive outcomes of the process. Even more problematic is that academics working at one institution may be part of the committee evaluating another one so that implicit collusion cannot be ruled out.

Beyond these two national levels, there are international accreditation options for business schools. Top institutions and/or their study programmes, particularly in the highly competitive MBA segment, targeting an international student constituency, can opt for the US-based AACSB certification, or the European counterpart EQUIS – both of which increasingly compete for the accreditation of business schools from around the world – and there is also the slightly less spread British AMBA certification. With such a world-renowned accreditation label, the bearers send out a message of top-quality business degree provision, with an international focus. Some prestigious business schools hold all three labels. This status is referred to as 'triple crown accreditation'. In Germany, only two institutions currently have that status: Mannheim Business School (a spin-off of the public university at Mannheim with non-profit business status) and ESCP Europe (a private transnational business school based in London, Paris, Berlin, Madrid and Turin).

Stakeholders' expectations

Universities at large, and business schools in particular, face various expectations of their major stakeholders. The previous sections have revealed that the government's expectations, vis-à-vis universities, are raising and becoming more specified. Increased competitiveness, more (measurable) output in terms of published research, more reliable throughput of students turned into employable graduates, and a contribution to the knowledge economy at large. On the one hand, the political actors demand more business-oriented conduct and governance even of public universities, which includes heightened efficiency in times of austerity policies. On the other hand, governments expect adherence to principles like academic freedom (rooted in the *Bildungsideal* of Wilhelm von Humboldt who reformed German universities in the early 19th century) and to defined quality standards. On top of that there is the political target to increase the proportion of high school graduates enrolling into higher education. As a result, universities have to handle more students without an increase in resources allocated.

This setting implies the need for private providers to absorb an increasing share of the young people who enter higher education.

Faculty members face increasing pressure: there is an increased workload, induced by rising student numbers, many institutions set ambitious research output targets, and student evaluations of teaching performance can have adverse consequences if internally defined benchmarks are missed. This provokes a mismatch with typical expectations of professors and university lecturers. These people are highly qualified; yet usually earn less money in higher education than similarly qualified employees in the business world. What they expect in return is the freedom to pursue research, according to their interests and their curiosity, the freedom to design lectures and to define taught course contents, and also more discretion in allocating their working time, at least during semester breaks. Most of these expectations are in line with the Humboldtian principles, but clash with the now dominant paradigms of competition, output orientation and efficiency.

The constituency around which higher education efforts (should) revolve, of course, are the students. It is noteworthy that their expectations have changed in recent times. The so-called millennial generation is entering higher education, and it is characterized as demanding and feeling entitled. Furthermore, these students tend to expect enticing, rewarding, and work-life-balance-promoting study, as well as (later on) employment environments. But students are also under pressure, as they are aware of a tough job market. They realise that they need a (good) degree, as a major credential to enter the world of employment. Many of them choose to take up business studies because of a perceived enhancement of opportunities with the corresponding degree. There are ambiguities and even contradictions, as the 'millennials' also tend to look for meaningful work, and they are prepared to contribute to society, even if they are insecure in how to pursue that broader goal. As a consequence, universities face the need to become more student-oriented. This tends to be easier for private providers, which have less bureaucratic structures, besides already being used to focusing on their clientele as their major raison d'être.

The demographic factor

As briefly indicated earlier, Germany is committed, like other European and OECD countries, to increase the proportion of university graduates, and this process is well under way. In the year 2000, the share of graduates, as a proportion of the population, was 15.9%; in 2012 it was already 29.9% so that it effectively doubled within a bit more than a decade. Furthermore, the percentage of high school graduates who actually enrolled in the year of their graduation from school rose from 28.4% in 2001 to 45.6% in 2011. The total number of students enrolling in their first semester in Germany rose from some 344,000, in 2001/02, to 495,000, in 2012/13 (see **Figure 17.1**). However, there may well be a decline in enrolment figures: a peak was apparently reached in 2011/12, when some 518,000 students enrolled into their first semester. Latest projections show a decline in predicted enrolments over the next decade (see **Figure 17.2**), mostly due to declining birth rates.

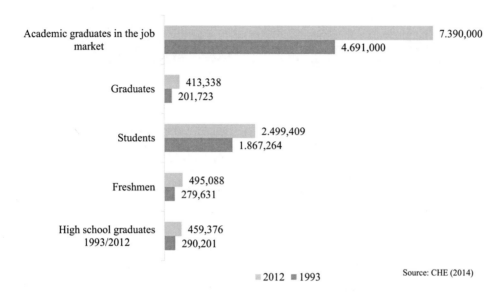

Figure 17.1: Overview of high school graduates, enrolment and academic graduates of the past 20 years[4]

Despite the political intent (and the related predictions) of widening participation in academic education, not enough places are provided for Master degree students. A major reason is that official projections were based on the expectation that no more than a third of Bachelor degree graduates would continue to pursue Master degree studies, because the other two thirds would be absorbed by the job market. However, many students seek consecutive Master degree education, partly due to perceived 'worthlessness' of Bachelor degrees alone, partly due to a lack of adequate job opportunities. Furthermore, many employers still struggle with the acceptance of the Bachelor as the standard degree to enter the world of work. Although industry associations called for shorter study times in Germany, earlier, now they are not convinced about the added value (or the specific skills) of very young graduates entering after three years of studies. If there are no adequate job offers, students of course seek to continue their academic education to obtain a consecutive Master's degree.

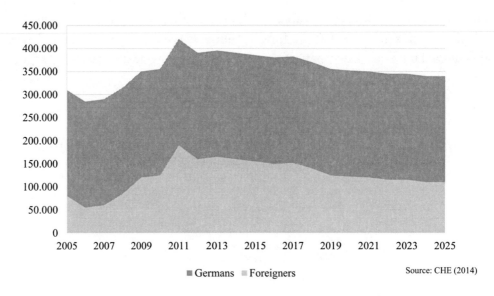

Figure 17.2: Freshmen at German universities *(incl. forecast)*

Private business schools in Germany

As of 2012, there were some 398 higher education institutions in Germany, 91 of which were privately owned. Hence, almost 25% of all higher education institutions are private (see **Figure 17.3**), but only about 5% of all students are enrolled at private institutions. More specifically, differentiated for the case of *Fachhochschulen*, some 12% of all students are enrolled at private schools. A veritable boom of founding private higher education institutions unfolded in the 1990s and in the first decade of this century. Almost 50 institutions have been founded since 2000, almost doubling the number of schools, and existing providers have also grown and expanded their capacities: enrolment figures have quadrupled in the same period and even multiplied almost tenfold from 1995 to 2012 (see **Figure 17.4** and **Figure 17.5**). However, private institutions remain significantly smaller than their public counterparts; they have, on average, roughly 1,000 students, compared to some 8,000 students, on average, at public universities. The range of subjects offered at private institutions is smaller than at public counterparts, and around 60% of students at the former type of higher education providers are enrolled in business-related study programmes.

Actually, the classification of private providers requires differentiation: there are organisations with a private legal form, but which are state-funded. There are also non-profit private institutions, such as those run by church. The German market for private business education has recently seen a substantial number and a wide range of schools opening, especially in the for-profit sector. It has also seen a first wave of crisis, entailing several bankruptcies or market withdrawals. Two prominent examples are the

International University in Germany at Bruchsal, founded in 1998, which ceased operations in 2009 when the owner decided not to cover up the losses any longer[5], and *Private Hanseuniversität*, founded in 2004, in Rostock, which also closed down in 2009 due to insufficient economic viability, with only very few students enrolled.[6] There are business schools owned by US-based private equity firms, usually specialised in higher education investments, such as *BiTS Iserlohn* as part of Laureate International Universities. Investor-owned models are usually multi-campus operations focusing on major cities; *BiTS* has also opened campuses in Berlin and Hamburg. There are also private nationally owned groups with multi-campus operations, such as *Hochschule Fresenius* (8 locations), *International School of Management* (5 locations) and *FOM Hochschule* (31 locations). However, most providers represent the wide range of one campus-based business schools. Besides the number of campuses, private business schools also try to differentiate along major positioning options (see **Figure 17.6**).

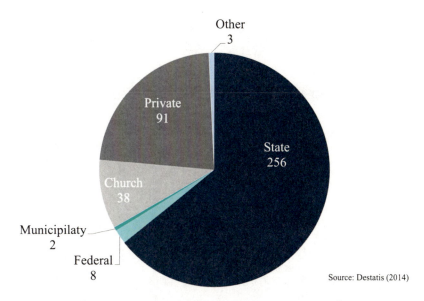

Figure 17.3: University ownership (absolute numbers)[7]

Due to the federal system outlined earlier, some *Bundesländer* offer more encouraging conditions for private institutions than others; differences becoming manifest in the varying deposit lump sums required (to provide for a bankruptcy case), as well as in varying policies of direct or indirect subsidies. The latter raise controversy in public, as the use of taxpayers' money is under heightened scrutiny in times of austerity. Recent cases of particular controversy include *Handelshochschule Leipzig* which reside in traditional public buildings for which the Land of Sachsen does not charge rent and *EBS Universität für Wirschaft und Recht* where an alleged case of misappropriated aid money has not been resolved yet. Besides - or arguably even more than - differing conditions in the federal states, the economic potential of a location drives the choice of campus location.

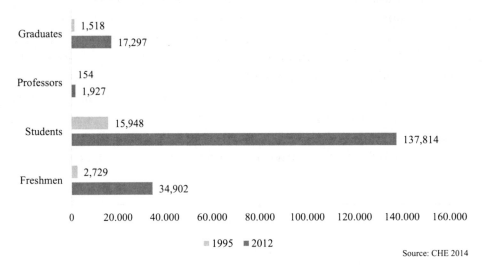

Figure 17.4: Expansion of private university capacities

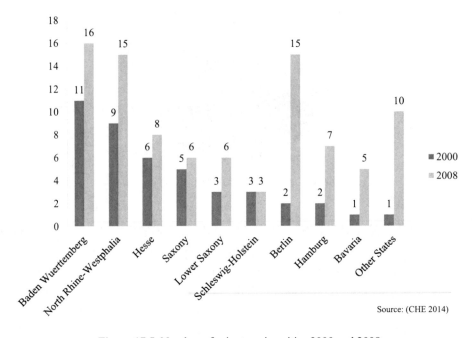

Figure 17.5: Number of private universities 2000 and 2008

Unlike public *Fachhochschulen*, many of which are located in small or medium-sized towns, which is, at least, in part owed to regional development policies, private business schools are almost exclusively located in big cities. These cities, such as Berlin, Hamburg, Munich or Cologne, promise to attract students, due to the strong appeal of metropolis regions and their urban flair, which is also an asset in gaining the attention of prospective students from abroad. In addition, economically strong regions surrounding these cities are required as a backbone in order to attract a critical mass of local or regional students who have sufficient purchasing power to enrol into private higher education. Private business schools charge substantial tuition fees as a major source of regular revenue. Typically, a three-year full-time Bachelor's degree programme has a price tag of 15,000 to 20,000 Euros.

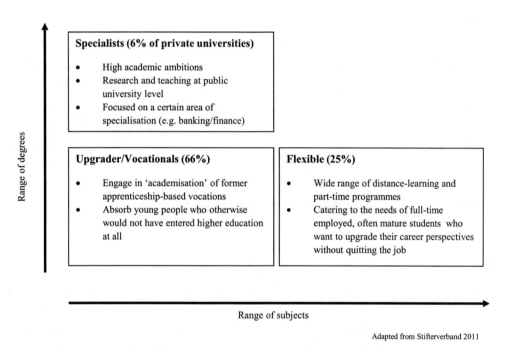

Figure 17.6: Strategic positiong options of private business schools[8]

Internationalisation

In the pursuit of growth (or other forms of added value), private business schools may have to look beyond the German borders. Attractive source markets of prospective students or image-enhancing research projects, as well as co-operation opportunities at large, arise abroad. There is already a widespread trend towards internationalisation of higher education, in general, also as a result of external drivers. On the one hand, there is increasing awareness of global interdependencies in the business world, where students want to work upon graduation. On the other hand, there is the political commitment towards opening up public higher education for international competition, which is meant to strengthen Germany as a location of high-profile science, as well as the preparation of future generations of protagonists for the manifold export-oriented businesses of the country.

One internationalisation option private business schools may pursue is the introduction of double degree programme schemes, in co-operation with partner universities. Under such a scheme, students complete their Bachelor or Master studies at their home institutions and then move to the partner university abroad to study for another year and, successful completion assumed, receive a second degree there. Hence, after a four-year period of full-time study, students are awarded two degrees, from two different universities, in two countries. In Germany such double degrees are increasingly popular.

Another option of internationalisation is to attract students, as well as faculty members, from abroad. Students from other countries can help to balance out the (projected) decline in German enrolment figures or allow further growth. Emerging markets such as China and India are especially seen as promising source markets for private business schools, as an immense number of young people living in those countries will also seek international business education, just like their German counterparts. However, major cultural differences and marketing barriers have to be overcome to succeed with student recruitment from such markets. Furthermore, most prospective students from abroad are not proficient in German and understand the language as a barrier, so that provision in English is a prerequisite to succeed with such a venture.

Researchers and teachers from across the border, or even from overseas, enhance the reputation of a business school and, of course, they add new perspectives and contribute to the enrichment of lectures, as well as adding a flair of diversity to life on campus. Furthermore, depending on their expertise or publication record, they can boost the scientific profile of an institution. However, the most reputable and talented academics are also in high demand in other countries and private business schools will find it difficult to compete with world-renowned universities in North America, Australia or Singapore for example due to a lack of reputation or status (in comparison with traditional universities that have been around for centuries). Furthermore, their limited resources tend to hinder truly competitive packages for high-profile candidates from overseas.

"ONE FISH IN THE POOL: BCSB'S POSITIONING"

Background and the early days

The roots of BCSB date back to the early days of the Maastricht Treaty. A predecessor organisation, specialized in training students in foreign languages, business knowledge and personal skills, within vocationally oriented, sub-academic and state-accredited degree programmes, supplied the industry of the region (also featuring multinational corporations headquartered in the city) with qualified graduates. A well-established regional business community network was part of the success of the predecessor organization of BCSB. High-level company delegates, as well as industry association representatives, were on the advisory board of this organisation, giving advice on various topics including business trends and business degree provision from the practitioners' perspective. Advisory board members' feedback emphasized the need for a more established standardized and internationally oriented education. Job candidates holding an internationally accepted higher education degree would better meet the demand of international companies, in terms of aligning job entry qualifications, compensation schemes and expatriate assignments around the world. The comparability of such candidates with those holding degrees obtained elsewhere in the world and already based on the Anglo-Saxon system of BA and MA degrees was an especially attractive aspect. Besides this industry-driven perspective, it soon became clear that graduates would also benefit through a better positioning on the job market, especially if they targeted multinational companies as employers. They could apply for better entry positions than graduates of non-academic schools and ask for better payment right from the start.

So BCSB started with a Bachelor's degree programme in International Business, even before this degree was officially introduced in Germany (see above for the Bologna process), and even before the market was opened wide for private business schools. As higher education is formally part of the service sector, and as the Maastricht Treaty grants free exercise of services within EU member states, BCSB went for the option of importing a successful Bachelor programme from a UK university, on the basis of a franchise agreement. Hence, formally BCSB became a German campus providing the programme of its franchisor, teaching the proven curriculum with its own teaching staff, under the strict supervision of the UK partner university. The advantage was to have a well-developed but unique product in the German market and, furthermore, to gain expertise concerning how to teach, design and manage BA programmes. Thus, BCSB became the pioneer of BA-style business education in Germany.

The implementation of the Bologna process led to changes in legislation covering higher education. The aforementioned *Hochschulrahmengesetz* was adapted to meet, among other purposes, market liberalisation policy goals. Based on this opportunity, the board decided to apply for a licence to open up a state-acknowledged business school, with the status of *Fachhochschule*. Thus, BCSB achieved legal and organisational independence from their franchise agreements; BCSB was now free to design new BA degree programmes. Because of the institution's history with the UK Bachelor, and also due to an ongoing co-operation with the partner university, even the new programmes were entirely taught in English. This turned out to be a unique selling proposition for a while. Another one has been the small class sizes, with a maximum of 30 students in any lecture and the strict open-door policy of professors, making them easily accessible for students.

Current profile

Several years further on, the management board realised that further growth was necessary to remain an independent business school and to sustain viable operations. More and more specialisation options were introduced and accredited as separate BA programmes, albeit always based on business studies. Quite recently, a German track was also introduced, so that there are now programmes taught entirely in German, accompanying the still larger base of degrees with English provision. With these moves, BCSB became a mainstream market player. To become more international, the necessity of attractive Master level education became more and more obvious. Very late, compared to the quickly evolving competition, BCSB introduced several Master degree programmes, which mostly mirror the corresponding BA programmes.

BCSB is now a self-standing, full-range provider of higher education in business. Its portfolio encompasses a wide range of BA, MA and MBA programmes. The two former are offered in full-time mode, and they split up into various specialisation options, reflecting job market trends or attractive growth segments. The latter is offered in three formats, including a part-time mode with weekend provision. Students entering higher education fresh out of high school (or international equivalents), those with a first BA or equivalent degree (including Diplom or Magister degrees obtained earlier under the previous German system), and mature students who re-enter higher education for a career transition or for an update in the latest business knowledge, build a heterogeneous and vibrant community on BCSB's campus. There are some 1,850 students in total currently enrolled.

An already significant and steadily increasing proportion of the student body are international students, who join BCSB for an exchange semester, including Erasmus arrangements, or increasingly even for the entire degree programme. The latter so far particularly applies to the Master's level. About half of the MA student body are internationals, and in the MBA programmes there are even almost 90% participants from abroad. A network of partner universities, in many countries on several continents, already provide the opportunity of gaining international study and work experience during studies, for both incoming and outgoing students at Bachelor's level. All BA students go abroad for one semester so that international exposure is firmly incorporated into the study experience. BCSB has gained visibility in Germany, as well as abroad, and it is committed to strengthen its international profile further. This is also achieved through double-degree programmes. Currently, three of those are offered with partner universities in Asia and in neighbouring countries, respectively, and further options are being investigated.

To meet practitioners' needs and to connect students of all levels with the business world – still a major promise of BCSB's programmes and still firmly established in the institution's philosophy – the business network and its outreach are continuously expanded and intensified. Symposia on business world topics du jour, guest lecture series and even customized executive training sessions for business partners are conducted and developed further. Some training programmes are offered in partnership with the regional chamber of commerce, others with more specialized industry associations. Even research projects, supported by business sponsors, have been initiated.

There was an ongoing discussion in the organisation of BSCB on how external funding could be obtained. A balanced and sustainable financing is considered a key competitive factor of private business schools, and so far BCSB, unlike some other private business schools in Germany, has neither obtained donations, nor has it received support from large foundations. There is currently an over-dependence on tuition fees. The dynamic growth over the last few years has spurred enormous complexity in administrative processes, requiring additional staff, and also new faculty members have joined, adding to the overhead. In addition, urgently needed infrastructure upgrades and further investments are unavoidable in the near future. And there is little hope of government support: a recent trend points to the exclusion of private institutions from tenders referring to public funding, despite the overall political avowal to competition. Several highly motivated professors at BSCB have been desperately looking for external research funding – but sometimes they just received the answer that private institutions were not eligible. There is a Higher Education Pact whereby the federal and state governments grant additional funding to universities to extend their teaching capabilities, in light of the recently increased enrolment numbers. For example, in the state of North-Rhine-Westphalia there was a budget of four billion Euro for the years 2011 – 2015.[9] While during the first round of finance only public institutions obtained money out of this fund, during the second period also private institutions received subsidies, according to the number of freshmen admitted. But the ministry for innovation, research and teaching of North-Rhine-Westphalia hinted at the intention of, once again, excluding private providers from future rounds of Higher Education Pact allocations.

The Science Roundtable, an initiative by the Lord Mayor of Big City inspiring dialogue among all institutions of the higher education and research sector of Big City (and also the chamber of commerce), no matter whether privately owned or public, was recently started. Its major goal is to better integrate the region's economic and scientific potential, to launch collaborative projects, and to define areas deserving promotional support. During one of the first meetings in the traditional council hall of Big City - where top-level university and research institution delegates, as well as the representatives of the city were present - it became immediately clear that there is intense competition among the institutions, and there are also tensions. In part that was certainly already owed to the above-mentioned EU policy induced changes toward competitive higher education in general, provoking claim-staking behaviour. But it also became clear quickly that thinking in terms of status plays a role. Distinguished professors of the venerable university in town look down on all other academic institutions, and members of other public institutions of 'lesser standing' still look down on the private newcomers. BCSB delegates repeatedly heard that their workplace was just a "money-grabbing teaching hut" unworthy of participation in the discussion of research matters, and only their vigorous demeanour, in combination with a few promising research projects initiated at BCSB, secured their position at the table.

Local competition within Big City had become very dynamic, contributing to the challenges at hand. New players, mostly big groups with multi-campus operations, keep entering town; a number of new campuses with a plethora of BA and even MA degrees have recently opened. It was hardly possible to use local public transportation any more without massive exposure to the ever-expanding advertisement offers.

Over the years the number of faculty members has increased. Academics with various backgrounds in the business world, as well as in academia, have joined, some of them coming from overseas. Many have gained experience at distinguished institutes of higher education and research. As mentioned earlier, the freedom to pursue research is an essential characteristic of the academic profession. Particularly the academics trained in an environment where the slogan of "publish or perish" counts feel the pressure of shaping their research profiles through top tier journal publications (ideally in, so-called, 'A*", or "A"-journals. In order to achieve such publications, they expect support for research projects (time and money) and coverage of academic conference participation expenses. Especially at a business school, research is expected to inform teaching, which should reflect the latest management trends. Faculty members acknowledge the teaching orientation and the ensued teaching workload at BCSB, which is significantly higher than at research-driven universities. But recently the pressure arising from the so far ever-increasing student intakes and also the very demanding student constituency has sparked some dissatisfaction. The time-consuming pursuit of high-level research, which mainly shapes the individual academic profile, on the one hand, and the tremendous effort of preparing meaningful lectures, satisfying the demanding student clientele, on the other hand, open an area of conflict for faculty members. From the perspective of the business school's management, there is cost pressure, leading to a focus on efficient resource use. The latter is particularly reflected in allocating high teaching volumes to faculty members and attempts to reduce operational costs. However, the research academics want to pursue, and actually do pursue, research at BCSB, entailing numerous hours of overtime to enable them to live their scholarly passion. This, of course, also aligns well with the school's interest: with acknowledged research (and corresponding publications), a business school can upgrade their profile and work towards meeting the high standards of international accreditation labels and rankings. Firstly, this also helps meet the expectations of (quasi-)governmental bodies and, therefore, strengthens the reputation of the private business school. Secondly, it helps attract highly qualified academics, as well as students, also from overseas, who are impressed by the competitive research performance attributed to BCSB. Thirdly, it improves the school's position in widely published national rankings, when comparing business schools and visible aspects of their performance. A favourable ranking position in turn reinforces the two former aspects.

The expectation of students has also significantly changed in recent years, especially with the millennial generation entering. Students expect value for money and display increasingly consumerist attitudes. Compared to a study programme at a public university they pay a total amount that would buy a brand new small car. The pressure for management, as well as for professors, is high at BCSB. There are a range of complaints among students - like the "entertainment factor must be right" or "why didn't I get an excellent grade for my paper or exam - I expect at least 90 out of 100 points". Furthermore, an increasing number of students would like to be served by professors and colleagues personally (and more or less day and night, as there is an inclination to send mails from smart phones directly from the nightclub, and immediate answers are implied). Students have questions and issues regarding the schedule or exam problems and have high expectations, regarding an individual solution. In times of a digital world and total consumer-orientation this seems to be the benchmark, that "clients" expect. But it is obvious that students are also under pressure, as they have to qualify for a merciless job market and, in many cases, in addition have to (or want to) meet ambitious parents' expectations, regarding their career path.

Rethinking the strategy

The annual board meeting in November was hectically planned to discuss potential reactions to the increasingly complex mélange of challenges, culminating in the recent unexpected decrease of 10% in student enrolment figures in the BA programme segment for the next academic year. Since the school opened its doors in 1993 it was the first time that enrolment numbers had dropped. Despite moderate growth in the other segments, this development was perceived as a severe backlash, considering the pioneer tradition of BCSB and the cash cow potential realized with BA degree provision over 20 years. Besides the unfavourable trend of the political and demographic developments it was also clear that the competitive environment had become very dynamic, contributing to the situation at hand.

There was silence in the meeting room as the President and the Chancellor of BCSB entered. Everybody in the room, including the Deans and the Director of Administration, were highly committed to the organization. They represented a rich set of experiences and diverse backgrounds from industry and academia, national as well as international. Their expertise and their strategic creativity were in demand right now. After a brief update of the development and a presentation of the recent figures from the Chancellor, an intense discussion of how to react to the recent trends and how to adjust the business school's strategy ensued.

Professor Winterbottom, the Director of Administration, who chaired the meeting, summed up the presentation and said "I have the solution: let's do more marketing and penetrate the market even more! Everybody in the region should know by now how excellent our education is. We need to increase the next marketing budget by 20%. – I will call the Head of Marketing immediately". Dr Autumn, the Dean of the Tourism faculty replied, "That's a good idea – this morning I saw only red" (the advertising colour of one of the main competitors, who have hard to overlook billboards all around the city). Professor Winterbottom, furthermore, pointed out: "We should be more aggressive in our action plan. We need a nation-wide advertising campaign, including television spots to be aired to reach the target group".

Erna Lupus, the Head of Accounting, was getting nervous. "Extra spending for marketing is not the right action. We need to be much more efficient in our operations and processes, to stay competitive in the future. I have looked into the numbers and see potential for major savings and dramatic cost cuts". This statement was fully supported by the Chancellor who said: "We could reduce overhead costs by replacing full-time lecturers, whose contracts will end soon or who will retire, with external lecturers paid on a freelance basis". Another option would be he added: "We can merge first-year BA classes to groups of 100 students to save teaching hours".

Prof. Tiaojong, Vice-President of International Relations, and polyglot as her name, reacted to that with a much more progressive idea: "We have to go for new markets and we should intensify our internationalisation activities. We can easily tap new source markets for all degree programme levels." Dr Autumn replied: "And then you have hundreds of students on campus who come from all corners of the world where they do not speak the language of academia and who overburden our student service capacities". "Nonsense", she reacted: "Contracts with international businesses to provide intercultural training weeks on campus for overseas executives will be a cash cow".

Prof. Dr. Dr. h.c. mult. Shurmetz arrived late to the meeting. He just returned from a major research conference in the US. He was very proud of the conference give-a-way he was carrying: a Yale-coffee-mug full with freshly brewed coffee. He put this mug in the middle of the conference table and said only one word - but this with emphasis: "Research"! After a moment of stunned silence, Prof. Winterbottom asked him: "What do you mean by that?" Shurmetz just answered: "Research excellence is the key to success. We need to devote more passion, more time and more funds for it."

Prof. Koblenz, one of the other Deans, replied to Shurmetz: "Research is a breadless art! Let's better focus on our bread and butter business – teaching!" And she suggested a fundamental change in strategy toward a high-quality profile: "We would then offer only a BA degree programme, limited to an intake up to 50 students who have to go through a tough assessment and would pay high tuition fees. Our MA/MBA programmes should focus on a more professional and affluent constituency." Prof. Tiaojong added: "But this would mean further investments to upgrade our infrastructure". After more than two hours of discussion the air was thin in the conference room and the President, Ms Ribeauvillé, was a little bit confused because of the variety of contradicting suggestions. What is the best strategy – how should she act?

•••

Setting of the case: 2014; last revision: 2014.

NOTES

[1] The Bologna Declaration of 19 June 1999, (1999): URL: http://europa.eu/legislation_summaries/education_training_youth/lifelong_learning/c11088_en.htm, accessed on 15 August 2014.

[2] Capano, G., & Piattoni, S., (2011): *From Bologna to Lisbon: the political uses of the Lisbon 'script' in European higher education policy*, Journal of European Public Policy 18:4, 584-606.

[3] Sperlich, A., (2008): *Theorie und Praxis erfolgreichen Managements privater Hochschulen*, Berlin: Berliner Wissenschafts-Verlag.

[4] CHE, (2014): *Hochschulbildung wird zum Normalfall: Ein gesellschaftlicher Wandel und seine Folgen*, (Report), Gütersloh.

[5] Gillman, B., (2009): *Privat-Unis fürchten um ihr Image*, [Private Universities Image Fears]. Handelsblatt. Online issue, 24 Juli. URL: http://www.handelsblatt.com/politik/deutschland/privat-unis-fuerchten-um-ihr-image;2436746, accessed on 20 September 2009.

[6] FTD, (2009): *Private Hanseuni in Rostock gibt auf*, [Private Hanseuni at Rostock gives up]. Financial Times Deutschland. URL http://www.ftd.de/forschung_bildung/bildung /:Hochschulmarkt-Private-Hanseuni-in-Rostock-gibt-auf/480003.html, accessed on 20 July 2009.

[7] Federal Statistical Office, (Destatis) (2014): *Private Hochschulen 2012. Wiesbaden*, URL: https://www.destatis.de/DE/Publikationen/Thematisch/BildungForschungKultur/Hochschulen/PrivateHochschulen.html

[8] Frank, A., Hieronimus, S., Killius, N., & Meyer-Guckel, V., (2012): *Rolle und Zukunft privater Hochschulen in Deutschland*, Eine Studie in Kooperation mit McKinsey & Company, Stifterverband für die deutsche Wissenschaft, Essen. URL: http://www.stifterverband.info/publikationen_und_podcasts/positionen_dokumentationen/private_hochschulen/index.html

[9] Ministerium für Innovation Wissenschaft und Forschung des Landes NRW, (2013): *Hochschulpakt*, URL: http://www.wissenschaft.nrw.de/hochschule/finanzierung/hochschulpakt/.

Authors

Prof. Dr. Sascha Albers	University of Southern Denmark Faculty of Social Sciences Alsion 2 6400 Sønderborg, Denmark Email: sascha@sam.sdu.dk
Dipl.-Kff. Lisa Brekalo	University of Cologne Department of Business Policy & Logistics Albertus Magnus Platz 50923 Cologne, Germany Email: brekalo@wiso.uni-koeln.de
Prof. Dr. Jan-Philipp Büchler	University of Applied Sciences and Arts Dortmund Faculty of Business Studies Emil-Figge-Str. 44 44227 Dortmund, Germany Email: jan-philipp.buechler@fh-dortmund.de
Svenja Clever, B. Sc.	University of Cologne Department of Business Policy & Logistics Albertus Magnus Platz 50923 Cologne, Germany Email: clever@wiso.uni-koeln.de
Prof. Dr. Carsten Deckert	Cologne Business School (CBS) Hardefuststr. 1 50677 Cologne, Germany E-Mail: c.deckert@cbs.de
Dipl.-Kff. Stefanie Dorn	University of Cologne Department of Business Policy & Logistics Albertus Magnus Platz 50923 Cologne, Germany Email: dorn@wiso.uni-koeln.de
Prof. Dr. Andreas Fries	Rheinische Fachhochschule Cologne Business Administration Schaevenstraße 1 a-b 50676 Cologne, Germany Email: andreas.fries@rfh-koeln.de

Roberto González
Amor, M. Sc.

Zalando SE
Tamara-Danz-Str. 1
10243 Berlin, Germany

Email: roberto.gonzalez.amor@zalando.de

Lukas Held, M. Sc.

University of Cologne
Department of Business Policy & Logistics
Albertus Magnus Platz
50923 Cologne, Germany

Email: lukas.held@gmx.de

Thilo Heyer, M. Sc.

University of Cologne
Department of Business Policy & Logistics
Albertus Magnus Platz
50923 Cologne, Germany

Email: heyer@wiso.uni-koeln.de

Felix Limbert, M. Sc.

University of Cologne
Department of Business Policy & Logistics
Albertus Magnus Platz
50923 Cologne, Germany

Email: felix.limbert@gmail.com

Dr. Alessandro Monti

Cologne Business School (CBS)
Hardefuststr. 1
50677 Cologne, Germany

Email: a.monti@cbs.de

Prof. Dr. Markus Raueiser

Cologne Business School (CBS)
Hardefuststr. 1
50677 Cologne, Germany

Email: m.raueiser@cbs.de

Volker Rundshagen, MBA

Cologne Business School (CBS)
Tourism Management
Hardefuststr. 1
50677 Cologne, Germany

Email: v.rundshagen@cbs.de

Lukas Seeger, B. Sc.

University of Cologne
Department of Business Policy & Logistics
Albertus Magnus Platz
50923 Cologne, Germany

Email: seeger@wiso.uni-koeln.de

Tobias Schmitz, M. Sc.	University of Cologne Department of Business Policy & Logistics Albertus Magnus Platz 50923 Cologne, Germany Email: tobias.schmitz@wiso.uni-koeln.de
Gereon Schumacher, B. A.	Cologne Business School (CBS) Faculty of International Business Hardefuststr. 1 50677 Cologne, Germany Email: g.schumacher@cbs-edu.de
Dipl.-Kfm. Bastian Schweiger	University of Cologne Department of Business Policy & Logistics Albertus Magnus Platz 50923 Cologne, Germany Email: schweiger@wiso.uni-koeln.de
Dipl.-Kfm. Markus Tandel	Vaillant Group CEO - Assistant to Dr. Carsten Voigtländer Berghauser Str. 40 42859 Remscheid, Germany Email: markus.tandel@vaillant.de
Dr. Carsten Voigtländer	Vaillant Group Chief Executive Officer Berghauser Str. 40 42859 Remscheid, Germany
Simon von Danwitz, M. Sc.	University of Cologne Department of Business Policy & Logistics Albertus Magnus Platz 50923 Cologne, Germany Email: von.danwitz@wiso.uni-koeln.de
Prof. Dr. Ingo Winkler	University of Southern Denmark Faculty of Social Sciences Alsion 2 6400 Sønderborg, Denmark Email: inw@sam.sdu.dk